Delivering Competitive Advantage Through
BPM

Real-World Business Process Management

Published in association with the
Workflow Management Coalition

Workflow Management Coalition

Edited by
LAYNA FISCHER

Excellence in Practice Series

Future Strategies Inc.
Lighthouse Point, Florida, USA

Delivering Competitive Advantage Through BPM: Real-World Business Process Management

Copyright © 2012 by Future Strategies Inc.
ISBN13: 978-0-9849764-5-4

Published by Future Strategies Inc., Book Division
3640-B3 North Federal Highway, #421, Lighthouse Point FL 33064 USA
954.782.3376 / 954.719.3746 fax
www.FutStrat.com email: books@FutStrat.com

For bulk orders, resellers, academic orders and extracts: please contact the publisher.

All brand names and product names mentioned in this book are trademarks or service marks of their respective companies. Any omission or misuse should not be regarded as intent to infringe on the property of others. The Publisher recognizes and respects all marks used by companies, manufacturers and developers as a means to distinguish their products.
Neither the editor, the Awards sponsors, nor Future Strategies Inc., accept any responsibility or liability for loss or damage occasioned to any person or property through using the material, instructions, methods, or ideas contained herein, or acting or refraining from acting as a result of such use. The authors and the publisher expressly disclaim all implied warrantees, including merchantability or fitness for any particular purpose. There will be no duty on the authors or Publisher to correct any errors or defects in the software.

All rights reserved. Manufactured in the United States of America. No part of this work covered by the copyright hereon may be reproduced or used in any form or by any means—graphic, electronic, or mechanical, including photocopying, recording, taping, or information storage and retrieval systems—without written permission of the publisher, except in the case of brief quotations embodied in critical articles and reviews.

Publisher's Cataloging-in-Publication Data
ISBN13: 978-0-9849764-5-4

Delivering Competitive Advantage Through BPM: Real-World Business Process Management

/Layna Fischer (Editor)

p. cm.
Includes bibliographical references and appendices.

1. Business Process Management. 2. Organizational Change. 3. Technological Innovation. 4. Information Technology. 5. Total Quality Management. 6. Management Information Systems. 7. Office Practice-Automation. 8. Knowledge Management. 9. Workflow. 10. Process Analysis

Fischer, Layna. (ed)

Table of Contents

INTRODUCTION   7
Layna Fischer, Future Strategies Inc.

Guest Chapters:

EVOLUTION OF BPM: COMBINING BUSINESS ARCHITECTURE, INTELLIGENCE, CASE
MANAGEMENT TO ACCELERATE PROCESS IMPLEMENTATIONS   17
Meera Srinivasan and Linus Chow, Oracle

TRANSFORMING THE BUSINESS FOR A NEW CUSTOMER SEGMENT: THE ROLE OF BPM IN THE
NEW BUSINESS MODEL   25
J. Bryan Lail, Raytheon

BPM CHANGE MANAGEMENT: SOME CONSIDERATIONS   31
Jaisundar Venkat, Wipro

INNOVATION IN HEALTH CARE: INSIGHT FROM FIRST FEDERAL HEALTH CARE CENTER   37
*Paul Lam, Captain James A. Lovell Federal Health Care Center and
Linus Chow, Oracle*

Section 1: Europe

AVIO SPA, ITALY   43
Silver Award. Nominated by EKA Srl, Italy

HANSEMERKUR INSURANCE GROUP, GERMANY   57
Gold Award: Nominated by Bosch Software

HOMELOAN MANAGEMENT LIMITED, UNITED KINGDOM   69
Finalist. Nominated by IBM, USA

JARDINE LLOYD THOMPSON, UK   77
Gold Award: Nominated by HandySoft, USA

TOYOTA ESPAÑA, SPAIN   87
Finalist, nominated by AuraPortal, USA

Section 2: Middle East and Africa

ECOBANK LLC, SENEGAL   97
Silver Award: Nominated by Newgen Software Technologies Ltd, India

RIYADH MILITARY HOSPITAL, SAUDI ARABIA   109
Gold Award: Nominated by Bizagi, UK

Section 3: North America

DANFOSS POWER ELECTRONICS, USA   117
Silver Award: Nominated by Aalborg University, Denmark

NATIONAL INSTITUTE OF MENTAL HEALTH, USA   129
Finalist: Nominated by BP Logix, Inc., USA

NAVAL SPECIAL WARFARE GROUP FOUR GOVERNMENT PURCHASE CARD PROGRAM   135
Silver Award: Nominated by HandySoft, USA

COUNTY OF SAN JOAQUIN, USA — 145
Gold Award: Nominated by Oracle USA

Section 4: Pacific Rim

AUDI JAPAN KK, JAPAN — 169
Gold Award: Nominated by Bizagi, UK

VITEOS CAPITAL MARKET SERVICES LTD., INDIA — 175
Silver Award: Nominated by EMC, United States

Section 5: South and Central America

CARBONES DE CERREJÓN, COLOMBIA — 181
Finalist: Nominated by Bizagi, United Kingdom

CONAGUA: COMISIÓN NACIONAL DEL AGUA, MEXICO — 187
Gold Award: Nominated by PECTRA Technology, USA

GRUPO HOSPITALAR CONCEIÇÃO, BRAZIL — 209
Silver Award: Nominated by H&R Consultores, Brazil

Section 6 Appendix

AWARD WINNERS AND NOMINATORS CONTACT DIRECTORY — 219

FURTHER READING — 223

Delivering Competitive Advantage through BPM

Some organizations significantly outperform others in their industry. They become more agile by adopting smarter work practices and transforming their business processes to be more dynamic, collaborative, and connected.

Often, the business processes themselves create competitive advantage. Increased revenue at reduced cost makes more money for a very effective business. Changing market opportunities, customer demands, new technology and calls for cost reduction can make it seem impossible to keep operational chaos at bay.

Competitive advantage is gained when companies reduce operational risk by making sure that internal guidelines and external regulatory requirements are fulfilled. Companies thus offer customers a faster, more accurate and consistent service.

To position your organization for success, you need the ability to continually optimize, streamline and align business processes to meet changing business needs for greater performance, competitive advantage and to drive growth.

The companies whose award-winning case studies are featured in this book have proven excellence in their creative and successful deployment of advanced and business process management concepts. The positive impact to their corporations includes increased revenues, more productive and satisfied employees, product enhancements, better customer service and quality improvements.

Read these detailed case studies to find out how these award-winners moved the competitive goalposts for their industry.

CRITERIA

The criteria for submitting an entry are fairly simple: the project should have been operational for six months prior to nomination, and have been installed within the past two years. The submission guidelines, however, are more detailed. To be recognized as winners, companies must address three critical areas: excellence in *innovation*, excellence in *implementation* and excellence in strategic *impact* to the organization. Details are at www.bpmf.org.

Innovation

Innovation encompasses the innovative use of technology for strategic business objectives; the complexity of the underlying business process and IT architecture; the creative and successful deployment of advanced workflow and imaging concepts; and process innovations through business process reengineering and/or continuous improvements.

Implementation

Hallmarks of a successful *implementation* include extensive user and line management involvement in the project while successfully managing change during the implementation process. Factors impacting the level of difficulty in achieving a successful implementation include the system complexity; integration with other advanced technologies; and the scope and scale of the implementation (e.g. size, geography, inter-company processes).

Impact

Impact is the bottom line, answering the question, "What benefit does BPM deliver to my business? Why should I care?"

Using BPM for Competitive Advantage

Examples of potential benefits include: productivity improvements; cost savings; increased revenues; product enhancements; improved customer service; improved quality; strategic impact to the organization's mission; enabling culture change; and—most importantly—changing the company's competitive position in the market. The visionary focus is now toward strategic benefits, in contrast to marginal cost savings and productivity enhancements.

While successes in these categories are prerequisites for winning a Global Excellence Award, it would reward all companies to focus on excelling in *innovation*, *implementation* and *impact* when installing BPM and workflow technologies. Companies must recognize that implementing innovative technology is useless unless the organization has a successful approach that delivers—and even surpasses—the anticipated benefits.

SUBMIT AN ENTRY

The annual **Global Excellence Awards for BPM and Workflow** are sponsored by WfMC.org and BPM.com. The prestigious annual Awards are highly coveted by organizations that seek recognition for their achievements. Now evolved into their 20th year, originally starting with, and moving through, imaging, documentation, knowledge management and more, as our industry moved forward, these awards not only provide a spotlight for companies that truly deserve recognition, but provide tremendous insights for organizations wishing to emulate the winners' successes.

General information and guidelines for submissions may be found at www.bpmf.org.

Contents and Chapter Abstracts

Guest Chapters:

EVOLUTION OF BPM: COMBINING BUSINESS ARCHITECTURE, INTELLIGENCE, CASE MANAGEMENT TO ACCELERATE PROCESS IMPLEMENTATIONS

Meera Srinivasan and Linus Chow, Oracle

Over the past five years, adoption of BPM has increased dramatically and customers using BPM tools for management of their business processes has also exploded exponentially. The primary focus of the majority of these BPM Projects is around automation and shortening the time taken to complete the end to end process. These BPM initiatives are largely confined to small footprint, departmental and tactical projects. However, BPM is much more than process automation, cost cutting and improving performance. BPM is about empowering business to take control, achieving efficiency in end user interactions with the process, monitoring key business insights for continuous process optimizations, attaining unprecedented agility to react to changing market conditions and improving customer satisfaction. This paper looks at some of the emerging new trends in BPM and how next generation BPM platforms support these trends to get higher value from BPM initiatives.

TRANSFORMING THE BUSINESS FOR A NEW CUSTOMER SEGMENT: THE ROLE OF BPM IN THE NEW BUSINESS MODEL

J. Bryan Lail, Raytheon

Extensive research across industries has shown that success in a new market or distinct new customer segment requires a transformation within the business driven by the value proposition, partnering approach and new types of revenue streams. This transformation does not happen easily, but has been achieved through development of a thorough business model[1] describing the new environment and the resulting changes necessitated within the business roles, processes and cost structures. An effective business model touches many aspects of customer focus, partnering, financials, human resources and business process changes.

There is a strong connection that can be made between a business process model focused on strategic levels of functional integration and the concrete execution of a new business model. This paper shows the general aspects of the business model canvas that can benefit from the rigor of business capability mapping and process modeling, then provides examples. The views shown will certainly depend on the audience for presenting the business model defining a strategic transformation, since executives are unlikely to benefit from a multi-hierarchal BPMN diagram, but the diagrams under the hood can provide the real structure and tactical path to a model that may otherwise become shelf-ware.

BPM Change Management: Some Considerations
Jaisundar Venkat, Wipro

As Business Process Management (BPM) becomes more mainstream and its adoption increases, the list of key factors that typically contribute to its failure as well as success are becoming more and more apparent.

Interestingly, one factor common in both lists is Change Management. The reason that it figures in both lists is because, not only can poorly addressed change issues lead to failure, but a well-managed change plan can actually *escalate* the degree of success from BPM. Change issues threaten and impact BPM implementation success much more than we would care to admit. Challenges along the BPM life-cycle are real and the nature of change can be complex. This paper discusses how a well-thought out Change Program can complement a BPM initiative and actually help in fostering collaboration and teamwork required along the stages of the BPM lifecycle by introducing a more positive influence on the outcome. Fundamentally though, there are some very crucial elements or *hotspots* if you would like to call it, that need to be appropriately addressed to ensure the Change Management program supports BPM optimally.

Innovation in Health Care: Insight from the First Federal Health Care Center
Paul Lam, Captain James A. Lovell Federal Health Care Center and Linus Chow, Oracle

Combine enormously complex data integration with the most sensitive, yet essential, case management processes run by two of the largest organizations in the world, and you have one of the biggest challenges facing the United States. Improving health care efficiency and effectiveness, while cutting costs, is the only way to solve the U.S. health care crisis. The pain can be especially acute for the U.S. Armed Forces, where both Veterans Affairs (VA) and the Department of Defense (DOD) are looking for ways to streamline operations to provide higher quality care while cutting inefficiencies in the system.

Section 1: Europe

Avio SpA, Italy
Silver Award: Nominated by EKA Srl, Italy

Avio is a world-wide leader in the aerospace industry. Based in Italy, Avio is a leading supplier of engine modules and components and it also operates in aircraft engines repair and overhaul with its Avioservice Division. In 2009, Avioservice Division started a new initiative for streamlining its Maintenance, Repair and Overhaul (MR&O) process of military engines in order to be able to sustain the new business and market conditions. The main objective of this initiative was to improve the performance of the process in meeting contractual SLAs in a new business environment where the repair and overhaul of several engines types, coming from completely new customers, is regulated by very different and very specific contractual agreements. As a result of the initiative, a system has been developed to govern the workflow of each engine in its company's "door-to-door" path and to collect actual performance measurements of the overall process which spans several organizational units.

HANSEMERKUR INSURANCE GROUP, GERMANY
Gold Award: Nominated by Bosch Software

The objective of the project was to implement a process-oriented architecture including the standardization and improvement of user interface ergonomics. The goal was to raise the degree of automation in claims processing to absorb an annual increase in gross revenue by 10-15 percent with an equal increase in claims, as well as to relieve clerks of simple routine tasks.

The annual increase in gross revenue could be absorbed by automated claims processes, which meant that the number of experts needed for processing was almost stable. This is an equivalent of € 0.75 million in cost savings per year and rising. In addition, the implementation of a rules engine for regulatory rules resulted in an increase of one percent in claims rejection or over € 1.65 million per year and growing. Claims processing time could be reduced from an average two weeks in the past to a few hours. The new automated process frees claims experts from routine tasks and lets them work on unclear or complex cases. On the other hand, simple tasks as obtaining missing data or correcting errors can now easily be diverted to less qualified personnel.

HOMELOAN MANAGEMENT LIMITED, UNITED KINGDOM
Finalist: Nominated by IBM, USA

HML is the UK's largest mortgage servicer, providing outsourced mortgage administration for more than 50 UK and Irish clients, and operating out of three UK locations. The company was established in 1988 and is a wholly-owned subsidiary of Skipton Building Society. It manages around £43bn for some of the largest players in the UK and US financial markets.

HML's first BPM initiative, the credit management workflow system (CREWS) was initiated to address these requirements and contain cost. CREWS delivered automated functionality for HML's pre-litigation department. Feedback was gathered from the business area to continuously improve CREWS over the next two years and ensure what was delivered was in line with business requirements, therefore eliminating any rework. From 2010 through 2011, HML delivered significant enhancements to the initial CREWS application, with improvements in query responsiveness, agile development methodology and improved process efficiency. In addition, in early 2011, a new credit management enhancement project was completed to augment CREWS with possessions process automation.

JARDINE LLOYD THOMPSON, UK
Gold Award: Nominated by HandySoft, USA

Formed in 1997 from the merger of Lloyd Thompson and Jardine Insurance Broker, Jardine Lloyd Thompson (JLT) is an international group of Risk Specialists and Employee Benefits Consultants. JLT is listed on the London Stock Exchange and is one of the largest companies of its type in the world.

The EB Group within Jardine Lloyd Thompson (JLT EB) made up £132 million of this 2010 turnover with 1500 employees in offices in the UK and India.

Between 2007-2010, JLT made more than 20 acquisitions globally across the group. JLT EB operations quickly became highly complex, distributed and paper-based. Employees were handling millions of documents annually covering Pension Administration, Payroll, Defined Contributions, Actuarial, Health and Risk, among other requests. Processes treated more than 16 million workflow elements, 300+ million rows of table data and 15 million SharePoint documents. JLT EB accomplished its goals of increased revenues with lower costs with continual investment in BPM. JLT EB has used BPM to streamline >200 processes. From an ROI standpoint, this work has provided a key business component, contributing to JLT EB's growth in trading profit by 50% in the last financial year.

TOYOTA ESPAÑA, SPAIN
Finalist: nominated by AuraPortal, USA

Toyota is a well-known, leading worldwide automobile manufacturer. In Spain it is represented through its subsidiary Toyota España, which has a broad network of dealers to cover the Spanish territory, providing selling and technical assistance to end customers. The Toyota dealers are grouped into an association, who, sponsored by Toyota, took on the BPMS project in order to build an Intranet to manage and control their own environmental best practices according to Toyota policies and the ISO 14001 standard. Thus, the BPMS allowed the more than 250 Toyota dealers within the network to meet environmental Toyota practices with less human effort and the fewer technical and economic resources.

Section 2: Middle East and Africa

ECOBANK LLC, SENEGAL
Silver Award: Nominated by Newgen Software Technologies Ltd, India

ECObank, the leading pan-African bank, was established as a bank holding company in 1985 under a private sector initiative spearheaded by the Federation of West African Chambers of Commerce and Industry with the support of ECOWAS. Spanned across more than 32 countries, the bank operates as "One Bank" with common branding, standards, policies and processes to provide a consistent and reliable service to its customers. Today, the bank operates in more than 755 branches and they have 779 ATMs and 888 points of sale (POSs).

RIYADH MILITARY HOSPITAL, SAUDI ARABIA
Gold Award: Nominated by Bizagi, UK

Al-Wazarat Health Center (WHC) is located in Riyadh City, the capital of Saudi Arabia. The center is associated with the **R**iyadh **M**ilitary **H**ospital Program. RMH is part of the Medical Services Department (MSD) of the Ministry of Defense and Aviation (MODA). The center is specialized as a Family and Community Medicine Department, with a large practitioner service and is currently incorporating a dermatology clinic, well women's clinic, and a pediatric clinic to accommodate the growing population and to further enhance the quality of patient care. In addition to the ordinary healthcare facility and auxiliary, the center also contains other medical facilities such as a Pharmacy Department, Radiology Department, treatment rooms, specimen rooms, resuscitation and ECG rooms, and a nebulizing room.

Section 3: North America

DANFOSS POWER ELECTRONICS, USA
Silver Award: Nominated by Aalborg University, Denmark

This case study presents the experiences of a manufacturing company with taking the first step towards adopting BPM. The company used process mining in SAP to tackle a highly turbulent inquiry-to-invoice process which hindered customer relationships and employee satisfaction. The case highlights the steps of getting from raw event data to business implications. It shows how using a combination of interdisciplinary skills and basic technology applications can be a springboard leading to a wider adoption of BPM in companies with a previously low process orientation.

NATIONAL INSTITUTE OF MENTAL HEALTH, USA
Finalist: Nominated by BP Logix, Inc., USA

There is a critical need within the government to manage IT procurements in such a way as to ensure compliance with organizational and governmental standards, to secure the appropriate review and approvals for all such procurements, and to account for procurements and expenditures. To achieve this objective, the National Institute of Mental Health (NIMH), part of the National Institutes of Health (NIH), needed a more effective methodology and a more efficient business process for acquiring, tracking and managing IT equipment procurement. NIMH was able to accomplish this goal by designing a procurement process that supported compliance requirements, while also providing a comprehensive review and approval process for all procurements. To develop and implement that process, NIMH licensed business process management (BPM) software to automate and streamline its IT Procurement system.

NAVAL SPECIAL WARFARE GROUP FOUR GOVERNMENT PURCHASE CARD PROGRAM, USA.
Silver Award: Nominated by HandySoft, USA

Naval Special Warfare (NSW) is a division within the U.S. Navy that includes more than 2,400 active-duty Special Warfare Operators, known as SEALs. All of these personnel are divided among "groups". NSW Group 4 (NSWG4) consists of three Special Boat Teams (SBT) and one international training command—all working together towards the common goal of fighting the global war on terrorism. In the past, NSWG4 always had more than adequate numbers of craft, engines and spare parts. However, with today's current high demand for combat operations, security force assistance (SFA) and fiscal downsizing, NSWG4 had to develop a different business sustainment model to complete missions with less assets.
The solution expertly weaves Lean Six Sigma, Agile, and dynamic BPM into a system called SWIFT—which successfully met this challenge, and exceeded expectations.

COUNTY OF SAN JOAQUIN, USA
Gold Award: Nominated by Oracle USA

The modernization of San Joaquin County's Integrated Justice Information System (IJIS) was a strategic initiative that started with setting our visions and goals to modernize interfaces and functions that continue to support the law and justice duties of the residents of San Joaquin County, Sheriff's Office, Public Defender, District Attorney and Probation Department, as well as the needs of other local, state and national law enforcement entities. We focused on reducing unnecessary redundancy and consolidating like functions to decrease costs and improve overall system performance. Additionally, new nationwide standards, such as National Information Exchange Model (NIEM) would allow us to collaborate more effectively with state and national law enforcement. This modernization is critical to San Joaquin's support of law enforcement and the public safety of over 650,000 residents. Our choice to modernize IJIS using Business Process Management (BPM) and Service Oriented Architecture (SOA) technologies aligned with our strategic vision of lowering our business risks by providing agility with phased modernization:

Section 4: Pacific Rim

AUDI JAPAN KK, JAPAN
Gold Award: Nominated by Bizagi, UK

At a certain point of business maturity, companies find it necessary to increase productivity and efficiency in order to stay ahead of industry standards. Audi Japan KK, importer of Audi vehicles and subsidiary of Audi AG, discovered that to reach operational efficiency it was necessary to gain more control and visibility over its core management and administrative processes.

A year ago, Audi Japan KK decided to begin the automation of several of their core back-end administrative processes within the financial department; processes that were found to be too manual and paper-based, which made them inefficient and difficult to manage.

They were also clear about getting a solution that was easy-to use, painless to implement and would automate everyday processes. The objective was to increase transparency and quality, and reducing reliance on paper-based trails and processes. This solution also needed to be replicable in other company departments and Audi subsidiaries around the world.

VITEOS CAPITAL MARKET SERVICES LTD., INDIA
Silver Award: Nominated by EMC, United States

Viteos Capital Market Services Ltd. (Viteos) is a hedge fund administrator and operations service provider for financial services companies. As a small, but quickly growing company, Viteos began to outgrow its systems and sought a solution that could automate manual processes, reduce paperwork, help the company meet compliance standards, scale up or down to meet changing demands, and remain cost-effective. The company arrived at a solution that combined an element of its existing system—Microsoft SharePoint—with a more robust business process management (BPM) and document-management solution—EMC Documentum xCelerated Composition Platform (xCP)—as well as virtualization with VMware. This combination enabled the company to meet its increasing document processing needs while maintaining familiarity for its users.

Section 5: South and Central America

CARBONES DE CERREJÓN, COLOMBIA.
Finalist: Nominated by Bizagi, United Kingdom

Cerrejon is the largest open-pit coal mine in the world, with 30 years in the market, and an integrated operation which involves a thermal coalmine, a railroad of 150 kilometers and a seaport able to receive ships of up to 180 thousand tons of capacity. Cerrejon was looking to improve the coordination and orchestration between several areas – the commercialization offices (Dublin and Atlanta),

For this, Cerrejon required a collaborative solution that besides bringing agility to the business, offered flexibility and would allow satisfying the requirements of local regulations. Cerrejon selected Bizagi BPM Suite to automate the coal sales process, which integrated to its ERP, would enable the management of all the transactions derived from the commercialization of the coal, consolidating a robust platform for the conciliation of payments and collections.

CONAGUA: COMISIÓN NACIONAL DEL AGUA, MEXICO
Gold Award: Nominated by PECTRA Technology, USA

As a result of regulations and initiatives of the Government of Mexico in 2004, the *Subdirección General de Infraestructura Hidroagrícola* of CONAGUA –*Comisión Nacional del Agua*decided to start a BPM project in order to standardize, organ-ize and control the management processes of budgetary resources for public works and procurement services (more than one thousand million dollars each year), through an online system of information available for public consultation by citizens. With over seven years of implementing BPM, the CONAGUA *Subdirección General de Infraestructura Hidroagrícola* reports multiple benefits: greater adoption of BPM (from 1 to 18 processes in place, with 700% growth in number of users and the incorporation 23 new states, 13 regions and 15 cities to the project), a recovery of the total investment in the first 18 months and savings in materials / supplies of USD340,000 a year and current expenditure of USD238,000, greater employee satisfaction (50 and 76%) due to a 67% reduction in administrative and manual activities -mostly reporting; improved citizen perception and credibility due to availability of information about the public works for hydro-agricultural infra-structure development; numerous awards received.

GRUPO HOSPITALAR CONCEIÇÃO, BRAZIL
Silver Award: Nominated by H&R Consultores, Brazil

Grupo Hospitalar Conceição (GHC) is the largest hospital complex in the State of Rio Grande do Sul, Brazil, and responsible for the admission of 59,900 people, 2.2 million appointments, and 36,100 annual surgeries. The group comprises four hospital units, twelve health clinics, and three psychosocial care centers.

GHC pursues excellence in providing healthcare to the population as we supply state-run health services given that we are connected to the Ministry of Health and are totally dedicated to users of *Sistema Único de Saúde* – SUS (the public healthcare system).

Besides providing the population with healthcare, Grupo Hospitalar Conceição is also dedicated to fostering education and research, thus becoming a center of knowledge and people training for SUS. To reach our mission of developing full healthcare actions with organizational excellence and efficacy, our group employs technological and human resources and education and research programs.

Guest Chapters

Evolution of BPM:
Combining Business Architecture, Intelligence, Case Management to Accelerate Process Implementations

Meera Srinivasan and Linus Chow, Oracle

Over the past five years, adoption of BPM has increased dramatically and customers using BPM tools for management of their business processes has also exploded exponentially. The primary focus of the majority of these BPM Projects is around automation and shortening the time taken to complete the end to end process. These BPM initiatives are largely confined to small footprint, departmental and tactical projects. However, BPM is much more than process automation, cost cutting and improving performance. BPM is about empowering business to take control, achieving efficiency in end user interactions with the process, monitoring key business insights for continuous process optimizations, attaining unprecedented agility to react to changing market conditions and improving customer satisfaction. This paper looks at some of the emerging new trends in BPM and how next generation BPM platforms support these trends to get higher value from BPM initiatives.

1. BUSINESS-LED PROCESS COMPOSITION

The "B" in BPM stands for *Business*. These are the people who interact with the process on a regular basis, people who understand the limitations and short comings and who have ideas for improving the process. BPM empowers these business people to take control and drive improvements to their processes by enabling capture of business process flows as explicit visual process models expressed in a common, standard notation such as BPMN (Business Process Modeling Notation). BPM platforms offer intuitive, business targeted tool for business users to model and analyze the business process flows for process documentation and discovery purposes.

The next generation BPM tools take this Business User Empowerment to a whole new level. In addition to business processes, business users can author and manage the business policies and rules surrounding the process in an easy to visualize spreadsheet like metaphor referred to as Decision Tables. Also, business user engagement is not just limited to modeling but also extends to other phases of the process development life cycle. In addition to creating process models that serve as requirements and a starting point for execution, next generation BPM platforms support business driven implementation or composition. Using next generation BPM tools, Business users can now design all aspects of a process like user interfaces (forms), data models and human task definitions. They can discover business services and tie it to system steps in the process, perform simple data mapping and complete implementation of the process for execution.

The role of the IT developer in this case is more of an enabler and their main job is that of a business enabler. They are responsible for population of the Business Catalog (library) with reusable, shared services, data types, and other such implementation artifacts. Tasks such as creation of complex mapping using XSLT or

XPATH mechanism, adapter services to integrate with backend applications and scripts to perform custom work are delegated to the IT developers. However, changes made by IT Developers can be shared back to business and viewed inside the business tool for further refinements by business. This seamless round-trip is possible because BPMN 2.0 is a model cum execution language and both Business and IT share the same metadata. Many next generation BPM platforms also go one step further and support the ability of stepping through or playing the process inside the business tool. This enables business users can do incremental development and validation of their business processes.

In short, next generation BPM platforms enable business users to compose and stitch together an end-to-end process inside their tool of choice with zero or minimal IT effort.

2. BUSINESS DRIVEN BPM

In a departmental BPM Project, the focus is on specific processes with the goal of automating them, improving their performance, lowering their costs and providing performance visibility. However, when BPM initiatives cross departmental boundaries and extend to the enterprise, we need to take account of the big picture. We are talking about hundreds of processes including mission critical processes instead of few processes that are typical of departmental BPM. In such cases, there is a need to capture the big picture view in a standard way starting all the way from enterprise goals and objectives to applications that implement them. This big picture view is referred to as Business Architecture (BA) and is the formal link between the business strategy and business processes.

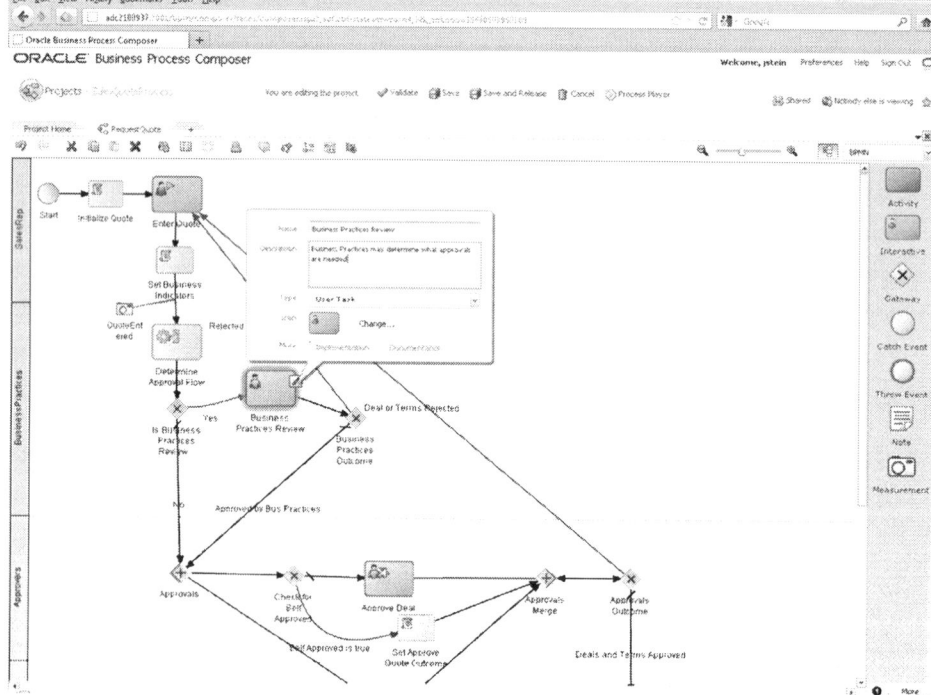

Figure 1: Business Driven Process Composition

BA captures the enterprise's core vision, the business goals that define the vision, the objectives that are decomposed from the goals, the strategies for achieving these objectives and their mappings to value chains and business processes. As part of strategy view, BA also captures the risks, success factors and KPIs for these above mentioned BA assets.

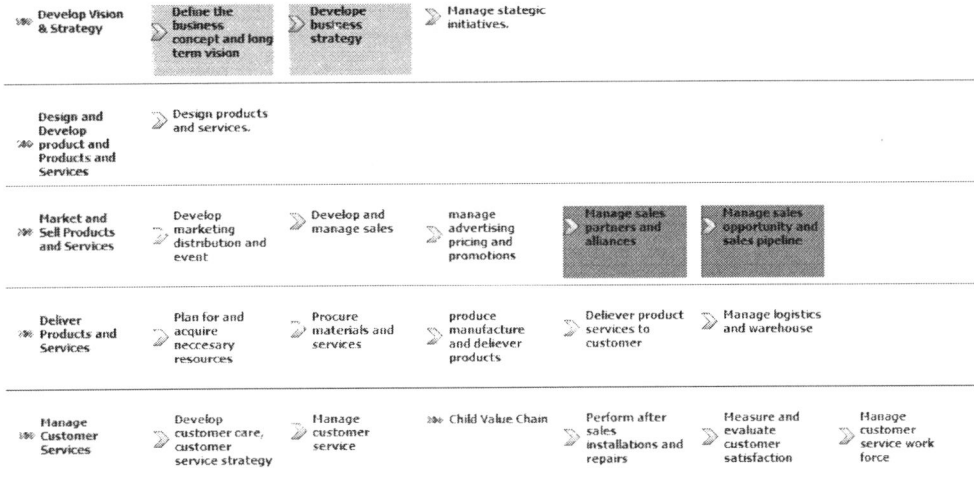

Figure 2: Value Chain Performance Dashboard

In addition to strategy based view, BA also supports Capability based views where Capability is an encapsulation of Business Function or value and tied to processes, applications, services and systems. BA not only provides capture of these assets and views in standard formats but also supports running reports based on the asset relationships for performing impact, gap and dependency analysis. In a nutshell, BA provides the ability to prioritize BPM efforts, understand which processes are currently most strategic to the company, and which services are most aligned with business strategy. Many maturing standards such as Zachman, DoDAF, TOGAF, and Semantic Technologies are being adopted by Enterprises; but only BPMN actually provides true native execution.

Traditionally BPA (Business Process Analysis) tools are used to capture BA but next generation BPMS platforms have started including some support for BA. A single platform that covers Business Architecture and BPM helps in tying the strategy to execution layers seamlessly.

3. DYNAMIC CASE MANAGEMENT

While companies have reaped substantial benefits and ROI by automating structured, repeatable process flows even greater benefits can be realized by taming dynamic, unstructured, ad-hoc processes. These non-linear processes are knowledge intensive and often performed by skilled workers also referred to as knowledge workers to coordinate the tasks. The outcome of the process is determined by knowledge worker rather than the system. In order to achieve better business outcomes, knowledge workers require greater flexibility, adaptability and control of their tasks as well as ability to collaborate with other experts for guidance. These processes are broadly referred to as "Case". Examples of case management processes are credit card dispute management, incident management and loan origination processes. Case processes are also document intensive and a Case is usually associated with different types of documents including unstructured content and media. To address the content requirements of a Case, a content management system is often included in the solution.

A "Case" typically comprises of case activities, case data, case documents, case rules, case events, case milestones and case outcomes. All these artifacts are surfaced to the case worker through a case interface. The case interface provides 360 degree view of the case and displays the history or the progression of the case. The progression of a case is indicated via case milestones. A case milestone signifies completion of a stage in a case and is useful as it provides high-level snapshots for management to validate the progress of a case. A case is said to be complete when a case "outcome" or "goal" is reached.

Traditional BPM platforms require a process definition and suited to handle only structured step-by-step process execution that are repeatable. Flexibility in traditional BPM platforms is limited to business rule controls and task-reassignments and makes it harder to implement untamed, ad-hoc processes. Dynamic or advanced case management platforms are specifically designed to support automation and streamlining of all aspects of a case. They have rich support for case activities. The case activities could be BPMN based process fragments or human workflow tasks or notifications or could be even an automated system step. These activities could be mandatory or optional and become available to the case worker at various points as the case progresses. The activation of a case activity can be manual or automatic based on case rules or case events or reaching of a case milestone. In addition to pre-defined case activities, most advanced case management systems also support creation of case activities on the fly by a case worker.

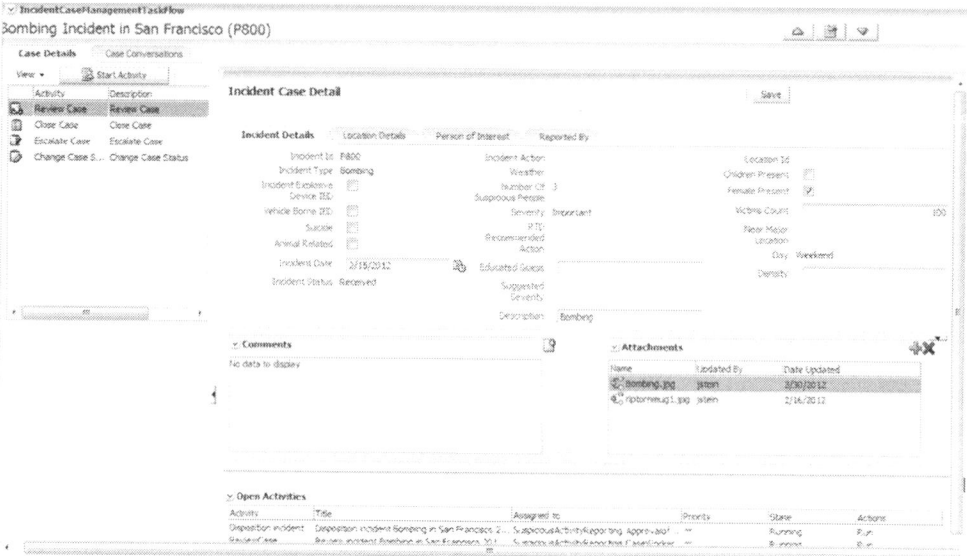

Figure 3: Sample Case Interface

Another key aspect of advanced case management is support for document intensive processes. The case documents are stored in a content management system under case instance specific folders. Advanced case management systems come with an embedded content management system and also support integration with 3rd party content management systems via CMIS (Content Management Interoperability Services) adapters.

Case events are a big part of the dynamic aspect of cases. The case events can be internal to the case (case reaching a specific milestone, case activity being completed, case rule being activated) or they can be external events as well. These events can alter the progress of the case and can change data, the timeline, reset a milestone or even cancel and terminate a case. A case event can also be tied to a case document being added to the specific case instance folder.

Lastly, in addition to being content-centric, a case is also collaboration intensive. Most case management platforms support collaborations within the case interface and facilitate the case worker to collaborate with experts via discussions, documents, wikis, etc. Since these collaborations happen with the case context, they are archived in case logs and can be traced to actions or decisions.

4. ACTIONABLE INTELLIGENCE

Though the letter "M" in BPM stands for *Management*, it could also be interpreted as "Measurement" or "Monitoring" since BPM is all about improving business processes. To facilitate process analysis, BPM Platforms usually include a Business Activity Monitoring (BAM) component for measuring performance via standard and wizard generated custom dashboards, for alerting when certain conditions are violated and for taking corrective actions in real-time. BPM is about continuous iterative improvements and the performance metrics gathered during process execution are fed back in to the modeling phase for further optimizations.

There are certain processes like credit card fraud detection, suspicious activity analysis that need to not only look at process events but also at external, seemingly unrelated, high velocity events in order to determine the process flow. Some next generation BPM vendors have addressed these requirements and support sophisticated analysis by integrating Business Activity Monitoring (BAM) and Complex Event Processing (CEP) product components. This integration enables performing advanced pattern detection of disjointed high volume events, filter out the noise, determine significant events, and surface these events to BAM dashboards as well as business processes for taking appropriate action.

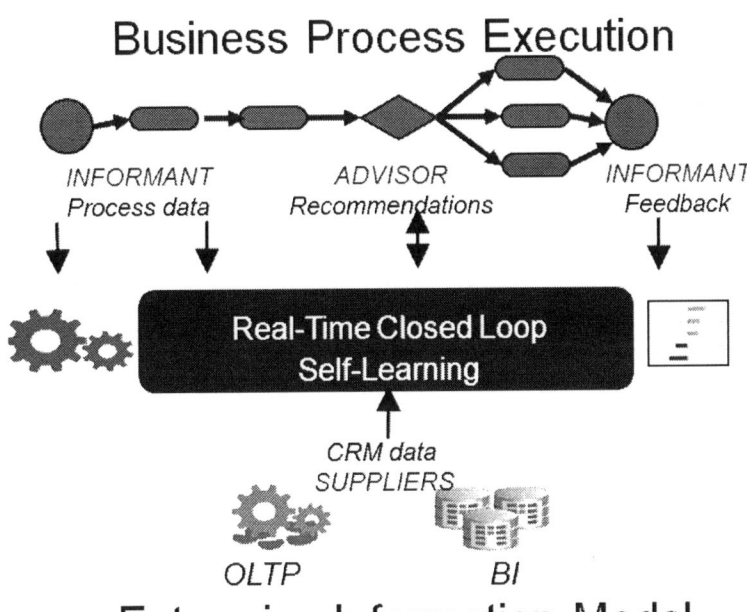

Figure 4: Interaction between BPM and Predictive Analytics products

Another key trend that is catching rapidly is predictive analytics and self learning systems. These self learning systems are also referred to as Real-Time Decision Systems (RTD). We have seen in the Dynamic case management section how a knowledge worker has more control and flexibility in doing case related work.

Freedom to choose the action also means that the knowledge worker has to piece together different sets of information and come up with an optimal decision. Some next generation BPM platforms integrate with Real-Time Decision systems to provide the next best action and guidance for the case worker. A Predictive analytics engine of the RTD is an automated self learning system and it combines dynamic rules and predictive models. It continuously updates the predictive model based on the data it receives, optimizes over time and then recommends the best action and predicts possible outcomes.

5. PROCESS ACCELERATORS

Today, companies do not re-invent the wheel but purchase off the shelf COTS Applications and tailor those according to their needs. The same approach can be extended to other business processes as well. Rather than building out processes from scratch, Organizations can get a jump start and accelerate the development and rolling out of their process driven solutions. Many vendors are now offering pre-built process solutions for common, well-defined processes across industries as well as industry specific vertical processes based on standard industry frameworks such as APQC's Process Classification Framework, SCOR, eTOM and ITIL. These accelerators provide a starting place, a common vocabulary, standard business objects that can be further customized to meet the company's needs and for providing a competitive edge. As an example, if there is an accelerator for HR On-Boarding process, you can use 60 to 80% of the process as-is and change the rest to meet company specific needs.

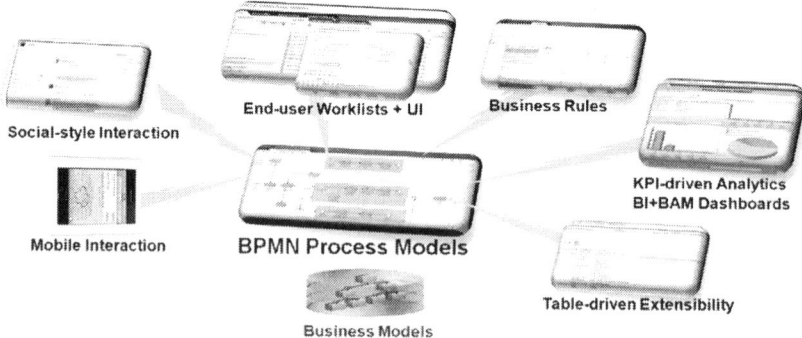

Figure 5: Components of Process Accelerators

There are a number of pre-built process accelerators offered by the different BPM vendors in the areas of healthcare, finance, insurance and public sector. These solutions go beyond just blueprint process models and are in fact execution ready. They often include library of reusable assets consisting of data models, process roles, business rules, pre-built dashboards and business services. These reusable components not only lower IT implementation costs but also embody business value and help organizations reach process excellence faster. The accelerators can be easily customized or extended using tooling and with zero to minimal coding. In addition to accelerating process development, these frameworks embody architecture best practices; reduce risk, decrease cost, increase consistency and reuse. In short, Process Accelerators lay a solid foundation for achieving process excellence and serves as a launching pad for developing business processes.

6. BPM AND THE CLOUD

BPM is the perfect technology for managing Cloud solutions.

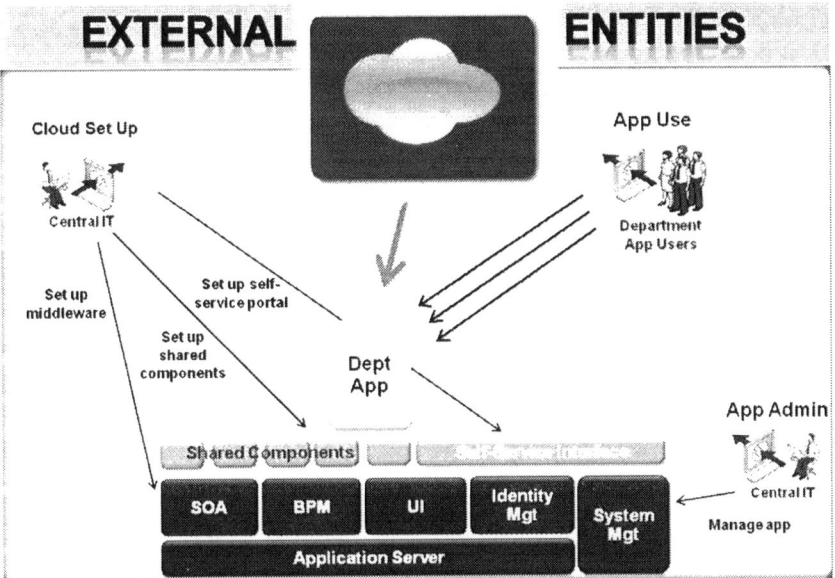

Figure 6: BPM Enables Solution as a Service

For solutions to truly meet the exacting requirements of specific departments or even external entities BPM is essential to enable sharing, interoperability and re-use. BPM allows the "Business" to "Manage" the "Process" while still taking advantage of shared components and assets of SOA. Mature BPM solutions are fully integrated and take advantage of SOA, Identity Management, Portal, Business Intelligence, Data (including Spatial and Semantic) and increasingly optimized High Performance Hardware and Network configurations.

7. CONCLUSION

Business driven BPM, advanced case management and intelligent analytics for optimal decision making are next waves of business innovation. Maturing BPM platforms are bringing People, Process, and Technologies together with Process Accelerators, Best Practice Methodologies, and Business Architecture capabilities. Many next generation BPM platforms provide rich support for these new trends. Business users can now sit in the driver's seat and design, analyze implement, and improve their business processes. By adopting these next generation BPM trends, organizations can up the ROI of their BPM initiatives and substantially improve their Time to Value.

About the Authors

Meera Srinivasan is a Director, BPM Product Management with Oracle and is responsible for Oracle BPM Suite and Oracle BPA Suite. She has 15 years of extensive experience in integration, SOA, BPM and EA technologies and represents Oracle at OMG, OASIS and other industry consortia. Meera joined Oracle in 2003, and was part of the SOA Product Management team managing Adapters. Prior to joining Oracle, she spent seven years with TIBCO Software, a pioneer in electronic trading, message-oriented middleware and enterprise integration. At TIBCO, she was an Engineering Manager involved in managing the development of various Adapters and EAI technologies. She holds a Master of Science degree in Computer Science from the University of Florida at Gainesville.

Linus Chow is the Principal BPM Champion (Public Sector North America) for Oracle Corporation. He has over 20 years of leadership and management experience in information technology with over 15 years in workflow, BPM, and SOA. He has played crucial roles in expanding the growth of BPM and SOA adoption first in the US and then internationally from Australia to Switzerland. Currently, Linus leads the adoption of BPM/SOA and E2.0 solutions for Public Sector customers in North America. He has helped organizations win many industry awards for BPM/SOA and E2.0 implementations. He is a published author and an active speaker on the Best Practices of BPM/SOA and E2.0. A decorated former US Army Officer, Linus has an MBA, a MS in Management Information Systems, and BS in Mathematics; and is a Certified BPM Professional.

Transforming the Business for a new Customer Segment: The Role of BPM in the New Business Model

J. Bryan Lail, Raytheon

1. INTRODUCTION TO BUSINESS MODELS

Extensive research across industries has shown that success in a new market or distinct new customer segment requires a transformation within the business driven by the value proposition, partnering approach and new types of revenue streams. This transformation does not happen easily, but can be achieved through a thorough business model[1] as shown in Figure 1, describing the new environment and the resulting changes necessitated within the business roles, processes and cost structures. An effective business model touches many aspects of customer focus, partnering, financials, human resources and business process changes.

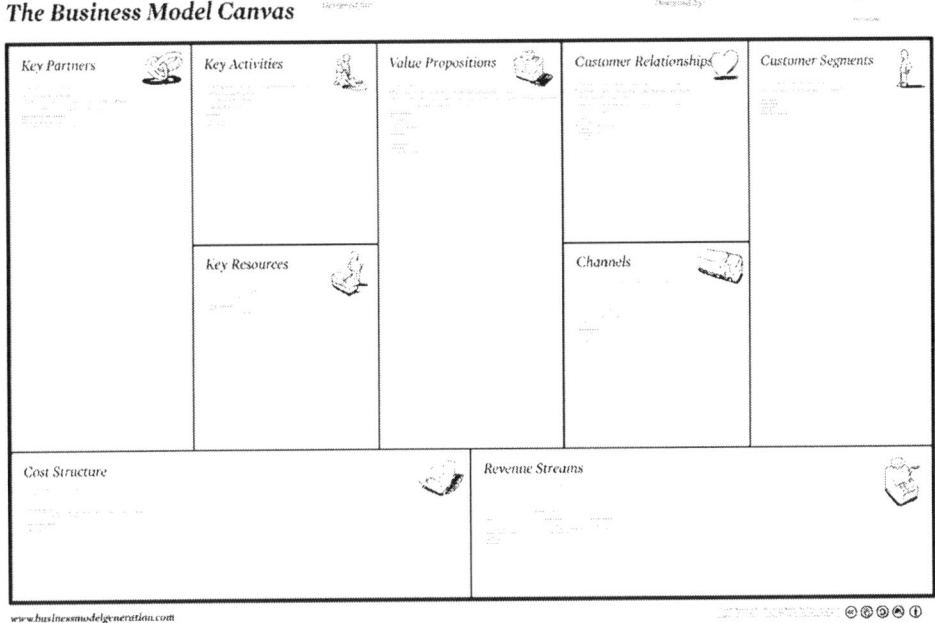

Figure 1. The Business Model Canvas

The starting point is generally the upper right area in the figure, first characterizing what has changed about the customer due to market or political forces, or driven by a desire to move into an adjacent market with a different set of customer concerns and new segments. These drivers for change necessitate an understanding of how to relate to and deliver value to the new cus-

---

[1] http://en.wkipedia.org/wiki/File:Business_Model_Canvas.png

tomer segment. Moving left, the company then has to address the value proposition they will bring outside just a product alone to break into this new segment or succeed in an evolving environment ("It's in my product bookings plan" isn't a value proposition for the customer). This explicit understanding, even if at a sketch level with rough notes, then creates the goal and focus for modeling how the company must change partnering, adjust internal costs and pricing, reassign resources and drive process changes to have any chance of delivering that value to that new customer segment. The model taken as a whole then allows a more realistic assessment of resulting revenue streams, enabling a trade across different markets, internal business models and expected return on investment.

The key point is that many companies across many industries have proven convincingly that having and executing a clear business model is necessary to successfully react to significant market changes. This is most often proven in the negative, partly explaining why there are so many more case studies on failures to move with changing times than successes.

2. THE ROLE OF PROCESS MODELS IN BUSINESS MODELING

This section covers the general aspects of the business model canvas that can benefit from the rigor of business capability mapping and process modeling. First, the development of a good business model is itself a process. As described in the introduction, it flows and builds in a sequential manner, initially with an evolution of key roles from marketing and selling, to functional planning, to operating the business. Changes in the market, by factors outside the company's control or due to a desire to tackle adjacent markets, act as the trigger for a new model of the customer segment and delivering a new value proposition to that segment. This new model to grow or sustain the business initiates the need for change internally, leading (for proactive companies) to an explicit model that accepts the need for new roles, resources, cross-functional tasks and cost structures compared to the organization built around the original business model. If implemented well, the company can then realize the new source of revenues.

Using B. Silver's methods around Process Levels[2], this work is best kept at Level 1 for clear executive communications with a master sequence all on one sheet. Relaying the steps and benefits quickly is not only important due to busy leaders, but also for simplicity to members of the modeling team who have never been exposed to methods for challenging the standard operating model of the company. In fact, once the process steps including roles, tasks and decisions are understood, it is best to keep the real process model as a backup and to communicate in block or animated form only as necessary to discuss how the business model flows from origin to results.

Second, the key to execution of a new business model is building and implementing the new business processes that must occur to deliver the value proposition to an evolving or new customer segment. All of the communications between capture (marketing), functional organizations (process owners), operations (executing the new model) and leadership is very necessary and the key work early on. Those communications and briefing materials, however, are not sufficient without also having the detailed diagrams under

---

[2] BPMN Method and Style http://www.brsilver.com/bpmn-method-and-style/

the hood that provide the real structure, tactical steps and metrics to a model that may otherwise become shelf-ware.

This is likely a Level 2 model with much more content than implied in the Key Activities cell of the Business Model Canvas. A thorough business process model will provide the focus for the key new changes required to succeed at the new market, in terms of different triggers, altered or completely new roles, new types of tasks or coordination across functions, new interactions with the customer and new metrics (measures of success). There will be many challenges to get to this model in terms of challenging the normal order of business and whether it supports the new model, obtaining leadership buy-in to invest in people and organization shift and adjusting ingrained policies, but forming the process model with this detail is the signal that there is a real execution path for the whole business model.

3. EXAMPLE OF DEVELOPING THE BUSINESS MODEL

This section provides examples of effective process modeling in the business model. The first is a Level 1 model and description, along with lessons learned, for the process of building the whole business model.

Figure 2 provides a process for building the business model. The swim lanes and black boxes provide the key roles involved, while the customer messages provide the trigger and final measure of success for the business model. Note the customer trigger can result from an overall market shift (the message is in the form of multiple news stories, budget plans and new directives), a need of the company to find and assess the needs of a whole new customer, or a more tactical issue such as change of direction by one specific established customer agency.

The capture or marketing organization is responsible for recognizing the trigger and pulling together an assessment of the market shift, defining the new or transformed customer segment (C1) and driving to the adjusted value proposition (C2) the company will bring to that new segment. The larger the environmental change, the larger the group the capture role should bring together to build the new business model to get a broad representation across impacted functions and processes.

The capture organization, working with business leadership and functional representatives (process owners for operating the business), must decide whether this new or transformed customer segment is addressable by the company. The reason this decision is critical at this point is that the team required to achieve the next steps correctly is going to be broader and the tasks are going to take longer. The next step (F1) takes the market and customer-centric need for change and translates those into a gap analysis between the current business model and what the future must be to succeed in that segment. Since the organization of the company is often part of what needs to change, a best practice is to step outside the current org chart as a basis for analysis and instead leverage an industry capability map from the APQC Process Classification Framework[3].

---

[3] www.apqc.org/process-classification-framework

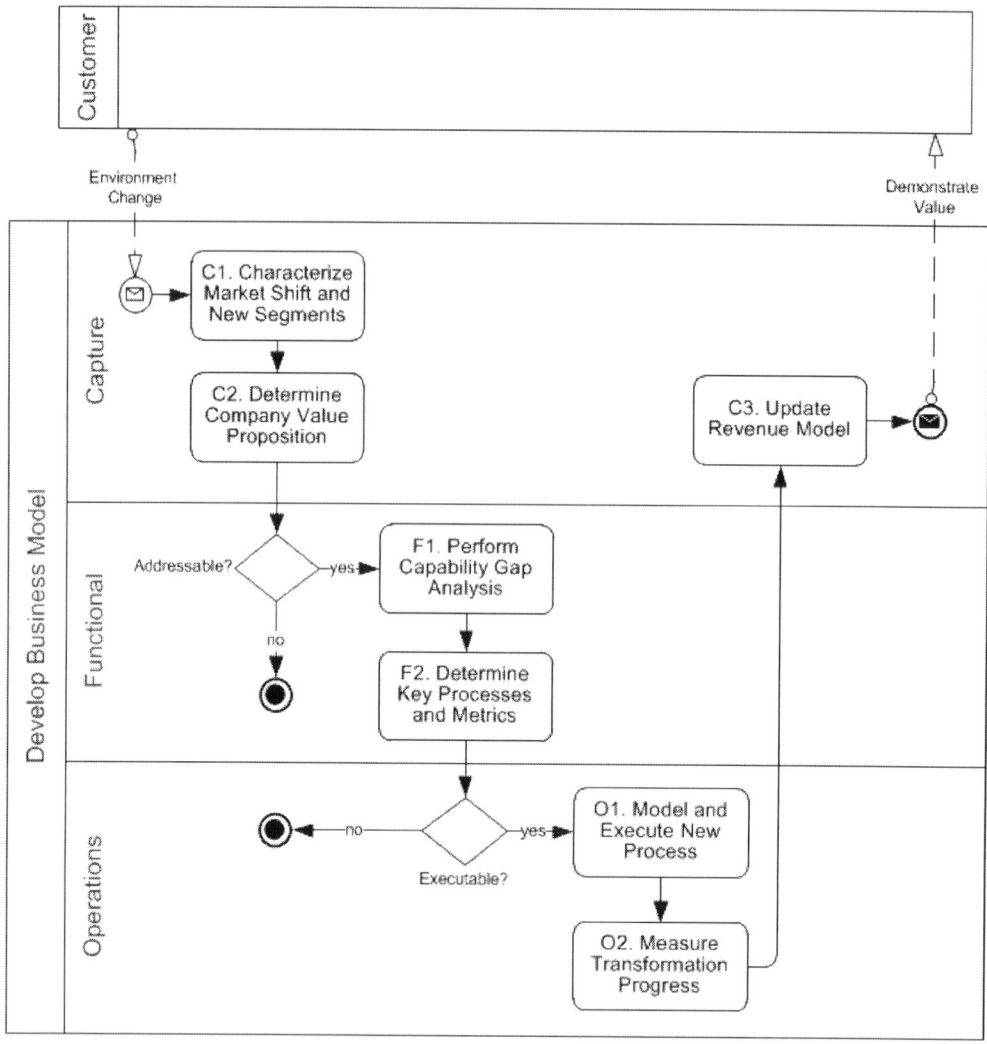

Figure 2. Develop Business Model Process

A solid capability mapping exercise then provides the basis for focusing the specific roles, key processes and key performance indicators that are truly critical to succeeding in the new environment, instead of making the common mistake of attempting to bite off too many change initiatives. A best practice is to look for the 2-3 key processes at the most that are at the heart of the change, with no more than 2-4 key roles for each that are central to executing that change.

Now the capture and functional leaders need to work with operations to assess whether the company is capable of executing the new processes and standing up the new (or evolved) roles within the timeframe required by the market. Since those responsible for operating the company day-to-day must buy in to the key functions that are impacted, they should be in the decision and own (O1) the more detailed Level 2 processes that result from this whole assessment. They are also then responsible for measuring and reporting the progress at executing the new business model (O2).

Finally, we arrive back at the purpose of the business model transformation, which is how to make revenue (C3). The capture organization now has a basis to justify how much of the segment is going to be addressable by the company based on what all stakeholders agree as the plan to execute on the new model. That new revenue model, compared to the case where there is no business change in response to the market, can now be tested by delivering a pilot for the new value proposition to the customer.

4. EXAMPLE OF FORMING THE TRANSFORMATIONAL CROSS-FUNCTIONAL MODEL

As a second example, we can look at the type of Level 2 process resulting from activities F1 and F2 in the generation of the total business model. The essence of the business transformation required to succeed in the new customer segment can be modeled in a new process, focused on the key roles that must do something different and then what is performed and measured differently rather than small tweaks to every standard process in the company. Before that model is built, however, we need to know which 2-3 processes are the key ones. Studying the Aerospace and Defense sector as described in a related article in the BPMN 2.0 Handbook[4], we find the APQC framework includes a capability map for that sector. This allows a company in this sector to benchmark against a general set of relevant business capabilities to study gaps, rather than limit the analysis by using one's own org chart.

Task F1 includes drawing together a group of experienced personnel from the functions most impacted by the market change, forming a team understanding of the new segment and value proposition, then performing a gap analysis on the business capabilities measured by achievement of the new market. With this information, a common mistake is to create initiatives (process improvements) for every one of those critical capability gaps. The best practice is instead to study the critical gaps as a group, then start defining the 2-3 integrated processes that weave through several capability gaps and, as a result, also integrate across multiple business functions. The more effective and higher impact answer is the harder one to implement, which is forming a customer-focused integrated process that focused across organizational barriers to focus on delivering the value proposition, rather than focusing on a politically correct model adhering to current organizations and charters.

With the combination of customer segment, value proposition, capability gaps and a rough definition of a small number of integrated processes, we have an excellent basis for forming the detailed models showing explicitly how to operate differently and measure progress towards the new or evolved market. Notice this also addresses an old problem of how to measure success at a new segment when the revenues may not be realized for years; the measured progress on the new integrated business process (for just the 2-3 key ones that move really move the dials) is the measure of success for the initial years of people and funding investment. The details of a new integrated business process will be competition sensitive to a specific company, but the essence is about forming a model that coordinates roles (or creates new ones if absolutely necessary), interacts with the customer in a way and at a time that creates value for them, and clearly describes the changes to the

---

[4] Business Process Integration in a Defense Product-focused Company, BPMN 2.0 Handbook 2nd Edition, Future Strategies Inc.

standard order of practice. Since senior leadership must be briefed on and sponsor execution of the big changes, note that the full business process model should be matched with a simpler briefing version that relays the key impacts and benefits (such as a table of roles, tasks and metrics).

5. SUMMARY

Business Process Modeling as a discipline applies at a couple levels in forming a comprehensive market-driven business model. Development of the total model is a process that requires key roles, tasks and metrics. There is also a strong connection that can be made between more detailed business processes focused on strategic levels of functional integration and the concrete execution of a new business model. Process modeling lives in the intersection of technical (product-focused) domains and financial domains achieved through a good business model.

About the Author

J. BRYAN LAIL

Business Architect Fellow, Raytheon, USA

J. Bryan Lail is a Business Architect Fellow at the Raytheon Company, leading the business modeling effort for a major new market segment. The pilot effort includes rigorous methods for building across the stages of the business model canvas and results driving business process integration across organizational functions. Previously he spent three years as the Chief IT Architect and nine years in engineering leading the application of netcentric technologies to tactical systems, including the formation of the Tactical Services Community of Interest for the U.S. Department of Defense. Earlier professional experience included ten years working for the U.S. Navy as a scientist at the Naval Air Warfare Center at China Lake. Bryan is a Raytheon Certified Architect, a program accredited by The Open Group to include Master Certified IT Architect status. He holds two patents in information management for tactical systems and multiple Excellence Awards from Raytheon. He holds an M.S. in Physics.

BPM Change Management: Some Considerations

Jaisundar Venkat, Wipro

As Business Process Management (BPM) becomes more mainstream and its adoption increases, the list of key factors that typically contribute to its failure as well as success are becoming more and more apparent.

Interestingly, one factor common in both lists is Change Management. The reason that it figures in both lists is because, not only can poorly addressed change issues lead to failure, but a well-managed change plan can actually *escalate* the degree of success from BPM. Change issues threaten and impact BPM implementation success much more than we would care to admit. Challenges along the BPM life-cycle are real and the nature of change can be complex. Being essentially about 'process change' automatically makes BPM initiatives very susceptible to challenges that come from causing a sort of disruption to people and their working styles. Many BPM initiatives also tend to span across multiple departments and functional teams making change even more challenging.

This paper discusses how a well-thought out Change Program can complement a BPM initiative and actually help in fostering collaboration and teamwork required along the stages of the BPM lifecycle by introducing a more positive influence on the outcome. Fundamentally though, there are some very crucial elements or *hotspots* if you would like to call it, that need to be appropriately addressed to ensure the Change Management program supports BPM optimally.

1. CHANGE MANAGEMENT FOR BPM PROGRAMS IS UNIQUE.

Change issues are not new to IT initiatives. Many enterprise IT initiatives—an enterprise ERP implementation for example, can have severe change implications. Several organizations support such large scale IT initiatives with aggressive change management programs running in parallel because these initiatives typically impact a large end-user base and therefore carefully planned and targeted change enablement programs become key to help ensure buy-in, adoption, and, more fundamentally, help manage the rather radical impacts such initiatives tend to have on the day-to-day work of end-users.

Change Management in BPM involves all this but its scope does not end there—the very nature of change itself in a BPM initiative runs wider and deeper—it is not just about change in the proverbial 'run-time'. BPM brings in a sort of disruption to the very approach that is taken towards an IT initiative—right from the time the project or program objectives are being discussed and in many cases, much earlier than even the selection of a BPM tool.

This big difference stems really from the fact that BPM is fundamentally a management concept first and then a technology. There are many case studies of BPM initiatives that have achieved sub-optimal benefits or even failed because this important difference was overlooked. This aspect is certainly being better understood today, but not sufficiently enough—it is really in the inadequate appreciation of this fact that many firms adopting BPM tend to have underwhelming benefits from implementing a BPM suite.

So essentially, when it comes to BPM, we are talking about managing two different dimensions of change implications:

1. Managing Change demanded by adopting BPM as a concept
2. Managing conventional Change issues as those seen in any medium to large scale IT initiatives

The change program to support BPM initiatives needs to clearly factor this in order to ensure optimal success. A BPM initiative supported by a change plan can still fail if it doesn't address either of these dimensions appropriately.

The two dimensions of change also address two different sets of employee roles that are part of a BPM implementation. These are

- The Core Team
- End users

The Core Team is focused on the strategic outcomes of the project and is firmly focused on exploiting BPM benefits most relevant to the organization. These outcomes are predominantly business outcomes, but it can also include IT outcomes. The team is comprised of carefully picked IT and business stakeholders who are committed to the Business Process Management vision that is driving the overall initiative. This team is concerned with establishing BPM the concept and so is primarily involved in all key initial strategic activities of a BPM program, for example

- Business benefits definition, BPM tool selection
- Process prioritization
- Process roadmap creation
- Process discovery
- Process optimization, modelling & design

The role of the Core Team is extremely important to ensure true success of a BPM implementation. Majority of the change activities involved in *Adopting BPM as a Concept* are predominantly directed at this team.

2. Adopting BPM as a Concept

As the US went into recession towards the end of the last decade, organizations went into a sort of frenzy to cut costs and improve efficiency. As a result IT budgets were slashed—strategic IT decisions were put on hold and we also saw reversals of budgets already approved. There was great apprehension about the future as fists clenched firmly around the dollar. However, one very interesting trend emerged. Interest in Business Process Management increased; many firms began to see BPM as a strategic tool that could allow them to reduce costs effectively and improve efficiency. They were in fact willing to invest in BPM even while they were cutting back on other IT initiatives.

Some of the industries hit most by recession actually invested more in BPM, the overall market spending on BPM increased and towards the end of the decade, many BPM vendors began announcing record growth quarter after quarter.

Return on Investments in BPM has been very tempting to organizations with value being delivered across several CXO priorities—costs, efficiency, control, effectiveness, agility and so on. Going by published success stories, BPM projects show dramatic returns that more than substantiate the investments made on licenses and implementation costs and in timelines much smaller than we have hitherto seen from conventional IT projects.

At the core of such a tempting promise of reducing cost, improving competitiveness and increasing profits, is a crucial fact that many firms overlook; that none of those benefits can be taken for granted. BPM really is no silver bullet by itself. The real power to unlock all those opportunities does not end with a decision to invest in BPM.

The effectiveness of the outcome is really the result of effective team-work and collaboration between business and IT, well thought out execution involving a convergence of carefully crafted and well-informed project scoping, model-driven BPM methods, technologies and guidelines. The ownership to drive these goes to the Core Team.

This is really the area where a BPM Change management program can be most influential—not in the execution *per se*—but in facilitating the collaboration, the mind-set shift and the knowledge that is required to help the Core Team keep business outcomes and the promise of BPM benefits always in sight from the time the first BPM project is being discussed.

This foundation is incredibly crucial for business and IT stakeholders to step out of years of thinking about and defining requirements in an certain way; involving screen flows, and functional-silo thinking, for example; and instead acquire a process mindset, which will enable them to effectively articulate current gaps and shortcomings and state requirements in the context of what and how BPM can really improve their process and its outcomes.

Much of the BPM Change Management focus would need to be invested here as the maximum influence on the outcomes and the benefits from BPM is from program/project objective-setting, process rationalization and optimization, and target process design.

3. IDENTIFYING CHANGE CHAMPIONS

The avatar that Change issues might take in any enterprise initiative is unique to each organization and this is no different with BPM. Issues could be a manifestation of one or more factors—those that may not be directly related to BPM or even business or IT. Organization politics can be a big source of friction, but not all issues will be evil, negative or willful. They could simply stem from a lack of appreciation, or awareness of the nature of change or its benefits.

So an important ingredient that goes into the creation of a Change Management program is deep insight into organization culture, people, and a sense of understanding of cause and effect—all coming from a great position of strength—that of first-hand experience gained from being part of the organization.

Systems Integrators and implementation partners may have great experience and track-record of successes in running a change management program, but it is important to nominate a change champion from within—someone who understands the pulse of your organization and can be an influential, driving agent of that program. At the same time it is important to exploit the fresh, detached perspective that an SI, external consultant or an implementation partner can bring in.

A good team of change champions will ideally be a combination of the two. The size of the team need not be big—a good approach would be to start small and grow as the program moves forward.

This team will need to additionally understand BPM themselves—both as the concept and as the technology to chart out the details of the Change Program.

The change champions will be key catalysts in identifying and engaging with various other teams and forging strong collaborative partnerships among them and guiding them along a common vision. One such crucial partnership that needs to be established is the Business-IT collaboration. The BPM way calls for a shift in the roles and responsibilities in the Business-IT equation. BPM expects higher influence and more active participation from business in the process design and conception phase—something not naturally a part of conventional projects.

The Change Champions will also identify target audience for the change program itself - the audience that will make up the Core Team and the End Users.

4. CHANGE IS HARD—COMMUNICATION IS KEY

Organizational change in any form evokes much the same feeling you have when you are on a diving board looking down at the cold water below. Although you know it will all be fine in under 20 seconds after you've left the board, before you take that leap though, it does feel like you are about to confront a most dreadful event.

That hesitation, that sense of apprehension, is not really about diving or about swimming. It is about those few moments when things can get incredibly jarring as your body splashes through that cold water. It shakes you up for a few moments.

Much the same way, employees really do not have a fundamental disagreement to the reasons why they need that 'change' that is being introduced—that new software, those process changes, those revised roles and responsibilities, those new user interfaces. It may not be any of those at all.

It may really be that 'jarring' effect of stepping out of one comfort zone into a new zone that they need to warm up to all over again.

Employees—especially End Users, need to feel a sense of motivation to step out their comfort zones, off their styles of working and, rather than remaining passive observers of the changes BPM will bring in, need to be engaged consistently through-out the program. They need to see and relate to the big picture behind the changes that are being introduced and they need to feel included and be a part of. Communication therefore is key, although it is only the beginning.

The Core Team, along with Change Champions, needs to address these in partnership with HR where possible. This could involve a range of innovative engagement activities that could include soliciting suggestions, providing updates, and so on. Further, employee effort on BPM can be rewarded too, for example, it can be tied to annual appraisals.

Not every BPM initiative calls for large Change Management support though. The nature and size of impacted processes and people involved should ideally decide the scale of change management support.

5. Sell the Idea of BPM Internally

This is one of the most important factors that will decide the degree of commitment and motivation carried by Employees, including those in the Core Team as well as the Change Champions. Employees need to appreciate the big picture and get the context and drivers behind the initiative. A vague idea of what change to expect and the meaning of that change will not do enough to drive motivation with momentum enough to last the whole program. Employees need to understand how the outcomes break down to tangible benefits for the organization, for their department, for people in their teams and eventually to themselves.

One other important factor that have a very positive influence on dealing with BPM Change is not just top management involvement, but equally, their buy-in. Support of the CEO and the commitment and continued involvement of senior management, easily trickles down as influencers and can have significantly positive impact.

All said and done, Change Management success hinges on one very important perspective; when everyone involved truly believes that they are a valuable, important and influential contributors to the initiative and that the BPM initiative and the 'change' caused by it can improve their own daily work life, and can indeed help them work smarter, easier and better.

About the author

Jaisundar Venkat is a process professional specialized in BPM and leads the BPM consulting practice at Wipro Technologies Ltd. Jaisundar's areas of interest include Business Process Management, Customer Relationship Management, SFA, Sales Performance Optimization, Corporate Performance Management and general IT industry developments and trends. He writes online and blogs on these topics at http://www.bouncingthoughts.com/

Innovation in Health Care: Insight from the First Federal Health Care Center

Paul Lam, Captain James A. Lovell Federal Health Care Center and Linus Chow, Oracle

Combine enormously complex data integration with the most sensitive, yet essential, case management processes run by two of the largest organizations in the world, and you have one of the biggest challenges facing the United States. Improving health care efficiency and effectiveness, while cutting costs, is the only way to solve the U.S. health care crisis. The pain can be especially acute for the U.S. Armed Forces, where both Veterans Affairs (VA) and the Department of Defense (DOD) are looking for ways to streamline operations to provide higher quality care while cutting inefficiencies in the system.

The National Defense Authorization Act (NDAA) for Fiscal Year 2010 authorized the Departments of Veterans Affairs (VA) and Defense (DOD) to establish a five-year demonstration project to integrate VA and DOD medical care into a first-of-its-kind Federal Health Care Center (FHCC) in North Chicago, Illinois. The Lovell FHCC was established on Oct. 1, 2010. This first of its kind FHCC incorporates facilities, services and resources from the North Chicago VA Medical Center (VAMC) and the Naval Health Clinic Great Lakes (NHCGL). The combined mission of the health care center means active duty military, their family members, military retirees and veterans are all cared for at the facility. The health care center ensures that nearly 40,000 Navy recruits who transition through Naval Station Great Lakes each year are medically ready and Lovell FHCC cares for nearly 67,000 eligible military and retiree beneficiaries each year.

Pioneering a dramatic change in People, Process, and Technology, the FHCC is the first true integration of DOD and VA facilities, a single chain of command, integrating staff, business process and practices to serve active duty personnel, their beneficiaries, and veterans at the same facility. And new technologies to run these processes and integrate VA and DOD systems had to be put in place.

FHCC is not business as usual. Not only did the organizational command have to change, but Business Process Re-engineering occurred making Health Care Providers develop new workflows for treating patients. Administrative support processes had to analyzed improved, and integrated.

Key to its success was the formulation of the FHCC standard Health Record that allows the sharing of information between the VA and DOD. This single, jointly created common health record for all DOD and VA patients at the FHCC proved that it is possible to build a joint health record system that could allow collaboration between multiple health entities.

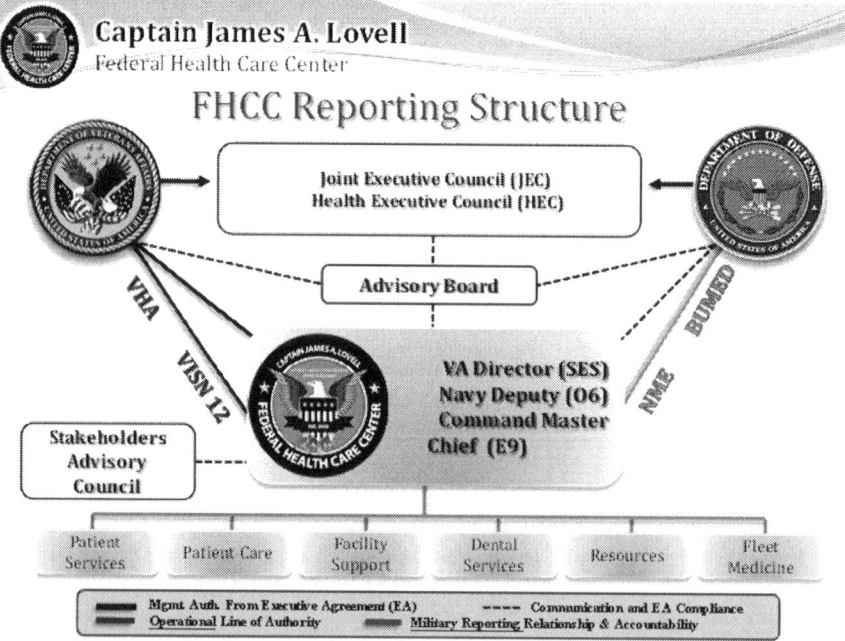

Figure 1: Jointly staffed and integrated chain-of-command.

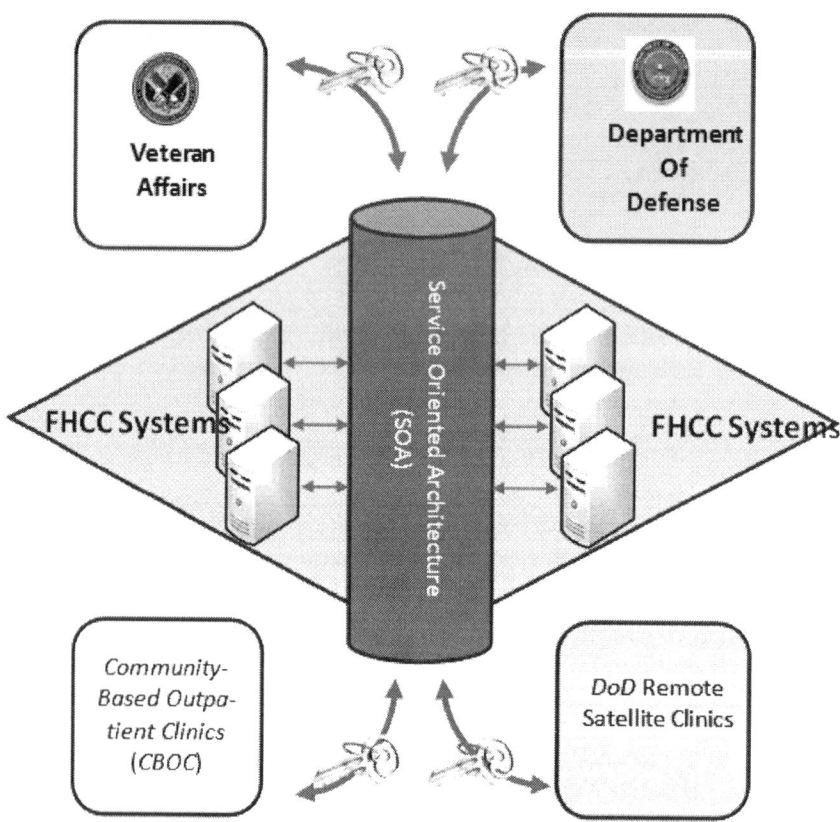

Figure 2: High-Level Architecture for sharing of Health Information

This common Health Record initiative, aiming to eliminate gaps and expand information sharing between the two systems used by the VA and DOD, is being pioneered at Lovell FHCC.

"This center is the first of a kind, a partnership between our two departments," Secretary of Defense Leon Panetta said on a visit to Lovell FHCC. "This really is a unique demonstration of effort to try to bring together the DOD and VA systems. It brings all medical care together into a fully-integrated facility that serves recruits, service members, military dependents, retirees and veterans. This facility is helping us chart the course for the future."

The successes and lessons learned at Lovell FHCC provide an opportunity to replicate an integrated health care system for our nation's service members and dependents with potential incremental model to follow. Additionally, leadership by the DOD and VA could uncover best practices in people, processes, and technology useable for the rest of the health care ecosystem, both public and private.

References:

http://www.lovell.fhcc.va.gov/http://www.lovell.fhcc.va.gov/features/Panetta_Sh inseki_announce_iEHR_milestones.asp

http://www.gao.gov/assets/330/321187.pdf

About the Authors

Paul Lam is the Chief Information Officer at the Captain James A. Lovell Federal Health Care Center, the nation's first integrated medical facility between the Department of Veterans Affairs (VA) and Department of Defense (DOD). Mr. Lam has 25 years of experience in Information Technology, including 18 years with the VA and 7 years in the private sector designing enterprise architecture and solutions for two major property and casualty insurance companies. He received his Master of Science in Business Administration degree with concentration in Information Systems from the Roosevelt University in Chicago, Illinois.

Linus Chow is the Principal BPM Champion (Public Sector North America) for Oracle Corporation. He has over 20 years of leadership and management experience in information technology with over 15 years in workflow, BPM, and SOA. He has played crucial roles in expanding the growth of BPM and SOA adoption first in the US and then internationally from Australia to Switzerland. Currently, Linus leads the adoption of BPM/SOA and E2.0 solutions for Public Sector customers in North America. He has helped organizations win many industry awards for BPM/SOA and E2.0 implementations. He is a published author and an active speaker on the Best Practices of BPM/SOA and E2.0. A decorated former US Army Officer, Linus has an MBA, a MS in Management Information Systems, and BS in Mathematics; and is a Certified BPM Professional.

Section 2

Europe

Avio SpA, Italy

Silver Award:Nominated by EKA Srl, Italy

1. EXECUTIVE SUMMARY / ABSTRACT

Avio is a world-wide leader in the aerospace industry. Based in Italy, Avio is a leading supplier of engine modules and components and it also operates in aircraft engines repair and overhaul with its Avioservice Division. In 2009, Avioservice Division started a new initiative for streamlining its Maintenance, Repair and Overhaul (MR&O) process of military engines in order to be able to sustain the new business and market conditions. The main objective of this initiative was to improve the performance of the process in meeting contractual SLAs in a new business environment where the repair and overhaul of several engines types, coming from completely new customers, is regulated by very different and very specific contractual agreements.

As a result of the initiative, a system has been developed to govern the workflow of each engine in its company's "door-to-door" path and to collect actual performance measurements of the overall process which spans several organizational units.

2. OVERVIEW

Avio is the leader in the development of subsystems and components, mainly turbines and gearboxes, for military and civil aircraft engines. The technological competences acquired in the sector make the company an accredited and reliable partner for the major OEMs (Original Equipment Manufacturing), such as General Electric, Honeywell, Pratt & Whitney and Rolls-Royce. The company participates with "design responsibility" to the main national and European programs, as the EJ200 for European Eurofighter-Typhoon, and represents an excellence in the propulsive systems with solid and liquid propellant, realizing 16 percent of Ariane 5 European launcher. Avio operates also in the MR&O of military engines with its Avioservice division. The division is located in the plant at Brindisi, in the South of Italy.

In the recent years, the core business of the Avioservice division has changed from a "single customer", the Italian air force, to a "many customers" business, up to about 30 customers distributed around the world and characterized by their own policies related to the management of MR&O activities and agreements.

In this new scenario, the company was forced to reorganize their way of doing the business in order to improve the quality of its MR&O services and meet customer expectations. Several issues, mainly caused by a lack of coordination between functional units, were threatening the overall management of MR&O activities in a process where most of the division's units take part. These process coordination issues increased the risk of late and poor quality delivery of engines.

With the sponsorship of top management, a BPM project was undertaken in order to address the problems Avioservice was facing.

As a result of the project, a new organization was conceived and a new information system was developed to support the process. The new MR&O system allowed for:

- the monitoring and control of the end-to-end MR&O process and,

- the integration of functional information systems.

The new process organization improved the control on the performance of the repair and overhaul activities and yielded a considerable reduction of MR&O cycle time. The BPM project team has been institutionalized to support the continuous improvement of the process and its sub-processes.

3. BUSINESS CONTEXT

The business of Avioservice Division was characterized for several years by an exclusive relationship with a unique customer, the AMI – the Italian military air force. The whole MR&O process of AMI engines, included the reception of engines, was managed in collaboration between Avio and AMI, which still has a warehouse inside Avio plants in Brindisi, South of Italy, where the repair and overhaul service is provided.

With the progressive rationalization of the national government expenditures and the related cuts to military procurements and services, Avioservice was forced to increase the number of customers served and to attract firms from all over the world. This opening to international competition pushed the company:

- to improve the quality of its services, especially concerning the repair and overhaul lead time and the traceability of the engine flow;
- to manage directly the communication with the customer and provide visibility on its processes;
- to manage different types of contractual agreements.

The pressure for changing how the MR&O process was carried out by the entire division was confirmed by the issues Avioservice was facing in the overall management of activities. These issues were mainly caused by the lack of coordination among functional units in a process where most of the division's organizational units are involved. Military Programs Management, Product Quality, Logistics, Planning, Engineering, Technologies, Repair and Overhaul Workshop, and Test Laboratory units, each using their own information systems, were also lacking the management of shared information about customer orders.

Changes to the organizational structure of the division had already been made in order to centralize the management of information in a newly created unit bringing together the Engineering and Technology employees (E&TU) so as to empower their managers. This new organizational unit has been operating as a supervisor on the whole MR&O process as it is involved in the main activities and decisions.

It became evident to E&TU management, who was struggling trying to feed the process pipe, that Avio was required to remove functional silos and applications in order to operate a transparent management of the customer order and to gain a clear understanding of the work in progress in operational offices and production shops.

It was the strong sponsorship from the E&TU Manager, which was later embraced by Avio's top management, that allowed the BPM initiative to be able to sustain the new competitive scenario.

Hence, taking advantage of the on-going collaboration in BPM industrial research projects with the University of Salento that supported the initiative, a major redesign of the MR&O process concerning both organizational and technological aspects was undertaken to improve the overall management of the division core process.

4. THE KEY INNOVATIONS

4.2 Business

The relationship between the Avioservice division and its customers is changing a lot, thanks to the results of the BPM project, and the reliability of the company is increasing from the customer's point of view.

All the work performed on the engine could now be made publicly visible to the customer at some points in the process, but, what's more important; the process audits are now more successful.

Some clients extended their requests and started to ask specific information about the conditions of the engine during several steps in the workflow (i.e. the pressure and humidity of the engine container during the entire storage phase, which could last months), while in the past the touch points with the company were very few, only at the approval of the order and at the final engine test.

Moreover the capability to provide reliable information about the division's productivity to the executive management has extremely improved.

4.3 Process

As of standard re-design practice, the BPM project started by analysing the As-Is situation of the process. During the As-Is analysis, three main activities was conducted in parallel by the BPM team:

- the analysis of the actual performance of the MR&O process;
- the analysis of quality procedures and instructions;
- interviews with managers and key people of the different business units aimed at discovering the real processes and at identifying the information flow, the supporting information systems, and the actual problems.

The BPM team was composed by a Six Sigma Black Belt, a business process analyst, the manager of the IT team. The team reported periodically to the ET&U manager about the project progresses and findings.

During the analyses, the BPMN standard and a free modelling tool were used to create high-level and detailed process maps. BPMN played an important role in the process discovery, especially during plenary sessions with the organizational units' managers when BPMN maps where displayed and discussed to understand the real workflow and to solve conflicts, bottlenecks, and misunderstandings.

A high-level process was depicted with BPMN and 22 more detailed maps of sub-processes, as shown in the figures below. These maps were developed by the BPM team after the interviews, reviewed with interviewees to receive feedbacks and approval, and discussed during plenary sessions.

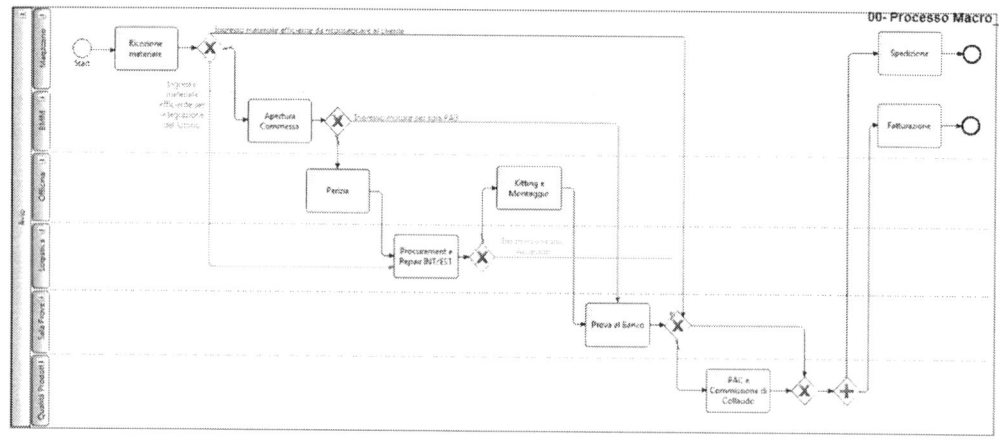

Figure 1 High-level MR&O As-Is process in Avio

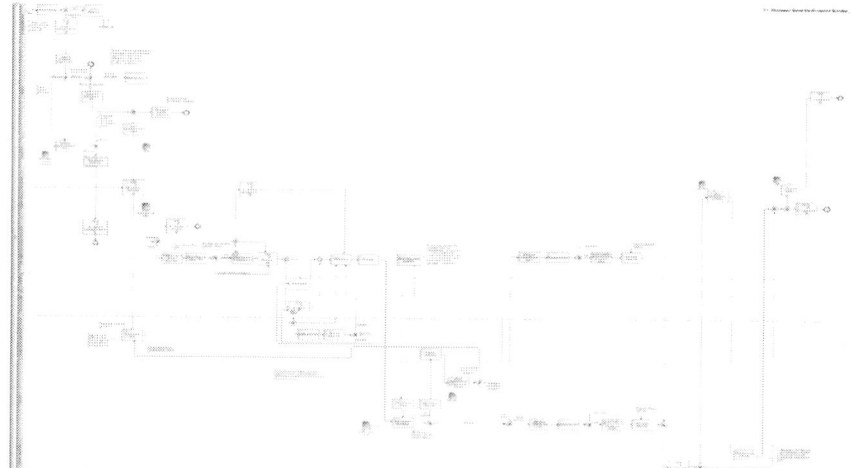

Figure 2 Resulting merge of detailed sub-processes

Five main phases of the MR&O process were identified for the three main types of products managed by the Avioservice division: whole engine, engine modules and accessories.

The key measure of success identified for this process was the cycle time KPI, therefore performance data from the available company's databases was gathered to measure the cycle time of every phase and the total cycle time. The 5 phases took into account the following sub-processes (see Figure 3):

- LT1 starts from the reception of the engine at the Logistics unit, includes the approval of the customer order together with the customer by the Military Program Management unit, the issuing of the engine work program to be sent by Engineering to the Repair and Overhaul Shop;
- LT2 registers the disassembly and the examination of engine conditions by the Repair and Overhaul Shop;
- LT3 encompasses procurement, repair and overhaul activities (performed internally and externally by suppliers of repairing services), assembly and tests in Avio's Test facilities; it involves the Planning, the Repair and Overhaul Shop, eventually Suppliers, and the Test Laboratory;
- LT5 registers the issue of the Quality Certificate by the Product Quality unit;

- LT8 includes billing and the start of shipment activities performed by AFC and Logistics.

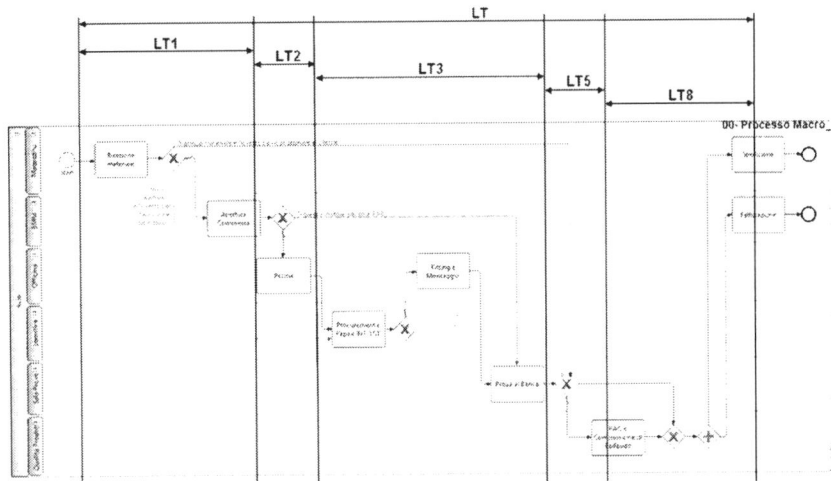

Figure 3 Main phases of the MR&O process

Avio has a 10 years experience in the use of Six Sigma. Every process improvement project is supported by the company's established Six Sigma procedures, methods and templates. Thus, the As-Is analysis was carried out using Process Capability, Pareto and others analyses (see figure below), in order to identify major defects affecting the lead time of the MR&O process and their causes.

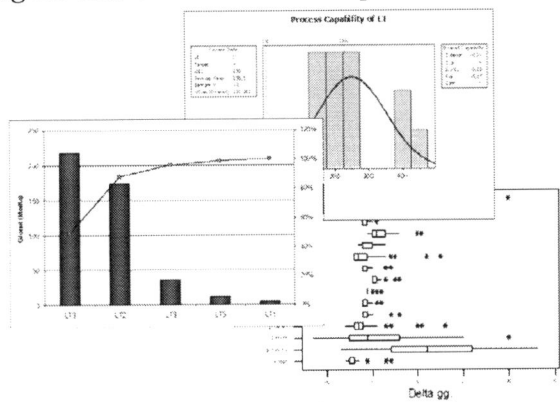

Figure 4 Six Sigma analysis of the MR&O process

BPMN maps, Six Sigma methods, the study of quality procedures, and interviews allowed to discover different types of problems but the most critical issues was related to order information management and task ownerships.

In fact, there were difficulties in the gathering of data since the early stages of the project, because each organizational unit was managing its own database and they were not neither consistent nor complete:

- the Logistics and AFC units managed the order information on the company's ERP;
- the Military Programs Management had an Excel register where information about the order status were updated on a voluntary basis by program managers;

- the Engineering managed the engine work program in an Excel file to be sent to the Repair and Overhaul;
- the Repair and Overhaul Shop used a legacy software system, developed in-house several years ago on a COBOL platform, whose name is MOS, that managed the complete engine BOM and the related work orders;
- the Test Laboratory didn't use any information system.

Having a clear idea of the internal customer requirements and of the problems to be solved, the To-Be phase of the project started with a 2-level QFD to translate the Voice-Of-Customer into appropriate solutions.

A new design of the process was conceived, including:

- new activities concerning:
  - o the management of a unique Return Authorization Number (RAN), to track the customer order and its related child-orders along the process;
  - o the execution of a preliminary examination of the engine conditions before the approval of the customer order (the second task in the figure above);
- 2 Toll Gates to review the status of the order and to obtain agreement on important decisions between the division's organizational units (the blue-colored None events): one coming after the newly introduced preliminary examination (LT1 phase) and the other after the complete examination of the engine (LT2 phase);
- major changes to sub-processes aimed at bringing forward or delaying some of the activities, or at introducing new activities;
- a new information system to monitor and control the overall MR&O process and to integrate legacy and ERP systems.

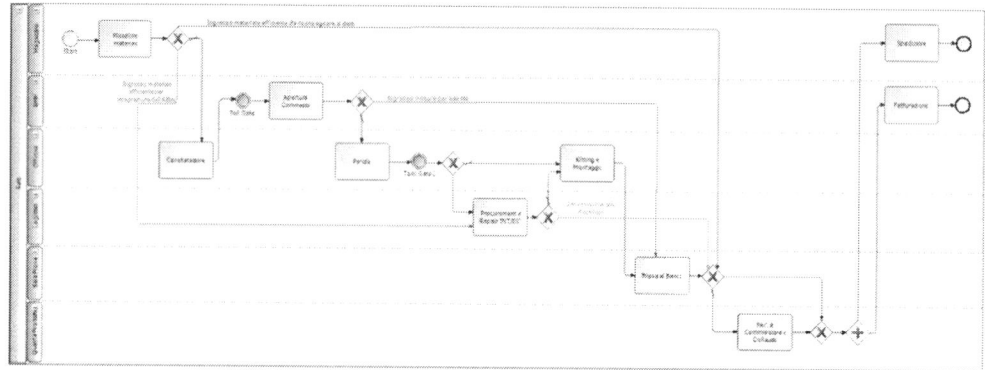

Figure 5 MR&O high-level To-Be process

The new MR&O information system has been conceived to store and track the RAN and the required order and engine information along the end-to-end MR&O process. An application integration with ERP and MOS systems, through direct interfaces and shared data folders respectively, has been developed in order to automatically retrieve information.

The user interface has been configured as a shared work list for all the users of the system (see Figure 6): the status of each customer order, that is the status of the engine identified by the RAN and of the related MR&O process instance, is visible to all users through 4 different work lists that are distinguished by tabs and represent the main positions of the engine: Reception, Storage, Repair and Overhaul, Shipping.

In every position, the engine has a different workflow which is specified by the underlying sub-processes. Every user of the system can add information about the engine/order according to its privileges. The privileges depend on the user role in the process and enable access to specific actions in the work list that allow updating the engine status. Some of the workflows are managed in the external MOS system and their logs are automatically transferred into the MR&O system for the sake of traceability.

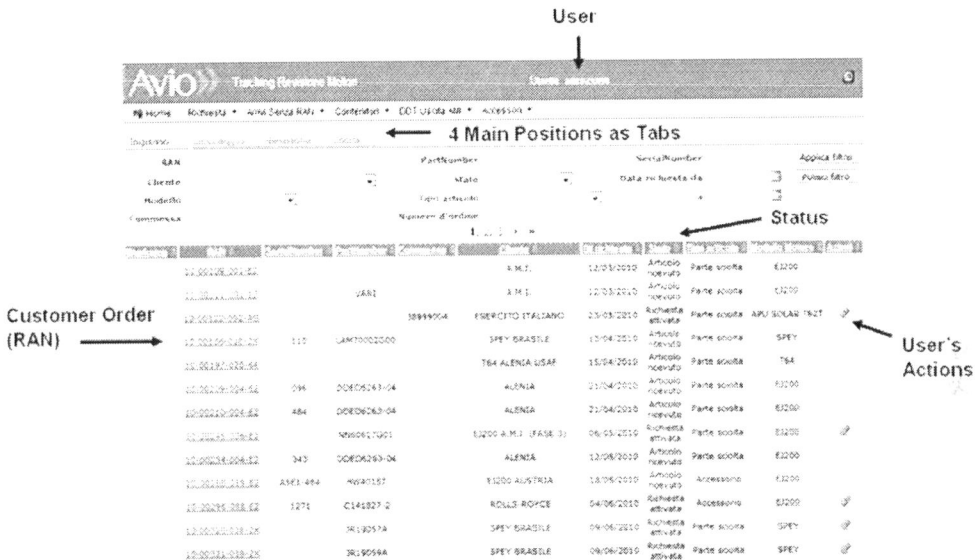

Figure 6 Shared Work list

While managing the engine/order workflows, the MR&O system can show the performance of the process in a back-office dashboard which is accessible only to process managers. This dashboard presents different types of aggregated analytics that span from the mean cycle time for engine type to the number of orders for a specific engine or type of product, and also include run charts, box plots and others.

The performance dashboard contains pre-defined reports requested by the Avioservice division and created during the implementation of the system. Reports can be easily added by using Eclipse BIRT which allows to aggregate data collected during workflows from the MR&O system's database.

The MR&O system plays a very important role as it allows the Military Programs Management to control the SLA for every order which is impacted by the cycle time. The SLAs are very specific and depend on the rules of the customer agreement. These rules determine the way the work stops are managed and how they impact the SLA.

Because the SLA is not managed by the system, the order has to be constantly monitored by the process managers.

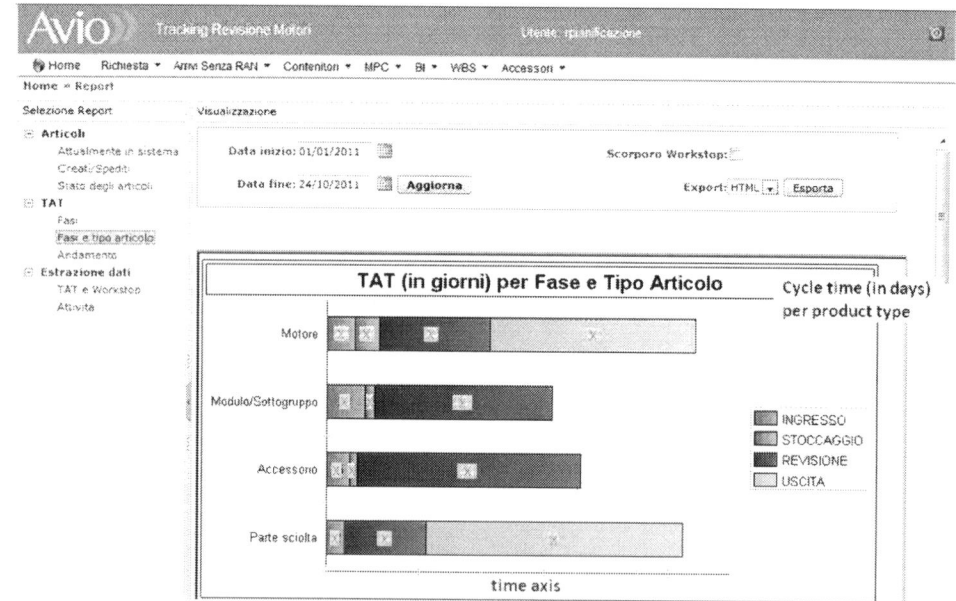

Figure 7 Example of process performance: MR&O cycle time

Push communications are also implemented into the system as e-mail notifications sent to specific users when the engine status is updated. These e-mails are used to notify the assignment of tasks to the proper roles according to pre-defined ownerships.

These notifications are very useful especially in recurring manual tasks that have deadlines, such as periodic controls that need to be performed on the engine when it is stored outdoors.

To sum up, the concrete benefits of the introduction of the MR&O information system in the Avioservice division are:

- Management of workflow and information updated in pull/push mode;
- Case management;
- Centralized work stop management;
- Quick centralized visualization of all articles, before and after repair and overhaul operations;
- Periodic controls management;
- Dashboard;
- Cycle time management.

4.4 Organization

The work of every division's employee has really changed. All the organizational units are required to enter their own information about customer orders in the common MR&O information system.

Military Programs Management and Planning can audit the work in progress for each engine; gaps in the process instances are self-evident. Task ownerships are visible through the system; they are enforced to the organizational units.

Accountabilities for delays are implied by the system's reports. The following is an example of report created by the system about the duration of each workflow activity.

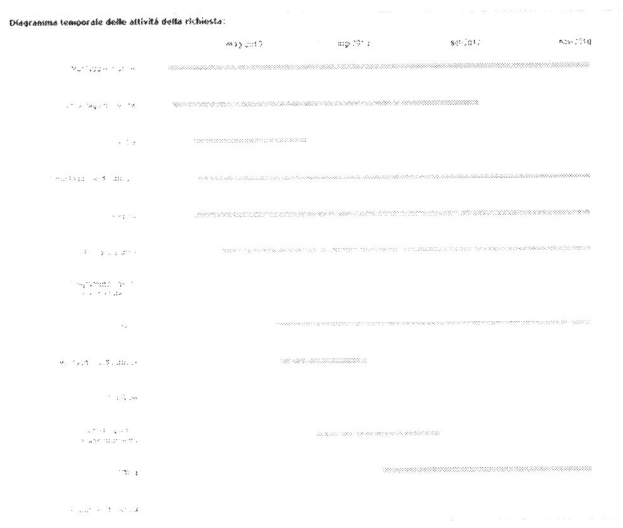

Diagramma temporale delle attività della richiesta:

Figure 8 Example of tracking of activities

The BPM project team has been institutionalized to support the continuous improvement of the process and its sub-processes, together with a Process Owner who is responsible for the supervision of the entire process.

The PO operates in support of the Engineering manager who sponsored the BPM initiative; he is in charge of:

- monitoring the major phases of the work,
- empowering users to use of the information system,
- collecting problems and users' feedbacks
- reporting major issues to the manager.

Depending on the type of issues, corrective actions for in-progress orders are put in place or specific process improvements projects are initiated by the BPM team. This team acts as a small BPM Center of Excellence managing a live BPM program.

5. HURDLES OVERCOME

Management

During the As-Is analysis phase of the project, difficulties were encountered to understand the real flow of the MR&O activities as the results of interviews with different people were contradicting. The discovery phase of the process required a huge effort in order to harmonize the information gathered from the different units; very often interviews had to be repeated after having discovered discrepancies in the resulting process. "Hot" plenary sessions with the organizational units' managers allowed to overcome these difficulties, by identifying real bottlenecks, and to reach a common, shared view of the process. During these sessions, BPMN maps were very useful to show the flow of activities, bring out problems and sum-up results of the discussion.

The introduction of the new MR&O system was carried out by iterations which implemented small parts of the process; this helped to sustain the change effort which was limited by the process scope of each iteration.

A new Process Owner was named to monitor and control the execution of the new process, to empower the process participants and to support the adoption of the system. The Process Owner, in collaboration with the IT team, acted also as a collector of feedback coming from the users during daily work. This allowed for the improvement of the MR&O system from the end user's perspective.

Business

No specific hurdles to overcome from the business perspective.

Organization Adoption

Every BPM initiative, like every change initiative, is rejected by the users for the same reason it is launched for: clear awareness of the process and its performances which are strictly linked to the performances of the single employees. The BPM in Avioservice was deemed to achieve transparency in the process from the management perspective by monitoring the workflows, controlling the assignment of tasks to the users and their performances.

Since the beginning, the Process Owner experienced problems with the "presence" of the system in the company. Users had to be incentivized to login into the system to insert the information about the work performed. In many manual steps the use of the system was perceived as additional but useless workload as it didn't add any assistance to the work to be performed. It was simply a confirmation that some work was done by the user, so that it was made visible "at the process or management level" together with the time elapsed and the name of the accountable person.

Besides the sponsorship of the top management, a sort of negotiation was started by the BPM team with each organizational unit to overcome these problems. The results were that additional functionalities for the specific units, in some cases not strictly related to the management of the MR&O process, were added to the MR&O system at each iteration in order to promote its use. Examples of these functionalities are: the management of DDT (delivery notes) for Logistics; the management of the engine work program for the Engineering and the Overhaul workshop; the implementation of the new WBS for the Military Programs Management.

6. BENEFITS

The project started at the beginning of 2009, about six months were dedicated to As-Is and To-Be analysis. As soon as the need for the new MR&O information system was evident, the specification of the software to be implemented was started. The release of the first iteration that allows the management of the Reception phase has been in the early months of 2010. The last major release which allows the management of the overall MR&O process was the end of 2010. The BPM initiative is still on-going to continuously improve the process and to add new features to the MR&O system.

The preliminary evidences of the benefits achieved with the BPM project started to be available in the middle of 2011, after "some tuning" made by the division on the use of the system.

Avio is reluctant to share the concrete data about the performance of the new process. The main reason is that data can vary a lot per order because they are strongly linked to the characteristics of the engine type and to the type of agreement with the customer. Moreover, the system itself can have a limited impact on the effective reduction of the process cycle time. The effectiveness of the MR&O process is mainly improved by implementing changes to the organizational and process structure, to the operational tools and to the capabilities and skills of the workforce.

However, thanks to the new MR&O system, reliable performance data of the entire process are now available and can be used to measure process improvement results, if compared to the old situation. Here are some qualitative measures of the benefits in the form of percentages.

6.1 Time Reductions

The *number of days* used to repair and overhaul an engine, that is the cycle time of the MR&O process, has been *reduced by 20 percent* approximately. The phases and total cycle time are constantly monitored and their performances are used to drive performance improvements in the sub-processes.

6.2 Productivity Improvements

After the re-design of the process, the productivity, measured as the number of engines that will be overhauled this year (2011), will increase up to the 10 percent approximately.

7. BEST PRACTICES, LEARNING POINTS AND PITFALLS

7.1 Best Practices and Learning Points

✓ *Use simplified BPMN models to represent processes and responsibilities:* the use of a simple process notation (we're not saying that the whole set of BPMN elements is simple), made of few and precise symbols, can facilitate the discussion about the process.

✓ *Validate BPMN models in joint meetings with all the organizational units involved in the process:* discussing the process under analysis together with organizational units involved in a process is a difficult but necessary task to avoid wrong process models and to prepare the deployment of the process.

✓ *Process improvement culture speeds up the BPM project implementation:* knowledge about process improvements techniques such as Six Sigma, TQM, etc. and tools facilitate the identification of issues and of proper solutions during a BPM project.

✓ *Involve end users of the system in the process analysis:* to reduce resistance to the introduction of a new system, that is developed to support a process, it is very useful to understand the needs of people performing daily work in the process.

✓ *Start small and iterate to release the complete process solution:* the release of small components of the software allows to reduce the impact on the current process and to gradually change how the work is done. Moreover valuable knowledge of the users' environment can be gathered during an iteration and it can be reused in the next.

✓ *Be prepared to give up something:* to attract users to adopt the system, it is sometimes necessary to change the initial plan and to consume project resources to add extra features for a specific key user.

✓ *Improvement drives improvement:* when a process is improved, linked processes (upward, downward, sub-processes) realize they are inefficient and are likely to be the subject of the next improvement effort in a sort of domino effect.

✓ *Get the Process Owner's hands dirty:* the process owner must abandon his crystal tower and walk through the process instances, interact with process participants, know the process information system, listen to users.

7.2 Pitfalls

✗ *Don't start without a sponsorship and a real commitment:* top management sponsorship has to be transferred to mid management that is in touch with the process. Changes imposed from the top rarely are successful.

✗ *The system is not the key to change the process outcomes:* if the process doesn't work, the new system won't introduce any improvement.

✗ *Don't rely on quality manuals:* very often processes described in the quality manuals and procedures are outdated.

8. COMPETITIVE ADVANTAGES

The Avioservice division improved the quality of its services by re-designing the MR&O process and by introducing the new information system. The system will be opened in the future to the customers worldwide to improve the communication about the customer order.

A BPM team has been permanently established to measure performances of the division's processes and to drive new improvements in order to increase the division's competitiveness.

9. TECHNOLOGY

The MR&O improvement was immediately recognized as a pure BPM project but, even if the project team had some experiences with open source BPM suites, a decision was taken by the BPM team to develop a custom workflow solution in order to manage the MR&O process. This choice was made for the following reasons:

- most of the activities in the process were manual;
- to manage the complexity of the MR&O process and its sub-processes, and the complexity of relationships among organizational units, only a state-based workflow approach was needed in order to be able to monitor and control the process;
- but most important, the system development effort had to be directed to the structuring of data about engines and orders that could replace the Excel databases and standardize the information coming from MOS and ERP systems.

Therefore the BPMN models were used as specification documents for the workflows along with the database and user interface design specifications.

Because of the huge organizational scope of the process, the project was developed iteratively. At each iteration a new phase or sub-process was further analyzed, and proper solutions was studied and implemented. The first three iterations was planned to fix main problems and they addressed the incremental implementation of Reception, Storage, Overhaul and Shipping.

After having put under control the overall process, the continuing BPM effort started to address parts of the process that were known as problems but had never been analyzed. In one of the latest iteration, a BPMS has been integrated into the system to improve the support to the process for approving customer orders. An old custom web application (WBS) has been replaced by a real BPMS to allow for a dynamic, easily changeable sub-process. In order to manage the approval process logic, only the workflow engine support from the BPMS has been integrated into the MR&O system; the user interface for WBS has been developed on the Shared Worklist already conceived for the whole MR&O process management. This process was modeled and implemented using Intalio BPMS 6.x, direct web services invocations to the Intalio workflow engine were developed to preserve the user from the need to access a new software system.

- The MR&O information system is a J2EE application that implements the monitoring and control of the process and the communication with several external systems. It is made up of the following components:
- the Web Application J2EE – Web front-end and the MR&O information and workflow management;
- the Intalio BPMS 6.x – Workflow engine for the execution of sub-process modelled in BPMN and stored in BPEL;
- the REALM – J2EE compliant service for the definition of roles and hierarchy;
- the Web Application DB – Database of the web-application;
- Eclipse Birt – an open-source business intelligence and reporting tool .

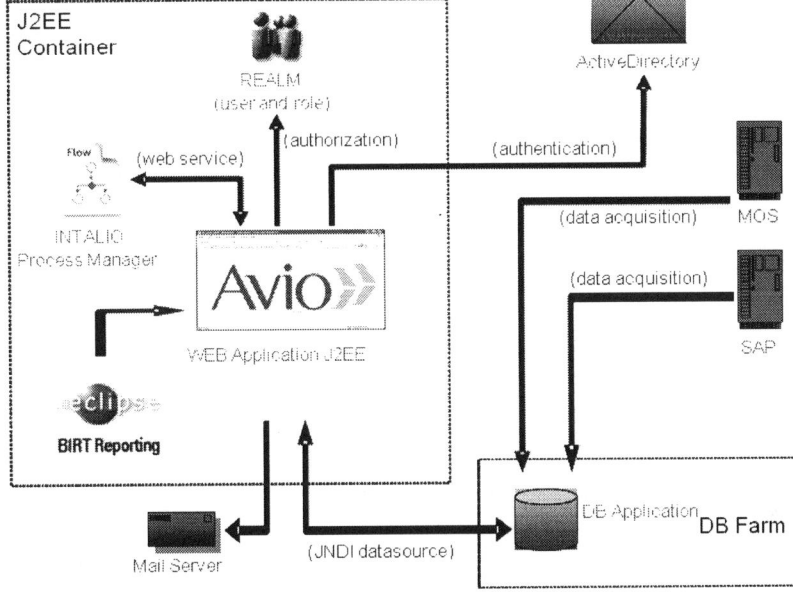

Figure 9 Technology Architecture

The external systems interacting with the MR&O system are the following:

- Active Directory – it provides the user authentication;
- Mail Server – it provides the push interactions with all the users involved in the process, at any level;
- MOS – it contains the information about work order for the Repair and Overhaul shop. MOS is a COBOL application. The communication between MOS and the J2EE application requires a shared file repository used in batch operations.
- SAP R/3 – it is the ERP system used in some steps of the process.

10. THE TECHNOLOGY AND SERVICE PROVIDERS

EKA Srl

EKA mission is to provide manufacturing companies with innovative services and ICT solutions aimed at improving the quality of products while reducing costs. EKA was born from the collaboration of the University of Salento with several industrial partners in PLM and BPM research activities. The company is able to help its customers at improving their development processes along the whole product lifecycle with its experience on several PLM systems and in process management methodologies that allows supporting operational units in the usage of ICT solutions and to design and implement new solutions.

(Web Site: www.eka-systems.com)

Center for Business Innovation @ University of Salento

Centro Cultura Innovativa d'Impresa - CCII (Center for Business Innovation) is a Department of the Engineering Faculty at the University of Salento. The CCII scientific and technological research activities focus on enabling Digital Innovation and its impact on processes and organizational configurations of firms, industrial clusters and institutions. The main strategic research areas concern: New Product Development in Aerospace, Product Lifecycle Management, Knowledge and Business Process Management.

(Web Site: http://emi.unisalento.it/)

HanseMerkur Insurance Group, Germany

Gold Award: Nominated by Bosch Software

1. Executive Summary / Abstract

The objective of the project was to implement a process-oriented architecture including the standardization and improvement of user interface ergonomics. The goal was to raise the degree of automation in claims processing to absorb an annual increase in gross revenue by 10-15 percent with an equal increase in claims, as well as to relieve clerks of simple routine tasks.

The annual increase in gross revenue could be absorbed by automated claims processes, which meant that the number of experts needed for processing was almost stable. This is an equivalent of € 0.75 million in cost savings per year and rising. In addition, the implementation of a rules engine for regulatory rules resulted in an increase of one percent in claims rejection or over € 1.65 million per year and growing. Claims processing time could be reduced from an average two weeks in the past to a few hours. The new automated process frees claims experts from routine tasks and lets them work on unclear or complex cases. On the other hand, simple tasks as obtaining missing data or correcting errors can now easily be diverted to less qualified personnel.

2. Overview

The German HanseMerkur Insurance Group, based in Hamburg, offers a wide range of insurance products, e. g. health and life insurance, car insurance, property insurance etc. The independent company is also the second largest travel insurer in Germany and the second oldest mutual health insurance company in Germany (established in 1875). Over the last decade HanseMerkur has more than doubled its total premium income and tripled the gross premium written in mutual health insurance. This had serious impact on their backend processes as well as the technical infrastructure.

The "KOMPASS" project to introduce automated claims processing in supplementary health insurance is a first step in implementing a new architecture concept.

Currently mainframe computers and sparsely standardized applications (known as contract management systems) dominate insurance companies' IT landscapes – and the HanseMerkur insurance company is no exception. The expectation from introducing a BPM platform to control all business processes was an increase in software development efficiency as well as more flexibility regarding business application modifications. A business rules management system (BRMS) complements the process management platform, thus constituting an important part of concept.

A vital element during the initiation phase of the project has been the proof of concept to the members of the board in order for them to approve of the necessary budget. Besides the corporate management, the insurance clerks affected by the change and the workers council also had to be very closely involved in the planning.

One of the enhancements the project provided was to enable the operating department to define business rules for process control in a graphical way themselves, so that they could be automatically applied to process execution afterwards.

Besides introducing a complete new architecture (SOA and process-orientation), the project organization was also changed completely as SCRUM was introduced. Furthermore, a complete development paradigm was created, covering all stages from functional analysis through two-step process modeling, object modeling and final implementation in an iterative way.

At present, around 25 percent of all claims in health insurance are processed fully automatically without user interaction. Of the remaining batches, around 60 percent are preprocessed and need no further inspection. This enables HanseMerkur to handle its growth in portfolio without adding personnel.

The technical platform created together with the new development paradigm is now used in almost every new project at HanseMerkur.

3. BUSINESS CONTEXT

Claims processing in private health care used to be a highly manual process. The customer sent his or her claim on paper to the insurance company via standard mail. This document was then passed through different departments within the insurance company, until finally a letter was sent and the money transferred.

Each step in this process was individual in that the experts had to decide which amount could be refunded and which had to be refused, which meant that the process was very expensive in terms of human resources. Turn-around time for this process was at least 14 days.

The motivation for this project sprang from the huge growth HanseMerkur was experiencing. With attractive products and clever marketing, new products could successfully be placed in the market thus considerably increasing the customer and contract portfolio. The aim was to handle the additional claims settlement processes with the existing work force at even higher quality. This required automation of as many process steps as possible, such as verifications against the portfolio management system to ensure coverage.

4. THE KEY INNOVATIONS

4.2 Business

First of all, the impact of the project on the customer was transparent, i.e. the customer did not experience any changes in the claims process. With the improvements made possible by the new architecture however, the changes are vast.

Turnaround time for claims processing was reduced from around 2 weeks in the past to a possible 1 day today and may even be reduced further in the future (see 6.2).

Furthermore, the new architecture enabled HanseMerkur to introduce new process steps such as online retrieval of claims data (see 4.3), thus minimizing errors, additional data input channels such as mobile devices, uniform settlements due to the introduction of business rule-based services for fee regulations and, soon to come, provision of tracking information for the claims process.

4.3 Process

The claims process used to be a highly manual process. The following picture provides an overview of this process.

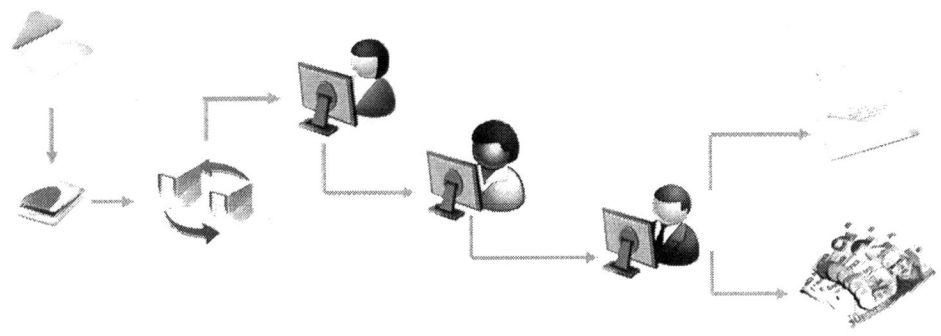

A customer usually collects doctor's bills and prescriptions for some time, and then sends them to the insurance company by mail. Here the data is either entered manually or scanned, and runs through character recognition software with optional manual post-processing of errors. Afterwards, the document is processed by several experts working on different aspects, checking different regulations or cases within a claims system until finally a settlement letter is sent to the customer and a payment is authorized. No documentation existed for this process.

To develop an automated process from this starting point required several changes in the way software is developed. One major change is that processes are now modeled within the department itself. As the first step in achieving this, the whole business had to be segmented into functional domains. Within these functional domains there are domain services, on which basis business services are created. These business services comprise the building blocks from which the processes are made. See below for a model of domains, services and processes.

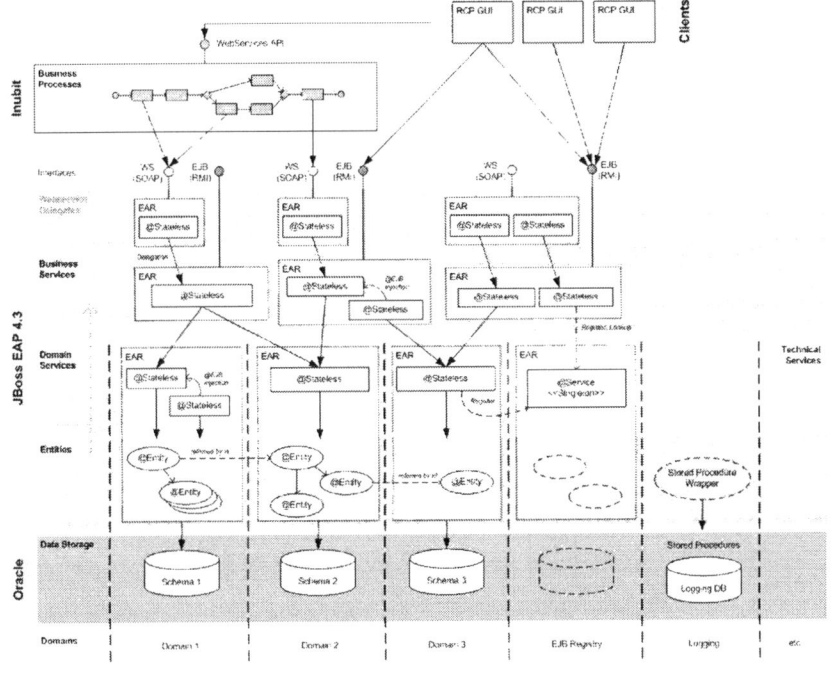

A process architect within the department or from a central service department (the organization's development department) then models the process in BPMN language or applies changes if required. This modeling capability is provided by the process engine, thus ensuring that there is always a connection between the functional model and technical implementation. The process model, in conjunction with subsequent object models, also provides a thorough documentation of process and service components. The resulting models look much more complex than the original ones, but also provide a much deeper insight into the process flow itself, showing exactly what needs to be adjusted in order to improve the process.

An automated process designed using these principles is shown below:

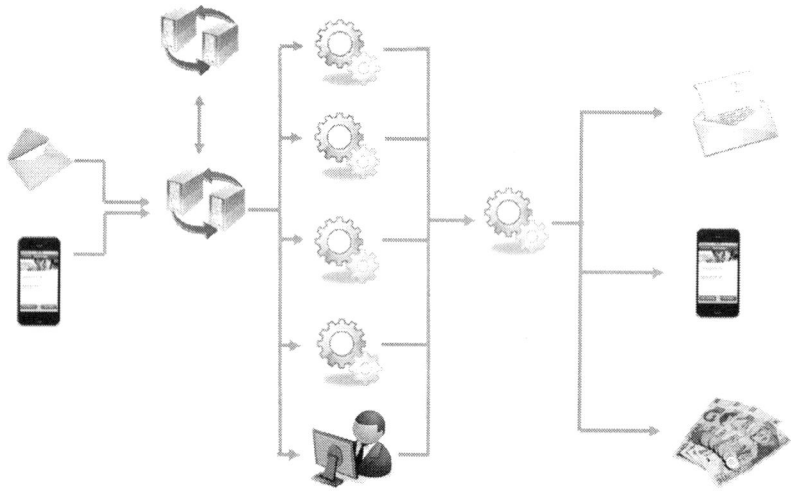

Today, the customer either sends the claims documents by mail in the usual manner or sends them directly as an iPhone-generated photo. However, this photo does not include the whole document, but rather the contents of a data matrix on the document by which the detailed data in it can be retrieved electronically from a data hub for private medical care clearing centers. (These clearing centers collect and process billing information from certain doctors working for the private medical care sector. They print invoices including the data matrix and send these to the patients. The data hub then in turn collects this data from the clearing centers and, if certain authentication requirements are met, sends this data to insurance companies on request.) By the same means, the data on the documents sent by mail can be retrieved without the need for data capturing.

The data from the documents is then sent to various automated processing channels depending on the type of document. For example, prescriptions are processed differently to bills for outpatient treatment or bills for hospital treatment. The allocation to these channels is accomplished using decision components based on a BRMS. Human intervention is only necessary if data is missing or unclear.

After these channels of regulatory business rules, the results may or may not be collected for the next processing step – again based on business rules. In either case the next step is the application of tariff rules and finally the same post-processing as in the original process with the option to send the settlement report electronically.

Due to the component services, architecture changes to this process are very fast. For instance the adaptation required for the new pharmaceuticals realignment law requires a couple of days (mostly taken up by optical recognition of a pharmaceutics code and process of transferring data to the pharmaceutical industry), whereas without this architecture it would have taken hundreds of days.

4.4 Organization

The new automated process frees the claims experts from routine tasks and lets them work on unclear or complex cases. On the other hand simple tasks such as obtaining missing data or correcting input errors can now easily be diverted to less qualified personnel. This leads to more distinctly differentiated job descriptions. There is no such thing as a claims expert any more.

Furthermore, a special group of the claims experts have been trained to work in process analysis and modeling. This is now a highly qualified group within the claims department which also acts as a link between the claims experts and the IT. These specialists are not likely to go back to their prior positions, however.

In the organization's development department, a new role of business process owner has been established. Here, all processes spanning several departments are accounted for. They also administer the central repository of business services from a functional point of view.

Within the software development department, the traditional branch-specific segmentation of developers is slowly dissolving as more and more services emerge that span the responsibility of several departments or branches. This leads to a disassociation between administrational leadership and functional leadership within the IT organization and management.

5. Hurdles Overcome

Management

Because taking a service-oriented view of processes was completely new to the members of the board and the next level of management, and also because introducing the architecture would cost a lot of money with no immediate benefit (i.e. in the first year or two), it took a great deal of marketing effort to make them believe in these principles. Once they were convinced that the approach was feasible, "only" results had to follow.

It was very helpful during the early stages to recruit external consultants who could report success stories of the architecture, albeit in other industries.

The next major step then was the going-live of an initial process with maximum gain. This demonstrated that it was possible to develop and install the architecture within a given time frame and afterwards to set up efficient processes in a very short period of time.

Another obstacle turned out to be the introduction of agile project methods (SCRUM), which resulted in an immediate loss of direct control from second level management over "their" employees. Only by redefining management roles by involving management in functional ways was this method and hence the project accepted.

Business

Fortunately the project posed no problem to business at all, because during development it had no effect on business and customer service subsequently improved.

Organization Adoption

At least three different parts of the organization were directly affected by the project: the department of the claims experts, IT and the department for organizational development, which had to adopt the role of process owners, especially for trans-departmental processes.

For the claims department, the whole method of operation changed. Whereas previously, they worked with a pull-principle by pulling jobs out of a workflow task list, with the new process it became push, where the clerk registered with a queue and then had his jobs allocated. Also the claims department was afraid that jobs would be cut. Both anxieties where smoothed by constant dialogue and early involvement in the project. In fact, a group of claims experts became central stakeholders within the project. Of course, the growth of the workload also helped as no layoffs were necessary.

For the IT department, the entire architecture changed, as did the software development process. This required a very steep learning curve for developers and architects. To introduce these new paradigms it was very helpful to have constant coaching in methodology from experienced consultants. The change in IT organization resulting from the SOA approach is an ongoing struggle and is being supported by the IT management.

Because the new processes span departments, it also became necessary to have process owners looking at the whole process. This role was adopted at an early stage by the department for organizational development. They became the drivers for process design and subsequent improvements. Without this new and crucial role, the whole project would not have been possible, because department leaders tend to optimize their own small areas without looking at the whole picture.

6. BENEFITS

6.1 Cost Savings

Although gross revenue increased by 10-15 percent each year, resulting in an equal increase in claims, the capacity of claims experts remained almost constant. The growth in claims was also amplified by another phenomenon: in 2005, 5 years prior to the going-live of the automated process, HanseMerkur became very successful in the market of supplementary dental insurance. The nature of these insurance policies is an annual increase in maximum refunds. This maximum becomes unlimited after 5 years, resulting in an increase in claims submissions after these 5 years.

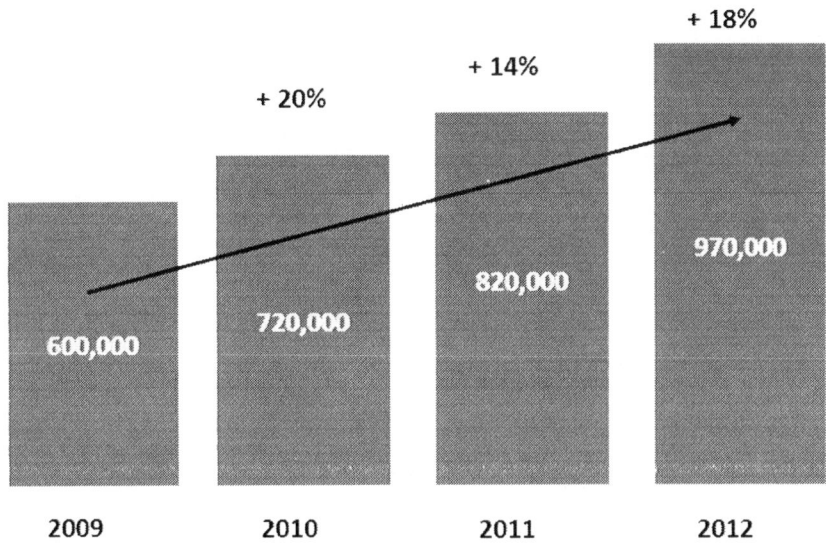

+ 18%

+ 14%

+ 20%

970,000

820,000

720,000

600,000

2009   2010   2011   2012

(Number of claims per year)

Both effects could be absorbed by the automatic process, which meant that the number of experts needed for processing was almost stable. This is an equivalent of € 0.75 million in cost savings per year and rising.

A third factor for recent cost savings has been a BRMS for regulatory business rules, which resulted in an increase of 1 percent in claims rejections or over € 1.65 million per year and growing.

With all these savings taken into account, the ROI will reach break-even after 5 years in 2013 and be increasingly positive afterwards.

6.2 Time Reductions

Claims processing time (counted from the claim being issued by the customer to the customer receiving the result) could be reduced from an average 2 weeks in the past to a few hours (with the help of an iPhone App). Without the host system (which is currently being replaced by a new settlements component) processing times can be reduced even further to a few minutes.

6.3 Increased Revenue

This project has not affected revenue so far, but will do so indirectly due to the increase in customer satisfaction as well as the possibility for faster product time-to-market (see 8).

6.4 Productivity Improvements

Although automation favors simple cases, hence the more complex cases are left to the experts and one would expect a decrease in productivity, in fact productivity has risen considerably.

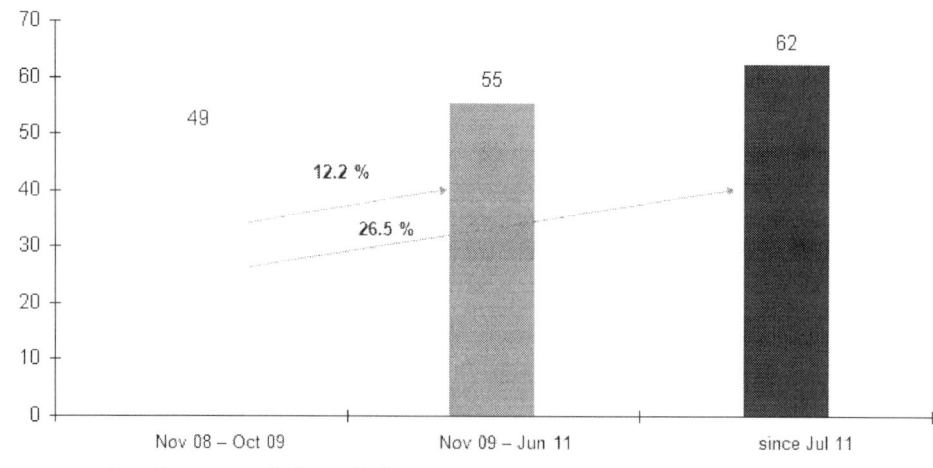

(Average number of cases per clerk per day)

Note that the first automation step took place in December 2009, followed by a major additional step in May 2011.

This improvement can be attributed to the fact that as a result of the service-oriented architecture, process steps can be routed according to skills, which means the experts can better focus on specialized tasks.

7. Best Practices, Learning Points and Pitfalls

7.1 Best Practices and Learning Points

✓ Ensure support of all parties involved up front. An SOA project is lengthy and costly and you do not want to alienate any party during the process. Constant marketing and persuasion is required.

✓ An SOA Implementation should be accompanied by agile project technology. When you enter unknown territory you have to explore where to go. There is no such thing as a recipe for SOA: you have to find your own model. Agile technologies best fit this approach.

✓ Use a sufficiently small goal with maximum gain for the first step. This usually ensures support from the board, but also boosts motivation within the team.

✓ Process orientation requires constant and close collaboration between functional departments and IT. The role of process owner has to be filled as early as possible.

7.2 Pitfalls

✗ Try to avoid dogma in applying SOA architecture and agile methods. Both have to be adapted to a company's existing architecture and culture.

✗ Prepare to have to defend the new approach. Classical architecture and development paradigms will seem faster and less expensive initially. Hence there is a trend in people to fall back to the "old ways". The expected gain has to be made plausible again and again, for example by successful extensions of the initial process.

8. Competitive Advantages

With a 25 percent automation rate (i.e. full automation plus 60 percent partial automation of the rest) HanseMerkur has a leading position among German private health insurers. This automation rate provides not just for cost-quota savings, but also enables highly standardized claims settlements, thus increasing customer satisfaction twofold by reducing the turn-around while making highly reproducible settlement reports possible. The following chart demonstrates the continual increase of the automation rate process improvements:

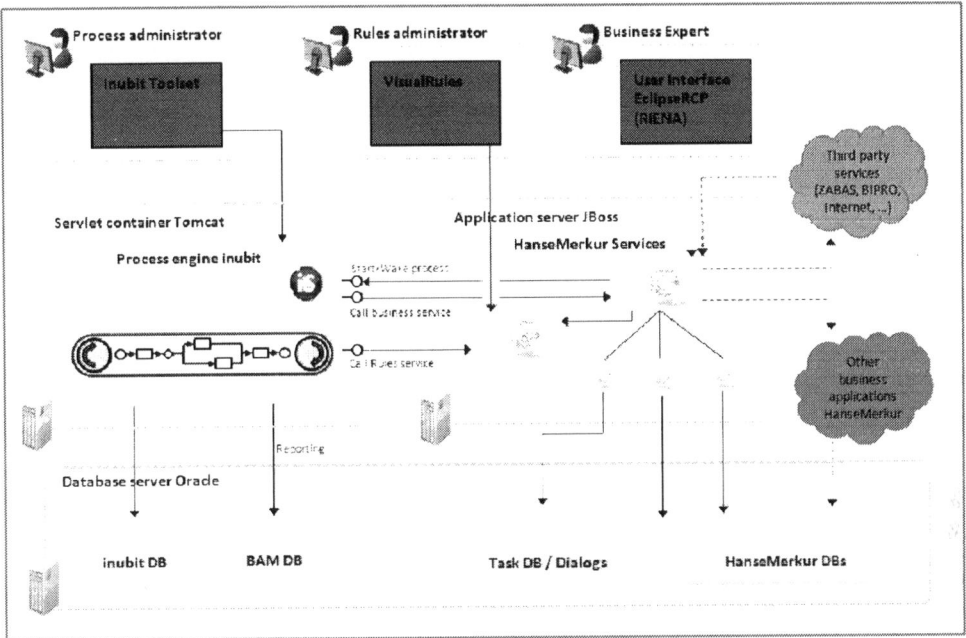

The underlying architecture also allows for rapid addition of innovative customer services such as the new claims app for iPhone.

Future plans include replacing the host based settlements core with a new one which can run fully automatically, based on product definitions from the policy module. This will further increase the automation rate, but will also provide for much more processing information, enabling for instance seamless process tracking for the customer as well as the HanseMerkur back office. Furthermore, this connection between policies and claims will allow for very high flexibility in product definition (an extremely short time to create and implement new products), which is a major competitive advantage in this time of rapid regulatory changes.

9. TECHNOLOGY

By introducing a service- and process-oriented platform, HanseMerkur achieved a broad range of goals. First and foremost, the SCOUT platform raises the efficiency of software development by introducing a unified architecture concept for all applications built on this platform.

The core of this application platform is a custom-made component / service architecture built on the JBoss application server. Standard JBoss features have been enhanced by concepts for hot deployment and multi-version support for services through a concept of class separation. Both features are necessary as processes with long durations are expected.

Process orchestration and execution are achieved using the inubit Process Engine as part of the inubit Business Process Management Suite. In this case the process engine was successfully tuned to high throughput in complex processes.

The inubit Process Engine calls services deployed into the component registry within the JBoss application Server. It is also used in the modeling process where the claims experts design the processes, and provides a link between functional process models and technical process models.

Usually, process flows are either batch or interactive (workflows). In this case a special requirement was the use of hybrid workflows, i.e. flows that contain process flows interspersed with human interaction.

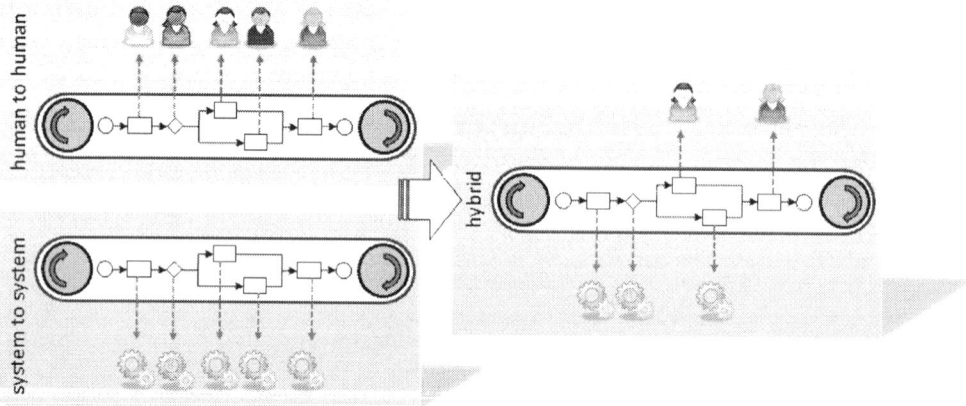

This could successfully be built into the process engine by designing means for suspending and waking a process.

One central set of services – known as decision components – are created by the BRMS (Business Rules Management System) Visual Rules from Bosch Software Innovations. The use of these components helps to homogenize validation and control rules. The model-based approach of Visual Rules displays the business logic graphically as rule flows or as decision tables. This helps to separate rules development from classical software development cycles and enables claims specialists to directly change, test and implement their rules.

The platform also includes the Eclipse RCP based Open Source project Riena as an application framework. Riena provides a clear navigation concept and ergonomic standardization of user interfaces. It also enables the user interface to operate like a service from the platform point of view.

Last but not least the technology stack is rounded off by the FIT framework for testing. This perfectly complements the built-in testing capabilities of the inubit process engine and Visual Rules, and the JUnit method within Java, thus providing a complete test suite from unit to system, integration and regression testing.

10. THE TECHNOLOGY AND SERVICE PROVIDERS

inubit AG (www.inubit.com), now a member of Bosch Group, provided the process engine of inubit Suite.

The inubit Suite 6 is inubit's core product. It is a comprehensive standard product for holistic BPM and is based on Java and XML technology. It supports all phases of processes management, from modeling in BPMN 2.0, simulation, pattern-based generation of executable processes, easy integration with legacy via more than 70 connectors, a full SOA foundation, business rules support, task handling, human workflow, portal integration based on the portlet standard and real-time monitoring with processes KPIs, dashboards and reporting. This is accomplished by a large set of enterprise and system management features including versioning, tagging, SNMP-alerting, monitoring of consumed server resources, multi-level staging and deployment plus support for clustering and high availability.

The inubit Suite is compliant with over 200 IT-standards and follows an open architecture principle in order to operate on multiple operating systems, databases, application servers, portal servers, and service registries. By default, inubit makes use of widely accepted open source components such as Tomcat, JBoss, and Liferay but is also prepared to run in commercial components such as Websphere and SAP Portal. This makes inubit very flexible in integrating with existing customer environments or operating as a stand-alone implementation.

inubit consultants helped in installing and optimizing its configuration.

Bosch Software Innovations (www.bosch-si.com) is a leader in Business Rules Management Systems and offers software and systems solutions for the financial services industry, eMobility, as well as companies in various industries.

The Visual Rules Suite offers proven tools and platforms, designed for technical and business software applications and completely scalable to meet customers' performance and agility needs. The rule-based integration concept establishes rules and rule modeling instead of programming as core elements of software applications. Rules define the business logic of applications, control internal workflows, and promptly react to defined events within the system environment. Rules are also used to integrate applications into heterogeneous and distributed system landscapes. Under this approach, sophisticated concepts come together with components based on mature technology and industry standards.

Holisticon AG (www.holisticon.de) is a management and IT consulting company from Hamburg, Germany. Based on a holistic consulting approach they assist customers in development projects on all technical, tactical as well as strategic levels.

At HanseMerkur, Holisticon consultants have contributed their core areas of expertise in Business Process Management (BPM), Enterprise Architecture and Agile Software Development (Scrum) to build a new service-oriented application platform, implement the first automated business processes on top of it, and establish a new paradigm of process-oriented, agile software development.

compeople (www.compeople.de) is an innovative IT-Service-provider. Their core competence is supplying modern, user-friendly IT-systems. compeople offers a complete range of services, focussing on software development, technology and architecture consultancy as well as consultancy on agile project methods.

As a solution member of the Eclipse Foundation, compeople have not only initiated the Eclipse RT project "Riena", but also lead the project within the Eclipse Community. "Riena" is a platform for developing user-friendly, multi-tier enterprise applications. Core to Riena is an OSGi-based Remote Services component that allows developers to easily create distributed client/server applications. Furthermore Riena provides an enhanced navigation concept for business applications with a focus on end-user usability. Typical users of Riena are companies which are interested in realizing complex enterprise applications and by doing so, attach great importance to a high usability of their applications.

Homeloan Management Limited, United Kingdom

Finalist: Nominated by IBM, USA

1. Executive Summary / Abstract

HML is the UK's largest mortgage servicer, providing outsourced mortgage administration for more than 50 UK and Irish clients, and operating out of three UK locations – Skipton (North Yorkshire – head office), Londonderry (Northern Ireland) and Glasgow. The company was established in 1988 and is a wholly-owned subsidiary of Skipton Building Society. It manages around £43bn for some of the largest players in the UK and US financial markets.

In late 2007 HML embarked on its Business Process Management (BPM) journey to improve, streamline and increase overall control of the credit management processes in response to rapidly changing market conditions and regulatory requirements. HML's first BPM initiative, the credit management workflow system (CREWS) was initiated to address these requirements and contain cost. CREWS delivered automated functionality for HML's pre-litigation department. Feedback was gathered from the business area to continuously improve CREWS over the next two years and ensure what was delivered was in line with business requirements, therefore eliminating any rework.

From 2010 through 2011, HML delivered significant enhancements to the initial CREWS application, with improvements in query responsiveness, agile development methodology and improved process efficiency. In addition, in early 2011, a new credit management enhancement project was completed to augment CREWS with possessions process automation.

2. Overview

The CREWS programme objective was to automate repeatable, efficient, consistent credit management strategies across the client base. The programme structure utilized closely integrated business and IT members all working collaboratively towards a common goal. The team worked closely with IBM, who implemented the business process management toolset, to ensure a robust and responsive system.

The workflow functionality enables us to operate in a multi-client environment by modeling and automating more than 50 different credit management strategies. The tool has 400 business rules, uses 100 data attributes as the basis for its decisions and is used by around 350 HML credit management consultants.

By moving more capabilities to this world-class platform, the credit management process is streamlined, more efficient and consistent.

The possessions automation enhancement was designed to provide a significant reduction in risk and costs for clients. This was achieved by automating cancellations, drain down and marketing processes for selling a repossessed property on behalf of a client.

3. Business Context

- HML's credit management function was heavily focussed on manual tasks to drive the collections process.

- Employees had to run reports from the core system and split the work by process area. The reports were exported to excel spreadsheets, manually manipulated and pushed out to staff.
- Report segmentation was used to identify data to populate outbound calling strategies within the dialler system.
- Operational management information was produced using reports and excel spreadsheets.
- Letter production was resource intensive with staff working from lists and manually requesting letters using screens in the core system.
- The high degree of manual intervention opened up risks around human error and the possibility of accounts 'falling through the gaps'.
- The possessions function also focussed heavily on manual tasks:
- Employees had to manually segment accounts for property possession.
- Management of the selling price and marketing of the property was inefficient
- Manual tasks for drain down, clean and clear were required
- With the extensive manual efforts, costs associated with debt recovery were significant.
- CREWS and possessions both directly addressed these shortfalls and moving forward, the IBM BPM project will further develop HML's BPM programme. Without the BPM project, HML would have faced rising costs in an industry where equity was declining, severely impacting its ability to compete.

4. THE KEY INNOVATIONS

4.2 Business

The CREWS and possessions projects have delivered a faster and more efficient credit management function that is less open to human error resulting in improved relationships with clients and trust in the credit management team internally and externally.

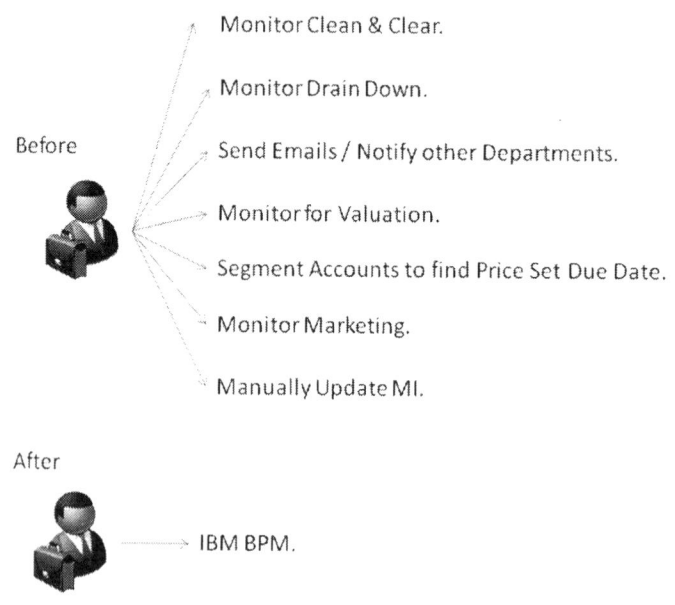

Before
- Monitor Clean & Clear.
- Monitor Drain Down.
- Send Emails / Notify other Departments.
- Monitor for Valuation.
- Segment Accounts to find Price Set Due Date.
- Monitor Marketing.
- Manually Update MI.

After
- IBM BPM.

4.3 Process

The improved possessions process has drastically shortened the amount of time HML employees spend on the process and fully automated reporting.

4.4 Organization

Training for new and existing employees is much easier because processes are clearly defined, and 'coaches' are used to guide employees through the specific task they are working on.

By automating non value add manual processes, such as the identification and distribution of work items, employees have more time to spend with customers to achieve positive results. This has delivered an increase in staff morale and improved overall engagement within the team. People also have a greater understanding of how the speed and accuracy of their work impacts on the credit management and arrears process.

Team managers have access to real-time dashboard reporting, which gives an instant view of key data, such as SLA reporting, enabling more informed resource allocation.

Below: Dashboards now available to managers following possessions project:

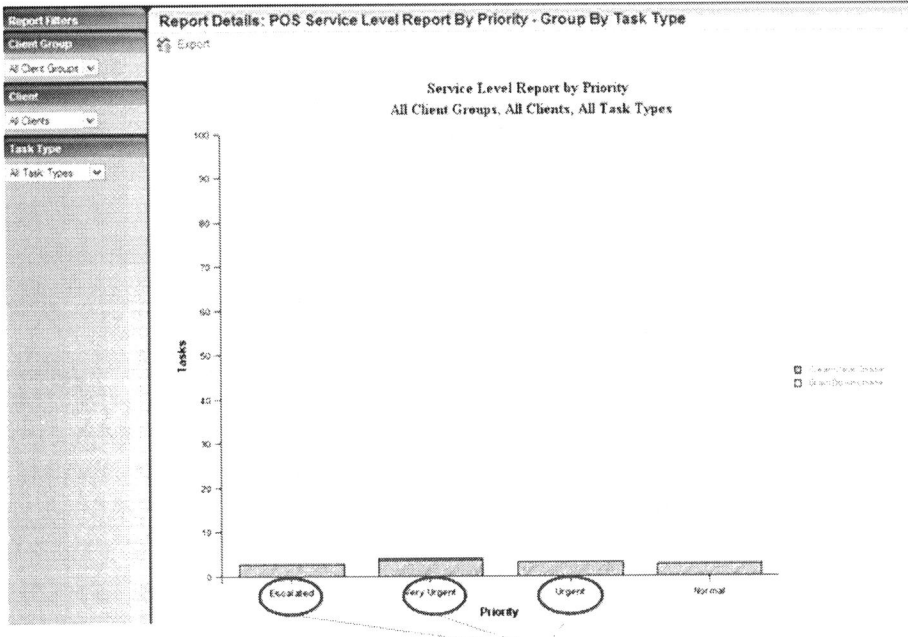

Managers can quickly identify problems and action changes

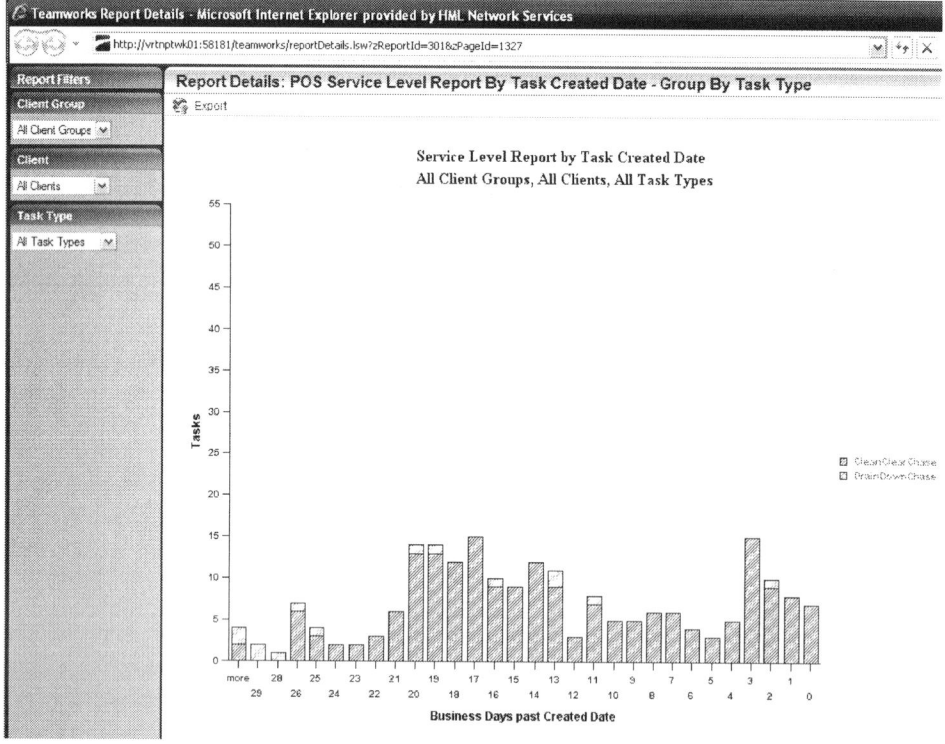

5. Hurdles Overcome

Management

- The key management challenge was rolling out the improvement to our clients within a set timescale and on budget. A single team enabled dedicated subject matter experts from the business, IT and testing resource to deliver on time and fulfill client expectations.
- To manage the cost challenges, HML uses an agile IT approach to change implementation. This fluid approach allows for planned changes, which are later proven to be ineffective, to be removed from the process saving money and resource.
- Business
- The key business challenge was convincing credit management and possessions employees that current processes could be improved and BPM was not a replacement for employees. To counter these issues, change champions were nominated from the impacted areas. They were provided with detailed information and involved in the business readiness activity, which in turn aided operational buy-in at the user level.
- Organization Adoption
- With CREWS being the first implementation of BPM technology in the organization, a centre of excellence (CoE) was created. This was made up of modelers, developers and testers following documented best practice and strict standards.
- With the CoE in place, the subsequent rollout of the possessions project was easier to deliver on time and on budget.

- At a high level, the organization has embraced BPM and sees it as an enabler for process change, control and efficiency which provides flexibility in resource deployment to manage workloads.
- To communicate changes, the project team provides monthly updates to employees. This way changes are bite-size and manageable and people can see the evolution of the project in stages.
- Following the success of CREWS and possessions HML has further committed to driving through process efficiency.
- In mid 2011 HML made the strategic decision to replace the current electronic document management system. In order to achieve this HML will create a digital mailroom with OCR capability, replace the existing document workflow system using BPM, and improve its image storage.
- The BPM solution will be a key component in the delivery and management of all incoming written correspondence and provide real-time reporting. Delivery of this capability is currently on track for early 2012.

6. BENEFITS

6.1 Cost Savings

The CREWS project has achieved savings of 22 FTE's due to the elimination of manual tasks translating into a cost saving of £400,000 a year.

The possessions project is anticipated to return equivalent financial benefits within a 19 month timescale and has reduced equivalent FTE spend by 10 - a further cost saving of £182,000 per year.

The Workflow programme has a target benefit potential of 12 FTE's attributed to removal of manual activity delivering an additional saving of £218,000 to the amount saved by HML since the adoption of BPM.

6.2 Time Reductions

Speed of change to strategies is key to HML's clients in the current market place. CREWS has provided a platform to quickly manage this change without the need for lengthy development, test and deployment.

The possessions project will realize the following time reduction benefits:
- Reducing the processing time for new possessions by up to 60 per cent
- Reducing the processing time for marketing and price set by up to 40 per cent
- Reducing the processing time for price reduction by up to 60 per cent.

6.3 Increased Revenues

HML's clients benefit from a number of features:
- HML can guarantee greater adherence to client strategies. This means HML has been able to eliminate the type of errors that arise from manual intervention, and ensure consistency and accuracy, making sure that all borrowers are treated in accordance with the clients' strategies, or those developed through HML's analytics, and within a strict Treating Customers Fairly framework.
- Elimination of manual intervention also means improved compliance reporting to demonstrate strategies and processing are effective and in accordance with the Financial Services Authority regulations;
- Clients benefit from better credit management results, with the aim of getting pre-litigation accounts to 'cure', where there are no arrears. Automa-

tion leaves our consultants more time to spend with customers and field counsellors to achieve positive results;

- IBM BPM offers HML increased flexibility, with the system able to respond quickly to any changes in client strategies by updating the relevant business rule.
- Better customer experience - a 'base-switching' problem meant customers were previously on a call for 45 seconds while a switch to the appropriate system was made

HML can draw the following benefits from the possessions project:

- Possessions information is clearer and more reliable
- Possessions will be easier to maintain in the future resulting in reduced costs and resource commitments

6.4 Productivity Improvements

CREWS has improved Business as Usual (BAU) support by raising the level of queries answered to 90 per cent within one hour.

This means 90 per cent of queries are answered comfortably within the SLA guidelines, and as such, a strategic rethink on SLA times has been proposed.

7. BEST PRACTICES, LEARNING POINTS AND PITFALLS

7.1 Best Practices and Learning Points

- ✓ Business Sponsorship
- ✓ Lean Agile development method
- ✓ Frequent iteration delivery
- ✓ Alignment with business needs
- ✓ Acceptance of system is ongoing
- ✓ Robust Change Control
- ✓ Integrated business and IT team is crucial
- ✓ Keep It Small & Simple
- ✓ Select a process that crosses humans and systems
- ✓ Measure the baseline process
- ✓ Speed – How long does the process take
- ✓ Cost – What is the cost of the process
- ✓ Experience – What value does the process bring
- ✓ Involve everyone the process touches
- ✓ Top-level buy-in
- ✓ Appoint a process owner
- ✓ Set Expectations
- ✓ Speed – What time improvements are expected?
- ✓ Cost – What cost reductions will be made?
- ✓ Experience – How will the user experience change?
- ✓ The person responsible for the process outcome has to 'own' the process
- ✓ Ownership is important for collaboration purposes
- ✓ Collaboration takes place when designing the process and within the process

✓ *Perform a dress rehearsal of the implementation in a controlled 'like for like' test region to increase confidence in the actual implementation process, timescales and flush out last minute bugs.*

✓ *Close partnership with your BPM provider and 3rd party resource providers.*

7.2 Pitfalls

✗ *Know your baseline to enable clear measurement of improvements.*

✗ *Perform meaningful proof of concept and pilot prior to full scale project roll out.*

✗ *Be prepared to manage the flexibility requirements versus the performance requirement. Manage both to arrive at a suitable level of each.*

✗ *HML is still coming to terms with the full scale of BPM's capability, so setting goals or targets too far in advance can lead to future inefficiencies.*

8. COMPETITIVE ADVANTAGES

CREWS has enabled HML to offer its clients a faster, more accurate and consistent service in accordance with regulations. Clients can save money through time saved in the possessions process by getting properties to market faster.

HML is currently replacing its existing task management system used for handling all mortgage related activities with IBM BPM. This represents further investment in BPM and is driven by benefits already realized through the CREWS and possessions projects.

HML anticipates a significant increase in the volumes of tasks per month over the next five years. IBM BPM has allowed project managers to plan for approximate annual increases of up to 50 per cent.

CREWS, possessions and IBM PBM have all created a more compelling proposition for HML's commercial team to take to the market. Increased efficiency and cost-saving projections play a big part in boarding new clients and cross-selling to existing clients, of which the credit management department is a crucial part.

9. TECHNOLOGY

The key elements of the CREWS and possessions solutions are;

- IBM Business Process Manager, Standard. This has been used to develop the Credit Management Strategies and fully automates the management of the processes that implement those strategies.
- HML's core system. This is the legacy system which maintains the detail of accounts, takes payments, registers arrears etc.
- HML peripheral applications. These handle such actions as sending letters and automatically dialing customers.

These elements have been fully integrated using Web Services, allowing each system to focus on what it does best. The systems exchange information in real time, ensuring that all decisions are made on up-to-the-minute data.

The credit management strategies and associated business rules are held in the IBM BPM system in the form of Business Process Definitions, allowing users to create and make changes to the strategies using the highly productive and intuitive IBM BPM graphical interface.

We have also developed a number of key, reusable components in IBM BPM, which, combined with the graphical interface, ensure that coding and development effort is kept to a minimum.

The data relating to the position of an account is held in the core system, and is passed, via Web Services to the IBM BPM system in real time. The IBM BPM system assesses the account and moves it through the relevant strategy, automating actions wherever possible.

Many of these actions involve interacting with other HML systems, for example sending a letter, or placing an account into the automatic dialing system – and again the integration has been completely automated using web services. Once in the IBM BPM system, an account will be fully monitored by the system until it is either cured or moves to the litigation stage.

10. THE TECHNOLOGY AND SERVICE PROVIDERS

IBM is the market leader in Business Process Management (BPM). IBM empowers organizations of all sizes to exceed their customers' expectations, anticipate shifts in their marketplace, and keep costs under control. It takes a process aware organization to achieve this level of agility and IBM has both the tools and the knowhow to transform you into one.

IBM Business Process Manager is a comprehensive BPM platform giving you visibility and insight to manage business processes. It scales smoothly and easily from an initial project to a full enterprise-wide program. IBM Business Process Manager harnesses complexity in a simple environment to break down silos and better meet customer needs.

For more information, visit: www.ibm.com/software/info/itsolutions/business-process-management/

Jardine Lloyd Thompson, UK

Gold Award: Nominated by HandySoft, USA

1. EXECUTIVE SUMMARY / ABSTRACT

Formed in 1997 from the merger of Lloyd Thompson and Jardine Insurance Broker, Jardine Lloyd Thompson (JLT) is an international group of Risk Specialists and Employee Benefits Consultants. JLT is listed on the London Stock Exchange and is one of the largest companies of its type in the world. JLT had a 2010 turnover of £746 million with 6500 employees across 34 countries.

The EB Group within Jardine Lloyd Thompson (JLT EB) made up £132 million of this 2010 turnover with 1500 employees in offices in the UK and India.

2. OVERVIEW

As far back as 2004, JLT EB started using BPM to streamline a limited set of business operations. Use was confined to about 30 people in a "model office". During that same time period, JLT acquired Profund, a leading provider of pension administration software in the UK. Customers included both in-house and third-party administrators. Profund had seen opportunities to expand its pension fund administration solutions into specific areas of process automation while helping customers to simplify the overall user experience. Deciding to use the current BPM tool, the company developed outward-facing solutions that rolled out to end customers in 2007. BPM usage at JLT EB and Profund grew to about 300 users.

Between 2007-2010, JLT made more than 20 acquisitions globally across the group. JLT EB operations quickly became highly complex, distributed and paper-based. Employees were handling millions of documents annually covering Pension Administration, Payroll, Defined Contributions, Actuarial, Health and Risk, among other requests. Processes treated more than 16 million workflow elements, 300+ million rows of table data and 15 million SharePoint documents. The BPM solution covers 14 active offices in Europe and India, off-shoring and massive amounts of regulations. The company knew that in order to continuing growing at the same speed while containing costs, it would have to do more with less.

JLT EB accomplished its goals of increased revenues with lower costs with continual investment in BPM. JLT EB has used BPM to streamline >200 processes. From an ROI standpoint, this work has provided a key business component, contributing to JLT EB's growth in trading profit by 50% in the last financial year. Revenue growth is enabled by more flexible solutions that can be highly tailored to internal client needs as well as end-customer engagements. Cost cutting is enabled through the use of process automation tied together with effective scanning, document handling and rule-based routing. Paper is largely removed, deadlines hit, and governance accomplished.

3. BUSINESS CONTEXT

Doing more with less requires innovative use of technology. Starting in 2004 JLT EB had been able to increase top line revenues by selling new solutions while lowering costs through process automation. This legacy of success became a critical asset when merging together multiple acquisitions between 2008 and 2010.

For example, in December 2009 JLT acquired HSBC Actuaries and Consulting Limited (HACL), a leading employee benefits and actuarial consulting firm with £40M in revenues. The acquisition was considered highly synergistic, extending JLT EB's capabilities in areas such as Defined Benefit, Defined Contribution and pension consultancy and solutions.

At the time of acquisition HACL had a complex, business-rule driven system and associated EDMS for process automation. JLT EB had its own BPM-based infrastructure. After doing a rigorous technology review, JLT EB decided to keep its current BPM platform and make a large investment in extending that infrastructure to enable both increased sales and reduced costs. Use would go from a few hundred people to >800 daily users. Expected savings proved high.

Expected ROI from Process Automation

Time Saved per Work Item	Hours Saved in a Year	Man Days Saved per Year	Working years	£££
1 second	4,444	593	2.7	£120k
30 second	133,333	17,778	80.8	£3.6m
60 seconds	266,667	35,556	161.6	£7m

Realizing these savings would put the company in a great position to grow both top line sales and bottom line revenues.

4. THE KEY INNOVATIONS

4.2 Business

BPM allowed JLT EB to innovate in the following areas:

- Sales – Employee benefits and pension fund schemes must be tailored to individual customer needs. Each scheme contains unique data and backend systems. With its BPM-based infrastructure, JLT EB can demonstrate to both current and prospective customers an ability to meet their specific requirements both quickly and cleanly. This inherent flexibility in technology architecture has been a component allows for product differentiation and supported the activities that have seen a 50% increase in trading profit.
- Document Handling – Looking internally, JLT EB has lowered costs per employee through process automation. Removing paper is one big reason for these costs savings. In the past, outbound document handling was printed and stuffed by a Post Handling Team (PHT). Through the integration of Scanning, EDMS and BPM, outbound documents are now directly integrated into the overall flow. Inbound document handling is likewise automated. Some of the incoming documentation (e.g., Checks and Certificates) are treated with special handling functionality. Streamlining and standardizing document handling alone has produced annual savings into the hundreds of thousands of pounds. Furthermore, it has ensured regulatory compliance. For example, regulators impose strict penalties if turnaround times are breached. BPM grants users visibility into work status as well as creates triggers for escalating and notifying users to get work done before regulatory penalties apply.
- Customer Service – Another innovative use of BPM is in the area of ad-hoc reviews. Within the structured workflow is a jump-off point for ad-hoc correspondence from the user to one or many colleagues. Keeping the work

within the application allows all users to collaborate to quickly resolve customer issues while tracking overall progress. It also removes the need for scattershot emails and calls, again reducing wasted time and resources. The ad-hoc capability has been particularly important as more work has been routed offshore where the implicit understanding of the UK pension rules and regulations is still maturing. In other words, BPM is a primer for KM.

- SLA Management – The use of BPM has also helped JLT EB to effectively meet SLA's and deadlines. The management of statutory deadlines often crosses the boundaries of natural processes. Knowing this is one thing, monitoring it is another. Using BPM, methods to manage SLA compliance were developed and reports created. Now missing statutory deadlines and breaches are rare. Improved performance and increased risk management have led to more sales and less legal costs.

- Compliance – As mentioned above, the employee benefits business is very highly regulated and all incoming and outgoing correspondence must be tracked. In order to accomplish this requirement while streamlining the entire employee benefits operation, JLT EB decided to integrate Scanning, EDMS and BPM components to create a highly sophisticated, large scale application architecture. The approach was to loosely couple BPM (BizFlow) with EDMS (SharePoint) whereby documents were directly accessible from workitems in the BPM user interface and/or forms. Integration was done using an API and sympathetic folder structure, but not direct coupling to the case in question. This approach has allowed flexibility and independent access to the EDMS documents using the EDMS front-end. The custom interface allows incoming documents to be 'indexed' with relevant meta-data and to have this data initiate relevant business processes. A Practice Engine is a time recording system used for billing and the workflow system updates this engine whenever a case is opened and closed. Accurate billing to the clients is managed through this interface.

JLT EB's commitment to BPM enabled it to on-board HACL with fewer people and a significant increase in the volume of daily transactions.

4.3 Process

With the HACL acquisition and subsequent development, JLT EB began to standardize its BPM methodology. In order to gain efficiencies, the business analysis and development was centralized in Manchester. Development was moved from a waterfall to agile methodologies.

While the lead business analyst in Manchester worked with other analysts across regions to gather requirements and specifications, developers started building process definitions and designing forms. Documentation was standardized so as to capture objectives, scope, flows, activities, rules, form elements, form design, and user experience. Process modeling was done in BPMN v1.0. Testing took place throughout the process life-cycle with the bulk of it along with user acceptance happening at the end. The methodology allowed project managers to distribute design and development work to offshore teams in Washington DC.

Over time, JLT EB established best practices and templates for their user experience. Templates included the UI, forms layout, and data structures. For example, many forms share the same headers. Applications can share functionality for ad-hoc joiners, ad-hoc reviews, and pends. These reusable templates have greatly reduced development timelines and have improved consistency.

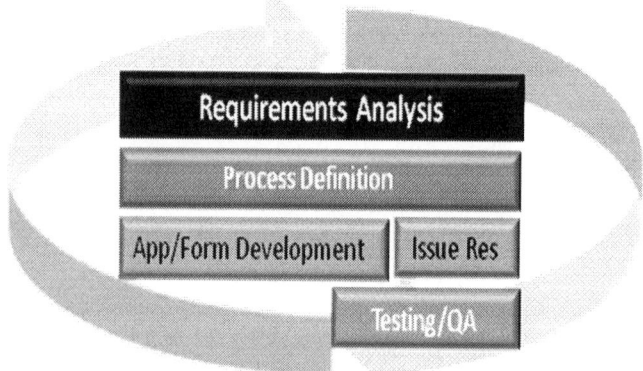

Agile Methodology for BPM Implementations

Since 2010, JLT EB has been able to streamline more than 127 unique processes. Overarching processes include:

Payroll:

When clients' employees retire their interaction with JLT EB moves them from the Pension Administration group to the Payroll business unit. Payroll is responsible for managing the monthly pension payments for many hundred thousand individuals and is a tightly regulated part of the business.

Payroll processes consist of a number of actions (e.g., Change of Address, Change of Banking details) that are initiated by the Payroll team or Pensions Admin team. The initiation occurs when a document is received, scanned and indexed by PHT and placed in SharePoint. The process can also be initiated manually by a user. Some processes are initiated by the Pensions Admin team and passed onto the Payroll Admin team for their input. Some of the processes involve other systems and other parts of the business.

For example, a Change of Address notification can be received and processed by either Admin or Payroll. However, if it is an oPen solution (a product of Profund) customer then the Admin must be informed about the address change and will have to amend the oPen record accordingly. These actions interface with certain backend systems like Cashfac and Propay. An example interface is the SharePoint wrapper that sits between Kofax (the automatic scanning software) and BizFlow. Kofax scans incoming documents and adds them to generic SharePoint document management libraries. From here they are indexed and saved in specific libraries which are linked to schemes. SharePoint then initiates a BizFlow process to manage the Action such as a Change of Address request.

Health and Risk:

JLT is a leading provider of health and risk management consulting and solutions. H&R processes include: Create Work, AdHoc Risk Joiners, Healthcare Renewals, Death Claims, Healthcare Joiners, Income Protection Claims, Appeals, Reviews, Leavers, Lost Schemes, Amendments and Switches.

Work is normally initiated automatically when a document is uploaded into SharePoint (either manually or automatically as an incoming scanned document). When an item of mail is received the PHT scans it and performs an initial Index/Coding that attaches metadata to the document using Kofax. The item is saved to a SharePoint document library and initiates the Create Work process within BizFlow. Other processes normally follow.

Defined Contribution Consulting (DCC):

The DCC application supports many processes, including: Create Work, Notice to Staff, Ad Hoc Requests and Queries, Direct Offer associated flows, Transfers, and Annuities. Subprocesses include Pending, Termination and Document Handling.

- Tasks are initiated by means of a 'Create Work' (Parent) process. This process is normally initiated automatically following the arrival of a scanned document. On the form, general information is captured (i.e., Scheme, Cli-

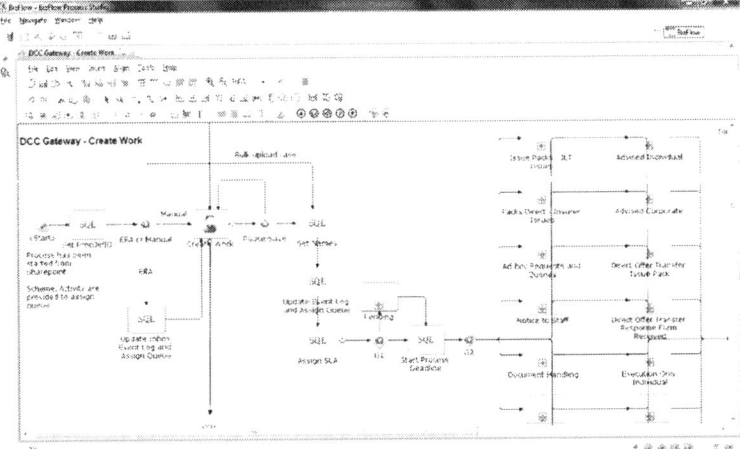

ent, NI, Type of Work), which is carried across as a Header on subsequent forms. When the 'Type of Work' is selected a 'Do Work' sub-process (Child) is initiated. The Child form consists of a Header (as populated in the Parent) and locked so that the information there is not user changeable. The Child form navigation includes tabs that correspond to specific activities.

- As a whole, the DCC process follows a "Doer", "Checker", "Completer" cycle where the Does and Checker cannot be the same person. Validation occurs to ensure all mandatory data has been added. The use of headers saves thousands of hours in data entry and validation.

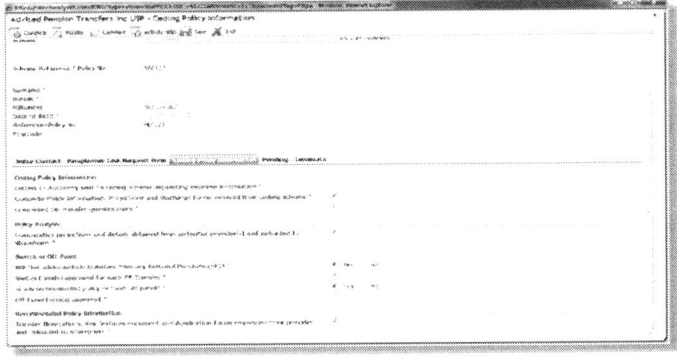

During this effort to expand BPM across the Employee Benefits group, JLT EB made many innovations in both development and user interactions. The overarching vision was that greater usability results in greater user efficiency, or in other words, design matters. Bringing together all elements of the process into one user experience would help users do work more efficiently and effectively.

Innovations include:

Adapting at Runtime – Forms have been created to allow users to modify flows at runtime. Whether through ad-hoc reviews, pends, terminations,

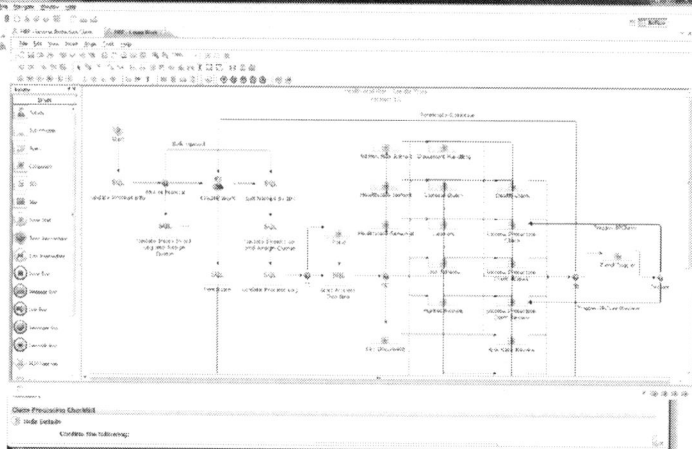

dynamically adding fields or requesting documentation, users have lots of flexibility to control work and change work in progress.

- Tabular Navigation – In order to incorporate more functionality and data access into the application while simplifying the user experience, JLT EB

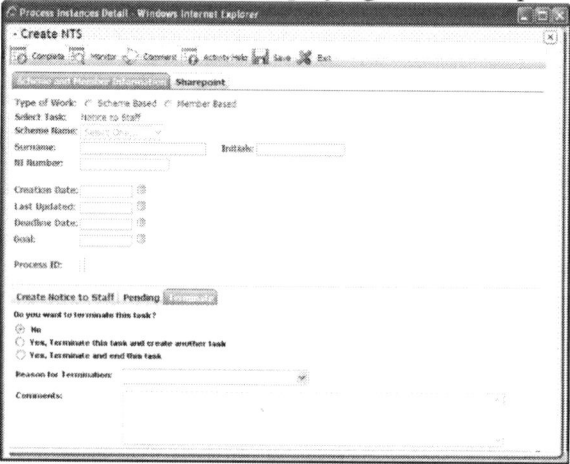

decided on a tabular form. As seen in the example below, JLT EB divided the form into top and bottom pieces each having associated tabs.

- Standardizing Common Elements – As there are many shared elements in each overarching process, JLT EB worked to standardize common elements for reuse. Elements include:

  - Headers – JLT EB uses Headers to collect common data that crosses over multiple forms and/ or sub-processes. The use of Headers eliminates data entry as well as ensures data accuracy.

  - Pend – Users can pend work at many areas in the workflow. Pend rules require users to identify a future date and reason. If the reason is internal, the SLA continues to run. If external, then the SLA is paused. BPM runs daily reports giving visibility to management of pended work with associated reasons.

- Termination – Users can terminate work during the process. Rules require users to state a reason (e.g., incorrect indexing, incorrect process selected, duplicate task) and determine any additional action. For example, when a work item is initiated in error it may need to initiate another in its place with the same header information.

- Routing – For DCC there are 12 different User Groups. Users are assigned to User Groups based on the Scheme/Member selected during the Create Work activity. Routing is done by means of Participant variables. Work can be started automatically and/or manually from uploaded and scanned documents to SharePoint via Kofax using metadata tags.

- SharePoint – SharePoint is used across the Group as a repository for ALL documentation including mail, email, and generated documents (e,g., Word, Excel, Visio, etc.). Each business has regions set up in SharePoint which spawns variants of the form: Client/Scheme/Member. The BPM processes have a tab on the top that when clicked points the User directly to the relevant hierarchy level (e.g., If it is a Scheme then it will point the User to the Scheme folder).

- Ad-Hoc Peer Reviews – During process execution users often need to ask associates for information to complete work. Rather than using email which leads to lost time and information, JLT EB added functionality directly into the application enabling dynamic collaboration. This capability is implemented as a separate tab along the top of the screen. The reviewer will be determined depending on what stage the process is at from a drop down list. A "doer" won't be able to review their own work. This innovation is enabled by the BizFlow engine.

- Document Handling – The 'Document Handling' tab allows users to follow a simple process to produce outbound correspondence and control valuable documents. Users can give instructions such as attaching a covering letter to a certificate and returning it to a client. The Document Handling flow

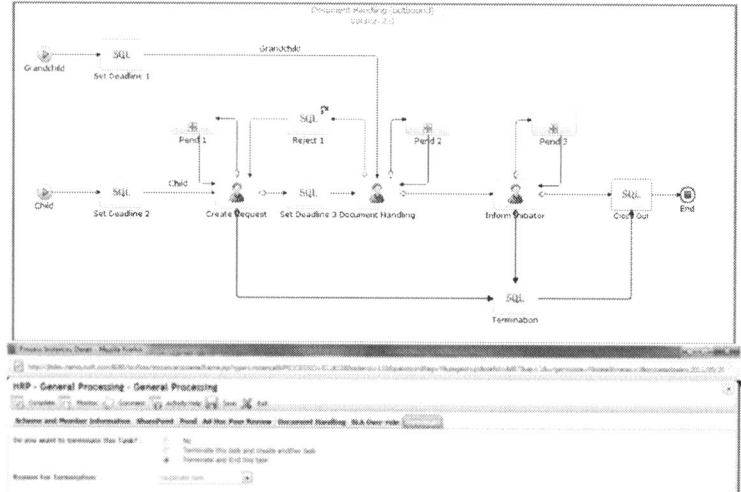

creates an item in the PHT Queue, displaying the instructions to be carried out. A work item can be terminated at any point. A reason for termination must be given. Reasons are captured in daily operational reports. Reasons include: Duplicate task, Incorrect indexing, Incorrect process selected, Not a H&R case, and Other. There are two categories of terminations: Terminate-End and Terminate-Continue. Terminate-End means nothing else needs doing. Terminate-Continue refers to where a process has been initiated in error and now needs to be replaced using the same Header information but a different Work-Type (process). This approach is also used when there is more than one task against the case (e.g., letter requesting a Change of Address might also mention a Change of Banking Details).

- Self-Triggering Processes – Some processes can trigger other processes. The relationships that exist between these processes are displayed below. The logic of the triggering mechanisms within each parent process is displayed against each process relationship.

BPM applications are now available to >800 people across multiple continents. Applications are becoming more sophisticated as the company adds more and more business rules and complex routings. JLT EB has integrated BPM with BI/Datawarehousing to run sophisticated reports.

JLT EB now is integrating a business rules engine to route work based on a very sophisticated list of rules to the lowest cost resource. Rules will pertain to users' skill base, experience, location, client relationships, etc.

4.4 Organization

The overall approach has been to incorporate dynamic checklists into the forms which has improved information available to the business and improved the visibility of areas of risk.

In 2010 JLT acquired a company using a different BPM-based solution. It was also tied to a different EDMS. After doing a study comparing BPM systems, JLT EB decided to use its own for cost and functionality reasons. The acquired system limited the way the employees naturally worked at JLT EB. It forced users to follow a very strict sequence of events which led to deadlines being missed and shortcuts being taken leading to risk for the business. With the replacement, the overall time taken to complete a case was reduced from days to hours. Furthermore, the development of new processes has been much faster and well received. For example, JLT EB was able to completely revamp work processes with half the process team and half the time as was originally accomplished at HACL.

Since 2011, JLT EB has been investing in a Center of Excellence. Based in Manchester, the COE works to establish standards associated with analysis, documentation, design and development. These standards help Business Analysts know what information to collect and how to document it. They help developers follow principles of agile development and user acceptance testing. The COE also sets expectations for training and resource development. JLT EB has matured from using a consultant in 2004 to having a team of Five Developers, 3 Business Analysts, two Project Managers and two Testers. A senior executive owns the budget and interfaces with executive management to manage development and rollout. Ultimately, BPM gets the backing of C-Level executives and a budget of several million pounds.

5. HURDLES OVERCOME

As JLT EB has matured the organization has overcome hurdles in three primary areas:

- Business ownership – It is vital to get the business involved. With business ownership, team members get refined requirements, locked scope, validated investment, and commitment to testing and use. Users more readily adopt solutions as they have had more input on features, functionality and design.
- Talent Development – Five large projects in 18 months required many people to learn on the job. Having a small group of true experts in business analysis and development helped to provide new team members with guidance and best practices as to requirements analysis, documentation, implementation and testing. All personnel also went through training and workshops to learn BPM products and best practices. Developers sat side by side to learn from each other as well as review and test functionality.
- Communication – There needs to be constant, real communication between the stake holders. Any business change project impacts a diverse set of people, roles and personalities, and assumptions need to be checked, re-checked and verified to avoid misunderstandings. There is also a need for a steering committee that has overview of the entire delivery to ensure that the intra-process interfaces and hand-offs are clean and continue to meet the requirements of the business. JLT EB have weekly project team calls as well as daily interactions through ad-hoc team meetings, calls, and Skype sessions.

6. BENEFITS

The BPM projects have resulted in many benefits. First and foremost, JLT EB was able to grow its trading profit by 50% in the last financial year. This was largely the result of doing more with less. JLT EB on-boarded new acquisitions with 50% fewer people despite a significant increase in the volume of transactions. And the company was also able to replace redundant systems.

The new methodology and best practices have enabled JLT EB to do work better and faster. For example, Business Analysts can do research and workflow design while developers focus on implementation and testing. This means that BA's can do about 50% of "development." Because the BPM suite is "codeless," they are saving time from not writing and maintaining code. JLT EB has also created a COE to ensure that team members learn best practices, get training, follow standards and get investment for new projects. Key reasons for success include: business involvement and user engagement, constant clear communications amongst stakeholders, and good vendor support.

7. BEST PRACTICES, LEARNING POINTS AND PITFALLS

On the road to automation, JLT EB has learned many lessons:

- Requirements – When reviewing requirements, talk through all scenarios, frameworks, and technical specifications. Lock down specifications as much as possible to create definitive scope and project plan. Involve end-users often during the requirements analysis so as to expose potential problems early.
- Project Management – Have committed project management. Ensure that team members are voicing concerns. Respond to questions same/next day. Watch scope creep. When outsourcing, ensure that both internal and external teams have active project management so as to avoid miscommunications.
- Resource Allocation – Assign a dedicated BA to the project to own requirements and make decisions on issues and change requests. Get technical resources talking to validate approach.
- Sponsors – Ensure that the business has clearly identified and committed sponsors and owners because any BPM project is about changing the "business."
- Documentation – Standardize documentation and isolate shared sections. "As little as possible and as much as is necessary" has been the ongoing motto whilst delivering many processes on numerous projects in parallel.

8. COMPETITIVE ADVANTAGES

The BPM infrastructure JLT EB has created enables the company to adapt faster to market forces, sell highly tailored solutions, and more efficiently service customers.

9. TECHNOLOGY

Core components include BizFlow, SharePoint, Kofax among others.

10. TECHNOLOGY AND SERVICES PROVIDERS

Project contributors include:

- **JLT EB IT Team** – Based in Manchester with staff located in Manchester, London, St. Albans, Bristol acting in roles of project management, business analysis, application development, QA/testing, and deployment.
- **HandySoft** – Based in Washington DC with team members in Washington DC and Manchester, providing BizFlow® BPM as well as professional services associated with project management, business analysis, application development, deployment and customer support.

Toyota España, Spain

Finalist: nominated by AuraPortal, USA

1. EXECUTIVE SUMMARY / ABSTRACT

Toyota is a well-known, leading worldwide automobile manufacturer. In Spain it is represented through its subsidiary Toyota España, which has a broad network of dealers to cover the Spanish territory, providing selling and technical assistance to end customers. The Toyota dealers are grouped into an association, who, sponsored by Toyota, took on the BPMS project in order to build an Intranet to manage and control their own environmental best practices according to Toyota policies and the ISO 14001 standard. Thus, the BPMS allowed the more than 250 Toyota dealers within the network to meet environmental Toyota practices with less human effort and the fewer technical and economic resources.

2. OVERVIEW

Toyota has been recognized as the top automobile manufacturer and one of the first to be concerned about the environment, driving a strong environmental best practices culture not only inside its own organization but also spreading it to its partners. Toyota is well-known for its market leading position selling eco-friendly hybrid cars that produce very low levels of pollution emissions. As a result, it created an ambitious project to have all of its dealers in Spain strive to achieve ISO 14001 certification and to demonstrate that their environmental culture is more than a marketing program. For this reason, Toyota hired a consulting firm with a leadership position in environmental practices in Spain in order to get the required advice for this ambitious project. With the external consultancy, the environmental system for Toyota's Spanish partner network was designed and implemented in tandem with Toyota's legal requirements as well as their internal audits and checks and balances. To make the project feasible, the consulting firm built an Intranet with all of the processes and documents involved, using a BPM Suite. The project was named GEAToyota, to coincide with the "goodness of the earth" and the initials of Environmental Managing in Spanish (GEA).

3. BUSINESS CONTEXT

All enterprises throughout the world have management systems related to environmental practices, some of them according to recognized international standards and some of them also with their own local policies and best practices. But the idea to extend these practices to a dealer network can be very difficult, because usually those dealers are small organizations without an environmentally conscious culture, and with limited economic resources. On the other hand, in Spain environmental laws and regulations are very complex, and there are several levels of environmental laws.

At the top, there are the European directives. Every country in the European Union can make specific laws according to this directive. Spain is a territory organized in an autonomous region of the EU, so, it can make its own laws which conform to the state laws. Ultimately, every municipality has its own laws and regulations as well, which are the most overriding. In this manner, a Toyota dealer have different regulations depending on the city where it is established, and all Toyota dealers must adhere to the environmental guidelines and best practices driven by the manufacturer. A traditional ISO project, without a BPMS to support it, would have failed. As a result, Toyota understood from the beginning that this project would need more than standard consultancy services, it would need a tool to manage the environmental system in order to normalize the processes and to automate the regulatory checklists individually for every dealer, keeping the amount of human resources in administrative tasks to a minimum, as well as keeping project costs at an acceptable level for the dealers.

In order to help the dealers, Toyota would subsidize and directly support part of the project, but every dealer would have to support part of the project to prove their involvement and commitment. The best way to achieve their goals for the project was with the inclusion of BPM practices and a BPMS product suite to build the management system.

To carry out the project, several actions where identified:

- To develop an environmental guide applicable to the dealers.
- To make an initial diagnose about the dealers' environmental practices and culture, and to split dealers in different groups according to their characteristics.
- To design the environmental system, according to the identified requirements determined in the discovery phase.
- To identify the legal requirements that every dealer should meet.
- To develop a process for maintaining the continuous changes in environmental regulations.
- To design and to create an Intranet using BPMS to support the system and legal requirements.
- To support every dealer certification.
- To regularly monitoring every dealer's activities and support them to maintain the system and the certification, using BPMS.

4. THE KEY INNOVATIONS

4.1 Business

This has been a large project, with several phases executed in order to achieve ISO 14001 certification for all of the dealers. The dealers where divided in four groups, starting with those who had a previous environmental culture or those who where most proactive with the project. It took nine months for this first group of selected members to become certified, but has been a complete success. The second group was certified one year later, and an additional year for the third group. As of today there are only a few dealers in the fourth and final group that are yet to be certified. So in about three years' time, 90 percent of Toyota's dealers in Spain have been certified and are using the environmental management system and executing environmental best practices every day.

4.2 Process

At the beginning of the project, no processes existed. All processes where created for this project, and they where created according to BPM standards.

The processes created were:

- Organizations (New dealer, new working center)
- Legal requirements
- Environmental Aspects (Identification and evaluation)
- Breaches (Corrective actions and non conformities)
- Emergencies
- Direction revision
- Documentation and registers

- Communications
- Events
- Environmental KPI monitoring
- Internal auditing
- Working center ownership changes
- Environmental responsibilities and training
- Objectives and goals

For every one of these processes, a detailed analysis was done, using ISO methodology and the consulting firm's own methodology, identifying the need for the process, how to solve it, players or actors involved, data to process and its sources and destinations, and KPI's for the continuous monitoring and improving of the process.

As a sample, figure 1 shows one of the processes regarding non conformities. This process can be started from the Internal Auditing or Corrective Actions processes or manually by the System Manager, and involves the following actors:

- RMA = ER: Environmental Responsible of the Working Center (every one of the dealers shops or workshops)
- AMA = ESM: Environmental System Manager
- GERENTE = MANAGER: Working Center Manager

When a Non-Conformity process is launched, the first step is to perform an immediate action plan by the ER. He or she decides who has to complete the action plan, if it will be completed by him or herself or if it needs the approval of the ESM. After the immediate action plan is registered, it could require the approval of the Working Center Manager or in the other case, it will launch a Corrective Action process immediately. After the corrective action process is launched, the system will monitor if a corrective action has been completed within 15 days. If not, the system warns the ER. Once the corrective action is performed, the ER must evaluate the effectiveness of the action. If it is not effective, a new Non Conformity process is launched. If it is, the Working Center Manager is informed and closes the process.

A total of 72 processes, most of them with similar complexity, were designed and deployed and are currently running in the environmental management system of the Toyota dealers.

Nonconformity Process – Level 2

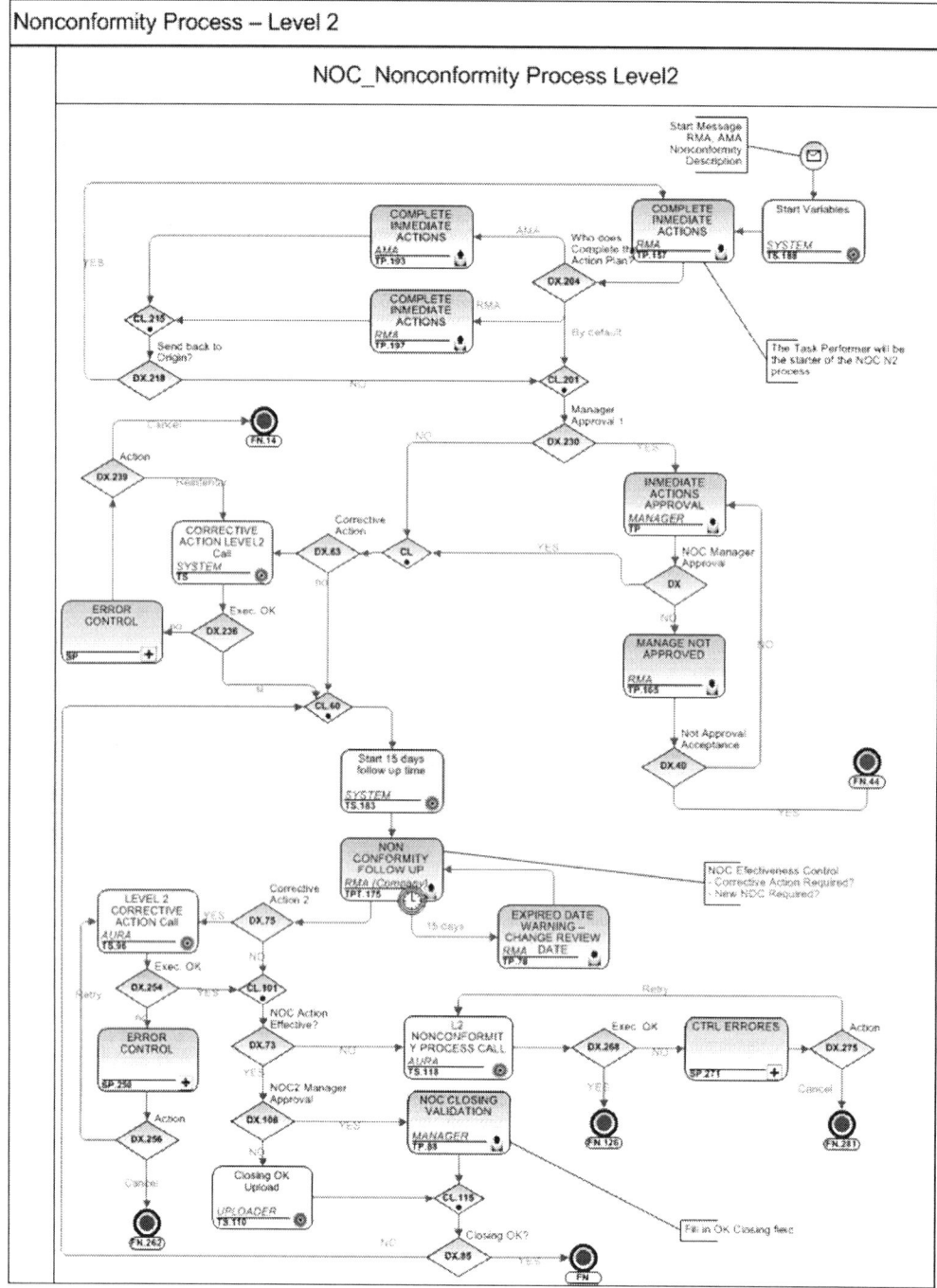

Figure 1. The Non Conformities Process Source: AUREN Organization

There are four types of employees using the system:
- Toyota corporate affairs users, who encourage the use of the system among the dealers, and who analyze the KPI's provided.
- The Environmental System Manager, who monitors the activity and support the dealers.

- Every dealer's Environmental Contact, who performs the actions needed for its working centers.
- Every dealer's Manager, who is informed about the actions taken and approves those actions that need an economic expense or modification in his Working Center.

For the corporate affair users, the use of the BPMS provides them the information they need to evaluate the degree of compliance to the environmental policies established. Without the BPMS it would have been very difficult to obtain KPI's and to know in real-time what the status was in each dealer regarding environmental matters.

For the Environmental System Manager, the BPMS is the way to keep all information up-to-date, and to easily receive all alarms and warnings. Without the BPMS, the alternative would be a large collection of unmanageable spreadsheets, a large database with difficult indexing for storing records, and a large collection of reminder notes, which would have been impossible to manage. Furthermore, there is the complexity to know which legal requirements apply to every working center. Toyota only has one person managing the environmental system of more than 200 dealers. Without the BPMS, more people would have absolutely been needed.

For every Environmental Contact, the system provides a portal where he can know what actions are needed, can make requests for support, and can store the records that substantiate best practices. Without that, he would have needed his own spreadsheets, database and notes without the support of a structured document repository. It should also be noted that in some dealers this job responsibility is shared with other duties by the same employee, so the more work that can be handled automatically for the ER, the more the project is valued by the dealers.

For every Working Center Manager, they can have a clear view of the status of their Working Center, using a tool that provides complete traceability and keeps all of the actions approved or not and all the communications with the headquarters, so again, BPM is reducing the burden on the organization.

5. HURDLES OVERCOME

Management

The most important hurdle anticipated at the beginning of the project was how to involve the dealers' owners. Within an organization, enforcing policies, processes and culture with all its employees is readily accomplished, but, how can this best be done outside the direct organization? How can a company convince more than 200 general managers working in autonomous dealer entities to adopt environmental practices according to the manufacturer's wishes?

At the beginning of the project this was a concern and a special communication plan was created. The project was presented at a dealer's convention, as a strategic plan of Toyota, outlining the benefits for the dealers. In addition, the corporate affairs personnel, along with the account managers of Toyota, worked together to convince and involve every single dealer, and visited them personally as needed. Throughout the project, regular dealer status meetings were held at each location in order to present the project status to the staff, including updates on dealers that have received their certification. Currently, regular workshops are held in several cities across Spain, allowing dealers that are using the system to orient new dealers that are not yet on the system. Through the support of Toyota, its certified dealers, and the participation of the consultants who built and help to maintain the system, these workshops help new dealers get answers to their questions and allow them to make suggestions for future enhancements.

Business

The business processes automated with the BPMS can be complex, but close attention was kept to keeping forms simple for the users and to maintaining a high level of usability for the system. After three years of use, experience has taught us that some processes can be improved, making it conceivable that the system can be made even easier to use in the future. During the last year, four processes have been modified to improve usability, and the other ten processes are planned to be modified in the coming months. As a result of Toyota's strong corporate support and promotion of the project, many major hurdles have been overcome.

Organization Adoption

As explained earlier, Toyota has demonstrated its leadership in environmental practices, particularly with the BPM project which has served a strategic initiative for the corporate office. Throughout the project, the organization as a whole has adapted to the project guidelines very quickly throughout its corporate culture. In addition, a special staff of Toyota Spain employees was created under the supervision of the Corporate Affairs Manager, including Corporate Affairs Staff, Quality Staff and an outsourced Environmental Manager for the dealer's network provided by the consulting firm. This staff has enough authority on the project, that if there is a dispute, the special staff's authority supersedes the authority of the dealer's account manager. Before the project deployment, internal presentations were made with the participation of the CEO and the worldwide headquarters deputy. This organization provided the right communication with the dealers and eased the dealer's adoption to the organization culture.

6. BENEFITS

The BPMS project can't be compared to previous systems that didn't exist, but we can imagine a comparative scenario using other tools to manage the system, one case using traditional single tools like spreadsheets, document folders, etc. and another case leveraging the development of a custom portal solution.

A primary benefit or requirement was to have a low total cost of ownership, including minimum cost to acquire and to maintain the system, the minimum number of people to manage the system and, equally important, the minimum time to deploy the system which implies the minimum opportunity cost.

Figure 2 shows the metrics comparative.

Metrics Description	BPMS	Single Tools 1	Custom Dev. 2	Cost Saving Vs. 1/Vs. 2
Number of people needed to manage the system for 250 centers (Assuming 1 person for 10 working centers)	1	25	1	2.400 %/---
Number of hours to obtain and aggregate KPI per month (not including working centers data registering)	4	500	4	12.400 %/---
Time to deployment, not considering opportunity cost	9 months	3 months	24 months	(66,67) % /166,67 %
Number of hours of system evolutionary maintenance per year, including training to final users	100	1000	500	900 % /400 %

Number of hours of system preventive and corrective maintenance per year	40	100	160	150 % / 300 %
Investment needed to build the system, including training of final users	1	0,1	3	(90) % / 200 %
Investment needed in infrastructures provided by working centers	1	10	1	900 % / ---

Figure 2. Comparative time and costs between different scenarios.

Source: AUREN

7. Best Practices, Learning Points and Pitfalls

7.1 Best Practices and Learning Points

✓ The creation of a project committee to sponsor the effort inside its organization and partners, with a close attention paid to project success and the support of senior management.

✓ The external support of a consulting firm with expertise in processes and technology.

✓ The detailed analysis of every process before its deployment.

✓ The implication of the final users along the project life cycle.

✓ The splitting of the users in several groups according to their profile.

7.2 Pitfalls

✗ The power of the system leads to an extensive number of KPI's, from the point of view of the amount of data produced by the users and the amount of data to analyze. Actually, the number of KPIs managed has been reduced.

✗ Some processes where tedious to some users without environmental culture. These processes have been simplified.

✗ The capacity planning for the records database repository was too limited. In three years the resolution available from picture devices such as cameras and smartphones has increased by 5 times, which has increased the data storage requirements, while most users don't mind photos taken at a low resolution. The process and database servers have been extended to support these new requirements.

8. Competitive Advantages

All automobile manufacturers are actually positioned to be environmentally conscientious, but only Toyota has really extended its philosophy to their dealers network. To maintain a leadership position in selling cars around the world requires many aspects to the business, but keeping this position requires a complete and never wavering commitment to environmental needs. Many manufacturers promote best practices along their dealer's networks, but only Toyota has provided a BPM tool to them, helping them to more effectively obtain individual certifications.

This experience in Spain has been very well received by Toyota headquarters in Europe, and it can be exported or leveraged by other subsidiaries in other countries. Due to the current recession, any good cost-saving initiative helps. Perhaps it is not the best time for car manufacturers to invest, but with the position of Toyota in environmental matters, it is helping them maintain its leadership in car sales. In addition, the project was presented to the Spanish ministry of industry and won an important economic award to help those dealers that joined the project, as a result of the important cost reductions and environmental benefits they contributed. In this manner, all the dealers that joined the project acquired the system for a very small investment, but with significant benefits.

9. TECHNOLOGY

When Toyota decided to carry out the project, the consultancy firm AUREN recommended AuraPortal BPMS as the platform to support the environmental system. Toyota evaluated another solution, offered by an ISO certification company, but the amount of customizations needed eliminated this option. Thus, AuraPortal BPMS was selected for the project. AUREN is a leading AuraPortal Partner in Spain, and decided to use AuraPortal BPMS in its projects due to the fast time to deploy the solution while offering a very high level of functionality and a very close and collaborative partner, regarding technical consulting and technical support.

A flexible self-maintained BPM technology was the basic foundation for determining the functionalities required for the Toyota´s BPM solution. The selected product was AuraPortal Enterprise Management platform including a full BPMS (Business Process Management Suite), considered by BPM industry experts as the world's most advanced, complete and easy-to-use; an Extensive **document management** facilities containing automatic generation of intelligent documents with automatic signatures and an agile file system; a new concept of **CRM** (customer relationship management) based on **process patterns** including 'marketing automation' with tailored **marketing campaigns** and **sales opportunities** follow-up; an enterprise **content management** system (ECM) with powerful publishing and broadcasting possibilities; and a revolutionary system for creating, by the user, an **online commerce** platform in his own web site including shopping cart and payment processing gateways; **all without the need of any programming experience required**.

A unique feature that differentiates AuraPortal is its automatic, on-the-fly conversion of modeled processes into executable processes without the need of any IT intervention or programming code, leaving the full control of the process creation and maintenance in the hands of business people. This core concept presents three advantages:

A) Eliminates the traditional communication difficulties between business people and IT people when designing and modifying processes.

B) Guarantees the right design and execution of all processes with no programming errors, therefore providing robust operations and processes that exactly fit the requirements of business executives.

C) Dramatically reduces process development time (and cost), with the ability to make process models changes easily, rapidly, and with immediate effect.

The executable model of any process is carried out using a diagramming tool based on Microsoft Visio and BPMN standard notation. Only some data such as the roles of the process performers and the forms design for each task needs to be defined before the process enters into execution mode. The automatic generation of executable processes directly from the model could lead one to think that the system is only applicable to simple processes. The vendor has demonstrated however, directly and via large customers using AuraPortal for several years with tens of thousands of users, in thousands of concurrent processes that the most complex processes (that in some cases are beyond the reach of other BPM products) run smoothly, with high performance, and that are error free.

10. THE TECHNOLOGY AND SERVICE PROVIDERS

AUREN was the consulting firm selected by Toyota to design and implement the environmental management system and the BPMS solution. AUREN is a leading consultancy firm in Spain, the first domestic professional services firm with other business divisions in Auditing and Advising, and with offices in other European countries and South America. AUREN is providing the technology infrastructure from the system, using it's own datacenter with a virtual server architecture, hosted by a prestigious provider: COLT TELECOM. This avoids the need for Toyota to invest in servers, communications, and security. More information about AUREN can be found at www.auren.com.

The BPMS used is AuraPortal BPMS. **AuraPortal** is a global BPMS (Business Process Management System) provider, delivering a solution that creates Business Process Workflow Execution Models without the need for IT programming. The **AuraPortal** solution has been proven in a variety of industries including: manufacturing & distribution, financial services, professional services, health care and federal and local government sectors.

The **AuraPortal** solution typically complements an existing ERP or CRM system, and is most beneficial in developing business process workflows across multiple disparate systems. AuraPortal is 100 percent Web-based, 100 percent Microsoft-based, and is complementary to existing ERP and CRM systems.

AURA has a presence in 50 countries with more than 400 customers including, among others: Coca-Cola, PepsiCo, Frito-Lay, Toyota, Yamaha, Petróleos Mexicanos (PEMEX), Carrefour, ArcelorMittal, Eletrobrás, Saras, Royal KPN, Bristol-Myers Squibb, Sodexo, etc., as well as a many Government Agencies and Departments in several countries.

More Information about AuraPortal can be found at www.auraportal.com

Ecobank LLC, Senegal

Silver Award: Nominated by Newgen Software Technologies Ltd, India

1. EXECUTIVE SUMMARY / ABSTRACT

ECO bank, the leading pan-African bank, was established as a bank holding company in 1985 under a private sector initiative spearheaded by the Federation of West African Chambers of Commerce and Industry with the support of ECOWAS. Spanned across more than 32 countries, the bank operates as "One Bank" with common branding, standards, policies and processes to provide a consistent and reliable service to its customers. Today, the bank operates in more than 755 branches and they have 779 ATMs and 888 points of sale (POSs).

The bank with their business in 32 countries faced some business challenges like: lack of process standardization- as the processes across 32 countries were not centralized, all the business processes were working in silos, manual intervention in business process was slowing things down, there was no process visibility and auditability. Also, the bank had to adhere to the regulatory guidelines given by the central bank for their business processes. The bank's forgery control policies were not strong enough. All these drawbacks together became a huge barrier to the bank's aggressive expansion plan.

To centralize and streamline the business processes, the bank decided to implement a BPM solution to work as a platform for all key core banking processes. The bank chose Newgen's Business Process Management (BPM) solution- OmniFlow™ with underlying Document Management Solution (DMS) - OmniDocs™ and Scanning and Digitization Solution- OmniScan™ , to automate their mission critical business processes like- Account Opening, Account Maintenance and Fund Transfer.

A Center of Excellence (COE) was created which takes care of continuous process improvement and allows further scaling up of new processes. The solution resulted in quick benefits. Some of those benefits are:
- Flexibility to incorporate changes in business processes as per market requirements
- Easy audit and tracking
- Minimal manual intervention for faster TAT and improved SLAs
- A one shop stop for all the key processes as they are connected via newly designed architecture
- Process standardization across 32 countries
- Centralized processes
- Better process visibility and control
- Leaner branches for quick business expansion

2. OVERVIEW

ECO bank had their business spanned across 32 countries and had multiple lines of Businesses (LOBs). All those business processes were controlled from the local or zonal offices. Even the same process was not connected or linked across multiple countries. All processes were run in the branch offices and this became a barrier to the bank for scalability. Only linear growth was possible (more headcounts for more business) for the bank which meant more operational cost and marginal benefits. So, the bank wanted to centralize all those business operations to gain economies of scale. Through centralized business operations, the bank wanted to get leaner branches for faster scalability and at the same time be able to monitor, measure and control its businesses across geographies from the same centralized location. Also, since the bank had one common branding standard, they wanted to standardize all their business operations that run across 32 countries. The bank had been using the core banking solution for all of their LOBs. To make any change in the business process meant change in core banking system itself which required a lot of customization, coding and hence a lot of process downtime. For this reason, the bank required a BPM solution which would work as a layer on the core banking system so that anytime they want to make a change in a business process they may do it from the BPM layer with no or minimal process downtime.

The bank had an aggressive expansion plan. But they found some operational and IT hindrances which became the barrier for them in achieving their target. Some of the key business concerns and challenges were:

- Lack of process visibility for measuring and monitoring
- Not able to incorporate quick changes in the process as per changing market scenario
- Physical document storage, tracking and management
- Adhering all the regulatory compliances as required by the central bank
- All the critical banking processes and systems worked in silos
- Higher process cycle time due to manual processing of tasks
- Customer satisfaction not up to the mark

The bank opted for Newgen's comprehensive BPM solution platform for their Account Opening, Account Maintenance and Fund Transfer processes. The solution solved the business concerns of the bank and became a game changer for them as it brought about the complete business transformation for the bank. The processes were made live in 22 days and the processes were rolled out in 35 branches in a single day.

The solution brought together all the processes and external business systems which were related with each other but were working on silos. Digitization of documents made it possible to take all the business decisions on electronic documents as documents are available anytime anywhere on the web. The BPM tool OmniFlow™ defines the workflow and the electronic document flow for every process. The electronic documents got archived in a centralized repository of OmniDocs™ and they were made accessible from there to the users as per the access rights given to them.

The solution was designed as per the strategic initiatives taken by the bank. All the customer requests and works are now processed in the central office resulting in leaner branch offices. The branch offices capture the customer documents and some of the key customer information by using Newgen's distributed scanning tool OmniScan™. After the de-dupe and blacklist check the customer requests for account opening or fund transfer or other requests were sent to the central office for further processing which effectively made the branch office more customer focused. The simplicity of operations made it easier for the bank to open a new branch quickly. The central office takes care of the opening of a new account, fund transfer or any other customer requests and do all the customer communications via email, SMS, courier etc. The welcome kit and the other related documents are sent to the customers by the central office.

A Center of Excellence (COE) was created which takes care of continuous process improvement and further scaling out of new processes.

Some of the key benefits accrued were:

- Solution helped achieving vertical and horizontal business growth
- Flexibility to change business processes as per market requirements
- Easy audit and tracking
- Minimal manual intervention ensures "First Time Right" for all the operations
- Faster process cycle time
- Ability to create and maintain account in bulk (up to 3000 accounts can be created at a time) aligns with their faster market capturing strategy
- Process and performance metrics for process visibility
- COE is enabled to faster roll out of new processes across the branches
- Improved customer interactions resulted in higher customer satisfaction
- Reduced operational costs
- Newgen is now doing process standardization across 32 countries. On completion this project will be one of the largest BPM implementation projects across the globe done by any BPM vendor
- Parallel work processing for activities like Customer On-boarding, Cheque Book Request, e-alert, Internet banking facility, Debit card automation which resulted in faster TAT
- Real time exception handling facility between the branch offices and the Central office like invalid documents, documents not attached, debit card not issued etc
- No data redundancy as single form template is used now for data entry replacing 8 different forms that the bank used before the implementation
- More flexibility in the business process as process route works automatically as per the type of work, like debit card request, internet banking request etc. or as per the amount associated with a certain work
- The Fund transfer process has become so comprehensive that it has been running in association with the referral system, the treasury module and the rapid transfer module without any toggling of screens between them
- A single platform for Interbank, Intrabank, Foreign draft and SWIFT (Foreign transfer)
- Better utilization of resources and high availability of system as solution runs smoothly even when the core banking system is down. Cases can be built and saved in the system and then can be uploaded to the core banking system when it is available again.

3. BUSINESS CONTEXT

Describe the initial state of the organization. Explain the driving motivation for initiating the change program.

The bank was in pursuit of expanding its business both vertically and horizontally. The bank wanted to open more number of branches and at the same time provide more products and services to its customers. They had an ambitious strategy for developing a common central processing Center (CPC) in Accra for all the affiliates. The bank realized that to achieve all these objectives they needed a solution platform which could not only bring complete automation and process visibility but also ensures adherence to regulatory compliance, continuous process improvement and improved quality of customer services. Some of the key business problems for the bank were:

- All the processes were running in silos and hence did not have any standardization. Situation became more complicated as all these processes had to adhere to the regulatory compliances given by the central bank
- Manual processing of all the customer requests which comes via multiple channels
- Manual hand-offs of documents made it difficult to track and manage the right version of the documents
- Managing all the physical documents and tracking of the same was a tedious and time taking process
- Managing customer communications via multiple channels
- Different business processes and systems worked independently and it resulted in data duplication and reworks
- Escalation and exception management process was manual and error-prone
- Tracking and audit facility was not comprehensive
- Usage of physical documents across departments and branches caused higher operational cost and higher process cycle time
- The core banking system works in silos from the banking processes
- No provision for Duplicate check and black list check which was a major issue
- No monetary policy and procedure for forgery control
- Core banking worked as point solutions for all the banking requests which created bottlenecks

4. THE KEY INNOVATIONS

The solution Newgen provided was built upon some innovative features and capabilities. Some of those out of the box features are:

- Dynamic work routing based on the job type and its severity. Right person or the right group of people with relevant experiences is assigned to a certain task.
- Automatic de-dupe check to make the business data consistent and non-redundant
- Automatic black list check and credit history check for forgery control and safer banking
- New business process structure was designed and implemented which did the process standardization across 32 countries
- Design and implementation of best of breed IT network that brought customers, bankers and other third parties together connected. The network made all the necessary documents available from anytime anywhere for faster & easier banking

4.2 Business

The business benefits, accrued to the bank, came from the changes, brought by Newgen's solution to their way of doing business. The number of customer interactions per sales agent and front-end executives in a day was below expectations and customers had to wait for long time to be able to talk to them. This resulted in loss of business generated. The Newgen solution did not bring mere automation to the bank's as-is processes but it completely changed their way of doing business.

After using the solution, the sales agents and front-desk executives started spending more times a day with the bank's customers and solving their problems.

So in this way, the bank started generating more business per day and because of the reduced waiting time they started getting higher customer satisfaction.

4.3 Process

Account Opening process- Pre-Implementation scenario:

Prior to implementing Newgen's BPM solution, the Account Opening process of the bank was time consuming and it required extensive manual intervention across various steps. Since, the Core banking System and other systems were working independently, the process required multiple data entry which led to data redundancy. Also, the manual intervention used to result into human errors which were difficult to trace and track. The process involved physical documents which used to move from one department to the other and many times from one branch to the other branches. Maintaining and tracking of all the physical documents was a major challenge.

There was no provision for Duplicate Customer Check, Blacklist/PEP Check and the Account Opening process had high dependency on other 3rd party applications for data and document verification and customer credibility checking. Also, the mandate cropping and uploading of the same in the core banking system used to be done manually. The cheque book or debit card requests from customers were registered manually. It was very difficult to track all the customer requests and maintain the SLAs. The customer requests were tracked and responded manually which resulted in delay in service and not-so-good customer experience.

Account Opening process- Post-Implementation scenario:

Newgen's BPM platform OmniFlow™ significantly reduced the number of steps (Almost 50% reduction) required for the Account Opening process. The cycle time of the Account opening process was reduced by 75%. The unified platform brought all the systems together on the same platform and all the systems were linked in such a way that they could talk to each other. Now, the entire process requires minimal manual intervention. System automatically checks for duplicate customer entry and prevents users from doing so. Also, the system automatically checks for blacklisted customers and prompts users the same if the customer is blacklisted. All the physical documents are converted into digitized documents which traverse across departments and locations.

The system also generates electronic data capture forms for the KYC process. The system performs automatic data entry by using the unique automatic data fill technique. The mandated cropping is taken care by the scanning tool-OmniScan™. The customer requests for debit card/ cheque book are now processed automatically and system ensures that the SLAs are maintained by giving automatic alert messages to the users. System sends automatic mails to the customer like welcome mail or request status mail etc for improved customer experience. The BPM platform supports auto-processing of e-Alerts, e-Statements and Internet Banking Requests.

The integrated document management system- OmniDocs™ and BPM platform-OmniFlow™, allow auto movement of all digitized documents from one user workstation to the other, and right-based access to documents for all level of users.

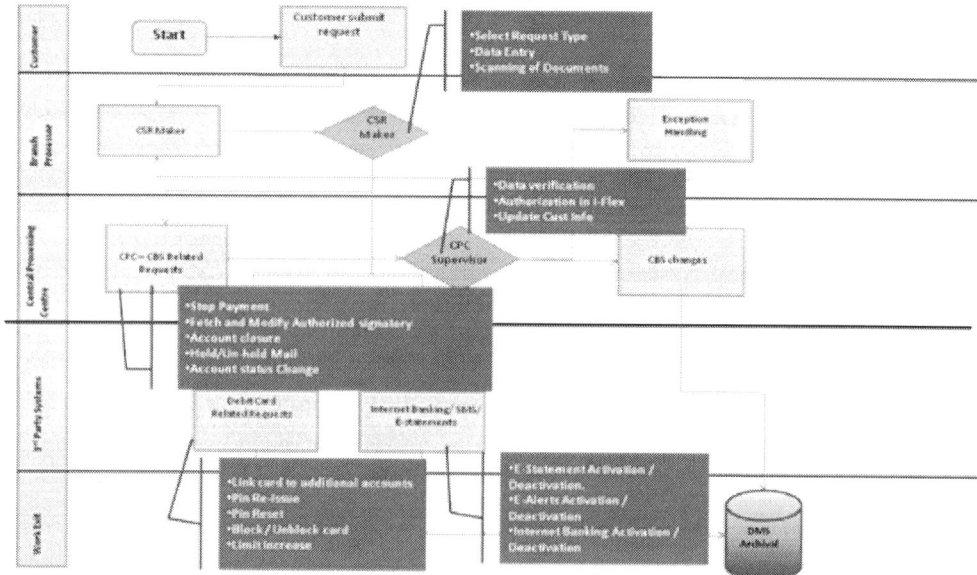

Fig: Account Opening Process Flow with Newgen's BPM solution

Account Maintenance Process- Pre-Implementation scenario:

Following is the highlight of the Account Maintenance process running in the bank prior to implement the Newgen's BPM suite-

- Decentralized Operations with multiple Processing Units
- Manual processing of account maintenance request in different applications
- No Escalation Management and Tracking of customer applications
- Manual mail requests were used to be sent to different departments for request processing
- Customization in accordance to the changing market strategies in the core banking system was a very time and effort consuming process
- Generation of MIS reports for regulatory bodies was cumbersome
- No integration with the core system and hence request processing in core system was tedious and error-prone

Account Maintenance Process- Post-Implementation scenario:

Some of the key highlights of the Account maintenance process after implementing the Newgen's BPM suite are as follows-

- The operations are centralized now with single Central Processing Centre and it requires minimal manual intervention
- Multiple reports generation to monitor and measure the process and the efficiency of branch offices
- Reduce process cycle time
- Processing of Account Maintenance requests is now done through a single interface i.e. OmniFlow™ interface, thus streamlining the entire process
- Automatic Escalation management and tracking of customer applications
- Automatic e-mails sent to different departments for request processing
- Customer Request management and tracking is now easier
- Automatic archival of customer documents in central repository, which can be used across products

- Flexibility to change the business process as per regulatory and market requirements
- Compliance fulfillment such as KYC in place without any extra man · hours effort

Fund Transfer Process- Pre-Implementation scenario:

- Users were unable to perform any transaction at the time when the system was not functional. This used to create a huge backlog.
- Rework was required due to the lack of system and data availability
- There are instances when some information was found to be on hold or missing for a transaction. Such transactions took a lot of time to process and often ended up going on the back burner
- Operational Reports were prepared manually

Fund Transfer Process- Post-Implementation scenario:

- Newgen's BPM solution has a higher availability as compared to CBS. So, even if CBS is not working users can just enter the data and save it to process later.
- A transaction can be processed later as someone can just fill minimal details and put the transaction on hold. This transaction can be retrieved later.
- Automatic report generation and distribution
- Better utilization of resources

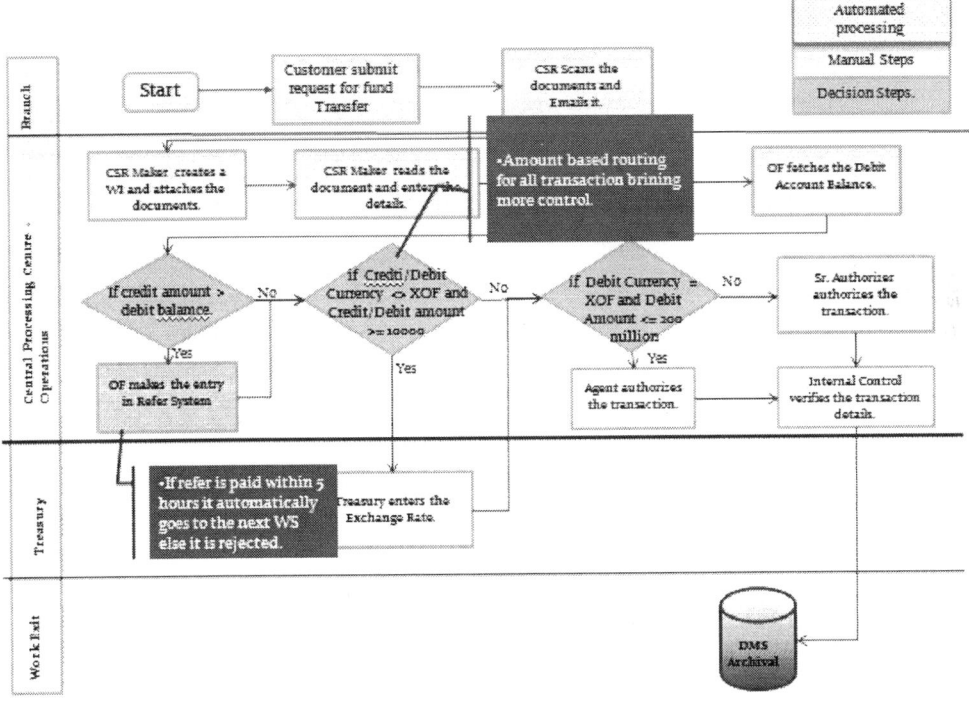

Fig: Fund Transfer process with Newgen's BPM Solution

Service Oriented Architecture Framework

The BPM solution designed by Newgen was built on a strong SOA architecture which has the following capabilities:

- OmniFlow has the capability of invoking any SOAP Compliant Web Service using Integration Step. Using Web services:
  - ✓ Integration workstep can be configured as 'Web Service' to invoke the methods of the remotely deployed Web services.
  - ✓ Both Synchronous and Asynchronous modes of invocation are supported
  - ✓ Connection through a proxy server can also be configured for calling to external web-methods.
  - ✓ Process Variables and Web-Method Parameters mapping need to be defined on Integration workstep
- Different ways through which OmniFlow™ can communicate with the Core Banking System
  - ✓ Invoking of web services from java based front end NGForm component of OmniFlow™.
  - ✓ Using the Integration workstep feature of OmniFlow™ for invoking the required web services through its Web service invoker utility program.
  - ✓ Java based auto utility program for executing the required user functionalities.

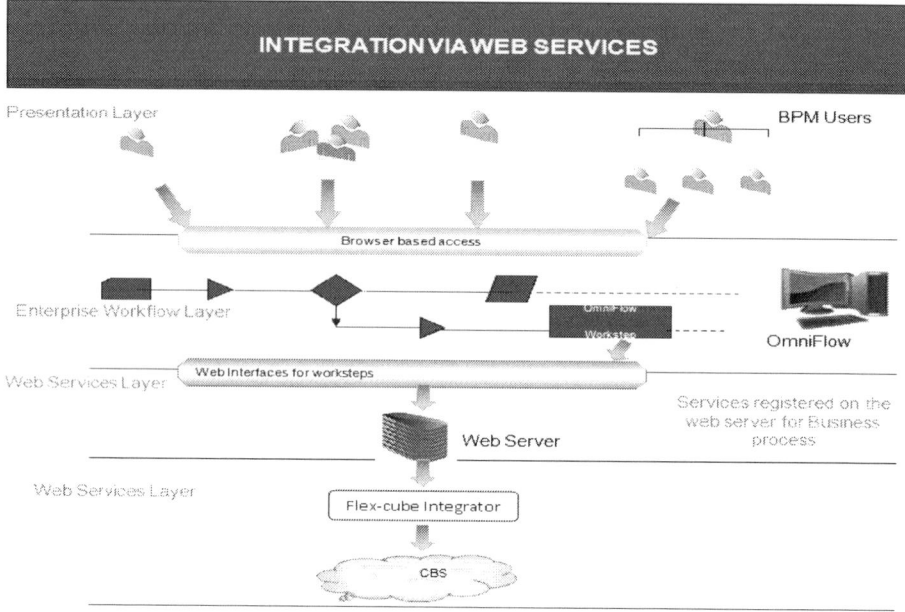

Fig: Solution SOA Framework

Fig; Solution Architecture encompassing 32 country Implementation

4.4 Organization

In the post-implementation scenario, the branch offices were responsible for the processing of A/O requests or any customer servicing requests and hence were heavily loaded with various day-to-day activities. As a result, they were not able to put a good amount of customer facing time.

The centralization of the banking processes made the branch offices leaner as they no longer had process jobs. They were required only to capture the customer documents and some key information about the customer. The distributed scanning tool digitized the physical documents and verifications sent across the documents to the central office for further processing. The branch office needs only a scanning tool for their day to day operation. So, using the solution, the branch offices started focusing on customers and they started interacting more with customers. The Turn-Around-Time (TAT) for customer interactions got drastically reduced as they had to capture only some basic information on the customers. So, this resulted into improved productivity and efficiency of employees with reduction in non-core activities, allowing branch executives to cross sell other products. The implementation resulted in improved customer satisfaction through quicker and better servicing, reduction in the requirement of physical forms, and reduced customer response time.

A COE was formulated which monitors the business process, makes quick changes in a business process as per the changing market scenario and works towards continuous improvement. Also, the COE is responsible for the fast roll out of new processes across all the branches. The COE was established with the cross-functional team from the bank and supported by Newgen consultants.

- Installed an automation system that automatically moves single piece of work across various disjointed base systems so as to improve efficiency and provide a way to match operating capacity with employees.
- It provided visibility to employees for all work items pertaining to a process. It helped in streamlining their activities in an efficient way.
- It provided easy access from desktops to all documents and processing status of the case. The previous actions taken are easily traceable from the extensive audit trails.
- Best in class operations and productivity standards were established through analysis of time and motion data coming out of the workflow databases rather than using traditional averages that could be skewed by idle time, low skilled staff and poor practices

5. HURDLES OVERCOME

Following are the hurdles we faced during the project:
- Employees' resistance towards the change: change in any organization is always difficult to manage.
- On time business/bank resources availability
- Third party coordination
- Integration calls not on time
- Change information not percolated to the lowest level
- Lack of affiliate support
- Local management was not serious
- Users were not so motivated to use the system
- Many users feared the loss of jobs

In the initial phase, Newgen helped the bank automate one its most critical processes, the Account opening process. Integrated with the bank's existing core application, the solution provides easier and faster data exchange across systems. Buoyed by the results achieved within a short time of deployment, the bank also implemented and automated a number of other key processes such as Customer and Account Maintenance, Fund Transfer on the BPM platform.

6. BENEFITS

6.1 Cost Savings

A greater number of transactions can be handled by each agent resulting in cost savings on agents. All the documents get digitized and the electronic copy of the document is used for day to day work processing. Before the implementation photocopies of all documents were taken for each application set, but with the new system no photocopies are required and this has led to drastic savings. Courier costs were also saved as applications need not be sent back. Also, all the customer communications are now possible via SMS, email or fax, which are integrated with the system. The Business Activity Monitoring (BAM) module automatically generates various complex reports for process monitoring which was otherwise time consuming and complex.

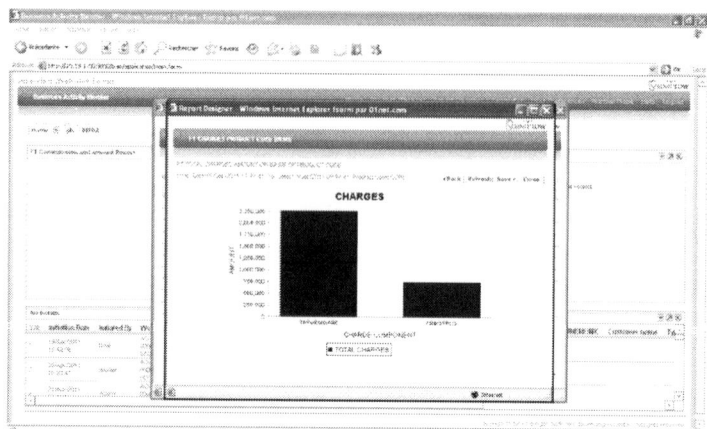

Fig: A BAM report showing the various types of charges collected against the product code.

Category	Pre-Implementation Scenario	Post-Implementation Scenario	Remarks
Compliance and Quality	50%	99%	• Each and every Account Opened through BPM is audited by a checker • BPM also ensures that cases without proper documentation are tracked and completed. • Inbuilt Controls in BPM process prevents Opening of Accounts with wrong data
Cost Saving by reduction in effort	-	USD (-)50 K /yr	• BPM has facilitated in enhancement of resource utilization, CPC is now enabled to handle more volumes with lesser resource bandwidth.

			• 1 hr =2.5 USD so (2.5 USD *15000 Account). • Expiry Report, Management Report etc was manually generated.
Document Handling	–	USD(-)13K/yr	• Mandatory checklist, Blacklist checks & seamless integration with CBS for end to end automation helps to identify compliance related issues thus rework possibilities are almost NIL.

6.2 Time Reductions

Reduced time-to-market, cycle time etc.

Process	Pre-Implementation – Avg TAT	Post-Implementation – Avg. TAT
Account Opening	3 hours	15 mins
Account Maintenance	2 days	1 hr
First Time Right (FTR)	50%	95%

6.3 Increased Revenues

The process has been running for three months now. We are expecting more than 250% of ROI at the end of the year. As, of now, the result is satisfactory.

6.4 Productivity Improvements

- Processing capacity increased by over 80%
- Completing the process first time right (FRT), improved by 95%.
- Adherence to SLAs improved by 99%

7. BEST PRACTICES, LEARNING POINTS AND PITFALLS

7.1 Best Practices and Learning Points

✓ *Starts with identification of actual pain areas and ends with resolution of the same*

✓ *Implementation, Flex, Ecobank and Newgen; good relationship in three parties*

✓ *Agile Implementation involving three different independent parties*

✓ *Teamwork involving excellent collaboration between the parties involved*

✓ *Project implementation on time with good customer feedback because of good PMP practices*

7.2 Pitfalls

✗ *User acceptance test should be done in parallel. It saves the implementation time and requires less iterations for modifications and easy change management*

✗ *High level integrations should be done at the very last stage of the project*

8. COMPETITIVE ADVANTAGES

By implementing the solution, the bank has provided a competitive advantage to its sales force as they are equipped with more time and facility to interact with more number of customers in a day:

- Scaling up of operational activities

- Enabling the bank to keep pace with business growth and demands
- Compliance and audit with easy KYC process adjoined with the Account Opening process
- Enabled real time movement of processing documents from all the branches to the central processing facility through OmniDocs™, while the workflow has enforced the process checks before the work item leaves the branch to ensure that it is processed "First time Right".
- Expanding the scope of the process to well beyond account opening and that too in a span of few months has resulted in it being embedded into the organization's "New" way of working

9. TECHNOLOGY

The solution was built on Newgen's BPM tool- OmniFlow™, Underlying Document Management system- OmniDocs™ and distributed scanning tool- OmniScan™

10. THE TECHNOLOGY AND SERVICE PROVIDERS

Primary Vendor: Newgen Software Technologies Limited.

Riyadh Military Hospital, Saudi Arabia

Gold Award: Nominated by Bizagi, UK

1. EXECUTIVE SUMMARY / ABSTRACT

Al-Wazarat Health Center (WHC) is located in Riyadh City, the capital of Saudi Arabia. The center is associated with the **R**iyadh **M**ilitary **H**ospital Program. RMH is part of the Medical Services Department (MSD) of the Ministry of Defense and Aviation (MODA). The center is specialized as a Family and Community Medicine Department, with a large practitioner service and is currently incorporating a dermatology clinic, well women's clinic, and a pediatric clinic to accommodate the growing population and to further enhance the quality of patient care. In addition to the ordinary healthcare facility and auxiliary, the center also contains other medical facilities such as a Pharmacy Department, Radiology Department, treatment rooms, specimen rooms, resuscitation and ECG rooms, and a nebulizing room.

The Family and Community Department aims to provide the best standard of healthcare services for its patients by meeting their expectations, and has full commitment to the principles of Total Quality Management. It also provides optimum support to all employees through effective training to further its management objectives.

Like any healthcare organization, WHC involves complex clinical and administrative tasks and processes to manage their daily operation which covers different specialty services. The clinical workflow varies from appointment registration, clinical procedures and investigation (e.g. laboratory/radiology), and may include a referral to the outpatient clinic or the emergency room. The various tasks and processes also involve healthcare providers, physicians, pharmacist, nurses, clerks and administrative personnel.

WHC developed a collaborative and process-oriented Business Process Management (BPM) system (eMedServe) built on Bizagi BPM Suite, which captures all of WHC clinical and administrative processes and activities, and automates them as they actually are. The aim was to enhance efficiency of health care delivery within a patient-centered interdisciplinary approach. Bizagi was able to provide the appropriate BPM system offering a robust, high-level and multifunctional application that would allow WHC to achieve faster results.

2. OVERVIEW

Al-Wazarat Health Center (WHC) is located in Riyadh City, the capital of Saudi Arabia. The center is associated with the **R**iyadh **M**ilitary **H**ospital Program. RMH is part of the Medical Services Department (MSD) of the Ministry of Defense and Aviation (MODA). The center is specialized as a Family and Community Medicine Department. This department has a large practitioner service for patients attending the center for medical treatment, which may involve treatment for acute or chronic disorders, ante-natal care, child welfare, vaccination programs, and care of chronic/acute wounds and injuries. A dermatology clinic, well women's clinic, and a pediatric clinic are being added to accommodate the growing population and to further enhance the quality of patient care. In addition to the ordinary healthcare facility and auxiliary, the center also contains other medical facilities such as a Pharmacy Department, Radiology Department, treatment rooms, specimen rooms, resuscitation and ECG rooms, and a nebulizing room.

The Family and Community Department of RMH offers medical treatment and follow-up to all eligible patients through the different clinics held daily from 07:30 a.m. to 23:30 p.m. The Family and Community Department aims to provide the best standard of healthcare services for its patients by meeting their expectations, and has full commitment to the principles of Total Quality Management. The Family and Community Department also provides optimum support to all employees through effective training to further its management objectives.

Like any healthcare organization, WHC involves complex processes that cover different specialty services. The clinical workflow varies from appointment registration, clinical procedures and investigation (e.g. laboratory/radiology), and may include a referral to the outpatient clinic or the emergency room if the particular case involved is of serious nature. The process involves clinical and administrative tasks which are handled by the healthcare provider according to the specialty-specific role which will alternate between different users.

The BPM system has helped to enhance the efficiency of health care delivery by improving health care interactions within a patient-centered interdisciplinary approach (e.g. physician to patient; physician to physician; physician to pharmacist). It encourages many forms of inter-partnerships to support patient care. A key factor in the success of a BPM system implementation is collaboration. While a data-centered application system tends to remain stable (i.e., unchanged) for rather long periods of time, a **process-oriented** application must be modified whenever the business processes they support change, and this may happen rather frequently in real working environments. The process–oriented system allows clinicians to update, manage and change a particular treatment protocol as new drugs are discovered or emitted, and shows new methods of application of how to treat certain diseases, including information concerning a course of a particular disease and its patterns. Other information such as a pre-planned treatment process, and organization policies and procedures are at the user's finger tips.

The challenges that the BPM system had to resolve regarding WHC´s operation are summarized in the following list:

- Increased patient waiting time
- Postponed or cancelled procedures
- Repetitive procedures
- Long treatment times
- Increased cost spends
- Inability to determine task times
- Allocation of resources on time
- Inability to estimate the needs for expansion
- Inability to maintain standards according to policy and procedures

Benefits and positive results regarding all these challenges were obtained with the BPM system developed with Bizagi BPM Suite.

3. BUSINESS CONTEXT

The process involves clinical and administrative tasks which are handled by the healthcare provider according to the specialty-specific role which will alternate between different users. Depending on the task; the initial process will be the registration of the patient by the clerk, and then the patient information will be reviewed by the nurse, and from there it will go to the physician for review. Once the information has been reviewed by the physician, he will input notations and send the information back to the nurse to complete certain procedures. Afterwards, the physician will make an evaluation/diagnosis dependent upon the test results.

The tasks in the work flow are performed either manually or by reviewing the results of an automated process in which new data is available for analysis and the next steps can be completed. The cooperation between different sections as well as between healthcare providers is crucial to accomplish the required process, since the work of each user (regarding a patient) is dependent upon accurate entries by the other user. Much of the value derived from the delivery system results from the effective communication of information from one party to another and, the ability of multiple parties to engage in interactive communication of information.

The (dynamic) planning of the patient flow is a very complex and error-prone task, since activities may be closely related to each other due to clinical, organizational, or logistic reasons; because of this, they can neither be executed sequentially nor completely independently of each other. For a particular patient, medical interventions may have to be performed in a certain order or with a minimum or maximum time distance between them.

Due to the complexity and size of the process, the sensitivity of the information that it handles and the accuracy with which it needs to be managed, the WHC decided and identified the necessity to implement a BPM system that would allow increasing efficiency and meeting service standards and policies.

4. THE KEY INNOVATIONS

The BPM project´s purpose was to map and automate the "Core Processes" of Al-Wazarat Healthcare Center (WHC), which is part of Family & Community Medicine (F&CM) Department at RMH. WHC has a total staff of 200 personnel in the following categories: Administration, Reception Areas (Clinical Reception Clerks / Appointment Desk / Referral Desk), Nursing, Doctors, Pharmacy, Laboratory, and Radiology.

4.2 Business

In order to provide a standards certified health service of the utmost quality to its patients (the military officers and their relatives) the Riyadh Military Hospital (RMH) embarked in a BPM initiative with Bizagi. This innovative project brought several benefits to WHC, including business agility and efficiency.

In terms of business and operation structure, the innovations include:
- Total of **4** Main Processes were **automated**
- Total of **6** Structural Sub-Processes were **created**
- Total of **67** Sub-Processes & Electronic Requests were **automated**
- Total of **41** WHC Printed-Letter Templates were **created**

4.3 Process

The BPM initiative is being led by the Technological Research and Development unit at the RMH, called MedIcen.

In its first approach, the MedIcen personnel have automated over 70 processes for the Wasarat Health Centre (WHC) primary care centre (PCC).

These processes can be classified in 4 main services:
- Walk-In process: Attention of patient that walk in to the hospital without any prior appointment.

- Short-booked: general service provided for patients that have booked an appointment.
- Speciality booked: speciality service provided for patients that have booked an appointment.
- Emergency: patients that come to the hospital because an emergency.

The project covers the complete life-cycle of the patient, from registration, triage, to diagnose and treatment and will be used by approximately 400 users serving approximately 2.000 patients per day.

Once the system was rolled-out, the BPM team at MedIcen initiated the definition and automation of the processes at the much larger RMH, where there will be several thousands of users serving no less than 6.000 patients per day.

Application Development Process:

The BPM system was built on Bizagi Business Process Management (BPM) solution. The eMedServe system is designed, developed, and implemented by the Medical Informatics Research and Development Center (MedICen), Riyadh Military Hospital (RMH). The purpose of eMedServe is to computerize the business of Al-Wazarat Healthcare Center (WHC) and automate its clinical practices built-on the Bizagi platform. The current release of eMedServe captures all of WHC clinical processes and activities, and automates them as they actually are.

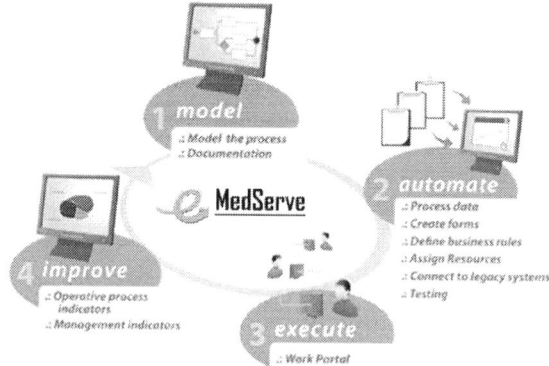

The following process model shows part of the Emergency Management process with some of its structural sub-processes such as: Treatment Room Process, Investigation Process, Referral Process…etc

The following image shows the stages of the project used to define the process architecture:

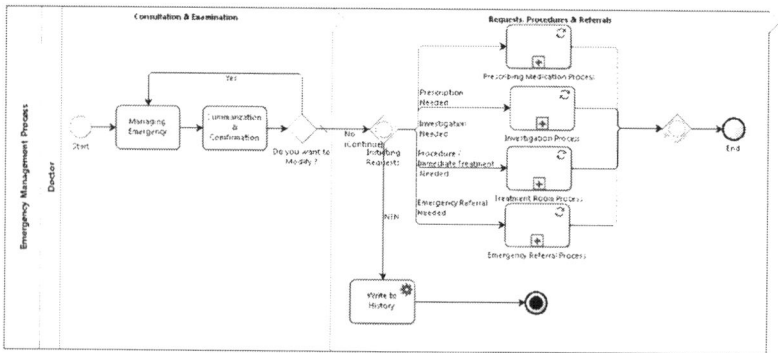

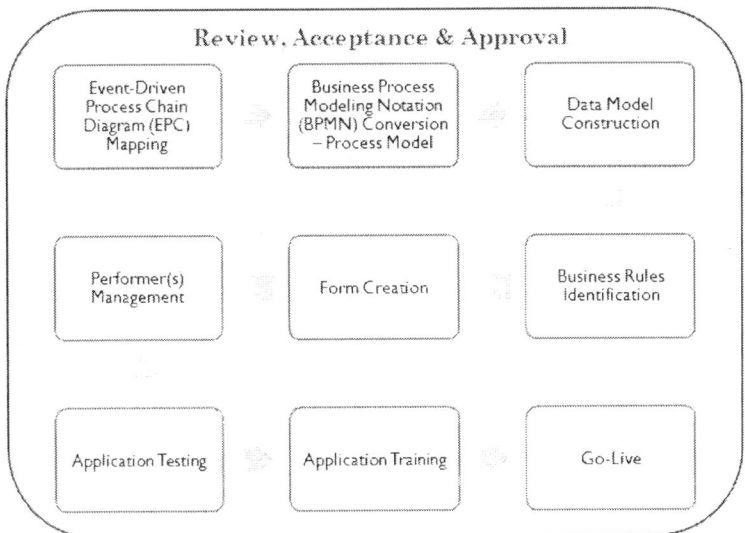

4.4 Organization

To help Al-Wazarat Health Center (WHC) with the appropriate technology, WHC management was in need of Business Process Management (BPM). This required changing their Health Information System (HIS) to a *process-oriented* system, which would help WHC management to streamline their processes so that they can deliver high quality care while at the same time reducing costs.

The Business Process Management - BPM system is responsible for keeping track of the practical tasks required and enables the user to perform a specific task, in a specific time, in the appropriate order. The system ensures the completion of the required task, and provides the flexibility to change the order of tasks (Business Process Reengineering or Improvement) when required without having to reprogram the system. It works by showing the user the function that is required to perform the selected task, and all necessary information is displayed in the proper sequence.

The system includes features that also allow the integration of functions and services of more than one system which is known as Business Applications Integration. It also supports the technology with Service Oriented Architecture.

5. HURDLES OVERCOME

The main challenge was to deal with the complexity of the process due to the large number of areas, stakeholders and actors involved. Also, the sensibility of the information handled by the process and the necessary coordination and interaction between tasks, activities and people were factors that had to be managed with care and detail.

Regarding the process itself, there were several challenges which needed to be resolved. These include:

- Increased patient waiting time for different reasons such as a healthcare provider not being present, or lack of resources like: medical equipment not available, or lack of an efficient systematic process.

- Procedures may not be performed, or may need to be postponed due to important information not readily available such as lab results, a missing file, or lack of preparatory measures, etc.
- Repetitive procedures which effect patients by exposing them to too many procedures (e.g. x-rays).
- Treatment time may take longer than necessary.
- Increased cost spends.
- Inability to determine the actual time needed to perform a task in order to evaluate the performance of the healthcare provider, and to be sure that high quality service is being provided to a patient in an appropriate time frame.
- The ability to allocate the necessary resources for each unit and distribute them according to the need in sufficient time.
- Ability to estimate the needs for expansion of the healthcare facility and to know precisely where the demands are needed most.
- The ability to maintain standards according to policy and procedure and update them as needed, and to apply a monitoring mechanism for adherence to the PPG's (total quality management standards and regulations).

To overcome the business and process challenges, it was necessary to develop the first stages of the project with special attention and detail, that is, the process definition and architecture design. This made it possible to perform an effective process modeling for a successful implementation and execution. Also, transforming the system to a process-oriented application was an important factor to guarantee meeting the project objectives.

6. BENEFITS

6.1 Cost Savings

Together with the aim of improving customer service and patient care, there was the need for reducing costs. Cost reductions are observed from the reduction of manual activities and paperwork as well as the optimization of resources and re-allocation of activities and people.

6.2 Time Reductions

The process and sub-process cycles have experience a significant reduction in time. The effective interaction and coordinated work between different areas as well as between healthcare providers and other personnel has helped WHC to deliver a faster and high-quality patient-care service. Effective communication, rapid data entry, and coordination from one party to another have been the key factors to obtain time reductions.

Other cycle time reductions are observed in: decreased patient waiting times, faster completion of procedures, shorter treatment times and quicker activity planning.

6.3 Increased Revenues

The main objective of this project was to enhance efficiency of patient care delivery within a patient-centered interdisciplinary approach and meet patient expectations. This objective has certainly been met and because new levels of efficiency have been reached, there have been indirect increased revenues. Specific revenue numbers are confidential.

6.4 Productivity Improvements

Healthcare providers are now able to perform their job more efficiently; data is available on time for analysis and revision, annotations from co-workers are included in the system and procedures are completed much faster. Eliminating manual tasks also helps to improve process tracking, visibility and control. This results in optimized access to patient records and increased productivity levels.

Productivity improvements are also observed from increased cooperation, interaction and communication between the areas and parties involved in the process.

7. BEST PRACTICES, LEARNING POINTS AND PITFALLS

7.1 Best Practices and Learning Points

✓ *Project development by phases*
✓ *Involvement and feedback from stakeholders*
✓ *Process-oriented system*

7.2 Pitfalls

✗ *Avoid solving problems during advanced stages of the project or late feedback from stakeholders. Try to look at all possible scenarios during the definition and design phase.*

8. COMPETITIVE ADVANTAGES

Staying ahead of industry standards has now become a necessity, especially in industries like healthcare where service levels will always be looked at with detail by patients and regulatory entities.

WHC has gone one step forward. With the determination of providing the best standard of healthcare services for its patients, WHC has definitely achieved a competitive advantage over other health institutions that haven´t recognized yet the value that agile and transparent processes, efficiency and reduction of manual tasks can bring for their patients.

9. TECHNOLOGY

WHC selected Bizagi BPM Suite for the automation of their complete clinical and administrative operation, covering processes, tasks and activities from several specialty services. WHC used Bizagi Process Modeler to map and design the process flow and then Bizagi BPM Suite for process execution/automation.

Bizagi is an integrated BPM Suite which enabled WHC to manage their complete process cycles and is flexible enough to support changes in business and market conditions. Bizagi is a robust, high-level and multifunctional process management system which can support mission critical operations and organizational growth.

Other technical aspects include:

a. Integration-Related (Web Services & Virtualization)
   - Patient Demographic Data
   - Drug History
   - Appointments
b. Platform-Related
   - BPMN Process Modeler
   - 100% Model Driven Architecture
   - Drag & Drop Forms Designer
   - Business Rule Engine
   - Service Oriented Architecture Integration

- Execution Engine
- Web Work Portal
- Process Indicators
- Business Activity Monitoring (BAM)

10. THE TECHNOLOGY AND SERVICE PROVIDERS

WHC selected Bizagi BPM (http://www.bizagi.com) for the implementation of their first BPM initiative. Bizagi is a leading BPM solution capable of empowering businesses of all types and industries around the world, providing them with unprecedented adaptability to changing business and market conditions through optimal business process automation (execution) and continuous improvement.

Bizagi is a business productivity tool for faster process automation. Bizagi´s built-in functionalities, ease of use and flexibility makes it the ideal BPM solution to obtain faster results. In Bizagi, most of the common and reoccurring requirements in process automation have been pre-built. These refer to:

- Control and visibility
- Alarms and notifications
- Performance analysis and reporting
- Auditing and traceability
- Workload routing and balancing
- Quality
- Mobility
- Robustness
- Integration
- Corporate features (multi-tenancy, BPMN process engine, multiple language support, time-zones, long lasting process transactions, enterprise data model, among others)

Bizagi is available in multiple editions to support the varying needs of organizations. The corporate editions are appropriate for mission critical and core business processes, satisfying the most demanding needs in larger organizations. Corporate editions (Enterprise .NET and Enterprise JEE) are similar in functionality, the only difference is the platform where they execute.

Danfoss Power Electronics, USA

Silver Award: Nominated by Aalborg University, Denmark

1. EXECUTIVE SUMMARY / ABSTRACT

This case study presents the experiences of a manufacturing company with taking the first step towards adopting BPM. The company used process mining in SAP to tackle a highly turbulent inquiry-to-invoice process which hindered customer relationships and employee satisfaction. The case highlights the steps of getting from raw event data to business implications. It shows how using a combination of interdisciplinary skills and basic technology applications can be a springboard leading to a wider adoption of BPM in companies with a previously low process orientation.

2. OVERVIEW

The context for the application is an overseas division of a large Denmark-based company. The organization had been managed in a functional manner, with little focus on processes outside of the shop floor. It implemented SAP in the mid-1990s, but it has been experiencing difficulties in using it to support execution of information-heavy business processes. As a result, the management of the division initiated a study in order to answer questions about the origins of the experienced problems, the performance of the processes and possible areas for improvement. The study progressed from scoping the process, extracting data from SAP, analyzing the process logs, using the results to make decisions and initiating a medium-scale process improvement project. It contributed three major benefits to the development of BPM in the company: (1) factual, unbiased insight into process performance; (2) launch of a process improvement project directly rooted in the information and (3) establishment of a BPM organization and adoption of BPM as a managerial paradigm.

The main challenges related to adopting process mining for developing managerial implications resulted from a process-immature technology platform, methodological learning curve and organizational set-up. Technical difficulties resulted from inconsistent data models in the enterprise system, which increased the complexity of data extraction and preparation. The project team also experienced low accessibility of guidelines related to data processing and difficulties in exporting the outputs of the analysis. Methodological difficulties were related to lack of guidelines on selecting the analytical methods and configuring the parameters of the analysis. The organizational difficulties stemmed from the lack of guidelines for interpreting the results from a business point of view, as the utilized BPI tool focused on processing data rather than on deriving meaningful interpretations of the results. Organization-wise, process mining required a situated application of systems and business knowledge and a blend of technical and business skills. Ensuring their availability was a key success factor during the endeavor.

3. BUSINESS CONTEXT

The study took place in an overseas division of a large Denmark-based company. The organization has heavily used SAP since mid 1990's and has developed deep expertise in using the system. However, numerous features and workarounds gradually added to the platform made it difficult to handle. The organization identified lack of consistent sales procedures as one of the main reasons for this situation. As one member of the management team recalls, *"We had a lot of complaints from the Customer Service people about the salesmen making up all kinds of new rules when they decided to take an order for either a new customer or an old customer with a new opportunity. They'd do things like make up new terms and conditions, tell them to do invoicing in a special way etc. [...] they were acting as if they were in the Wild West running their own show and there was no Marshall telling them what to do. It was never clarified [...] what the rules were."*

This way of conducting business increased complexity, caused errors in the systems, lead to low customer satisfaction, lengthy throughput time, eroding margins and employee frustration. With a strong business growth, the issues started to become a barrier to expansion.

In order to tackle the problem, the management initiated a process study. The reason for taking a process-oriented approach was that the initiatives limited to particular departments of the division could not tackle the problem. Many problems originated in a different part of the organization than the one in which they surfaced. A process approach was not widely used at the time and the study was aimed at answering a number of fundamental questions:

- What are the root-causes of the problems experienced?
- What do the processes look like?
- In which areas should the organization focus on reducing workflow complexity?
- How to permanently resolve the issues?

In order to commence the project work, the project team needed to answer several questions. First of all, they needed to know what problems they were supposed to solve. Although the management had examples of issues and pain-points, the project team wanted to have a complete and exact list of what they were trying to address. The second question concerned the exact process the project was supposed to consider. The mandate from the upper management was general in nature and referred to the sales process, but the team noted that some of the issues related to shipping and invoicing. Finally, the organization had not had much experience with a business process management (BPM) approach and the project team needed to get up to speed with it before applying it. Luckily, the Headquarters was able to provide an external consultant to assist with the process part.

In order to answer the questions about what issues were to be solved, the team conducted a snowball interview round in the organization. The interviews led to the identification of a number of issues directly stated by the employees and resulting from an immature process. The documentation of the process which was generated during system's implementation was only theoretical. The employees did not use it, nor did they know how to access it. With a more careful inquiry, the project team realized that the workflows in the system were outdated and did not correspond with the business requirements of the organizational processes. As a result, the employees queried external databases, made phone calls, communicated by email or even conducted manual numerical calculations in order to feed the system with the necessary data. The process was inefficient and error-prone.

The interviews also provided foundation for a process mining study which allowed recreating process models from transactional data stored in enterprise systems. The process mining approach consisted of four main steps: (1) preparation (described above), (2) extraction of data from the system, (3) analysis of the process log and (4) deriving managerial implications.

Data extraction

It was decided that MXML was going to be the target format for the log. The reason for that decision was that this format is compatible with the freeware PROM platform whose flexibility and wide selection of plug-ins was found to be a good match to the explorative nature of the study.

In order to recreate a process model based on the data, the project team members had to extract data from the system and prepare it for subsequent analysis. The sales related document flows we analyzed were grouped according to a predefined 'sales structure' in the system rather than by a specific process logic. In the analysis, the relevant system flow could be determined based on the catalogue of issues and the system documents used in the process, as identified by the respondents. The document flow included the process selected for improvement, with a significant amount of redundancy. Data extraction was performed using the SAP ABAP Query with both the Query and InfoSet components. In order to go through the complete document flow and all relevant change documents, a series of extract iterations was performed. The output of this step was three tables containing

- the document flow, consisting of the documents identified as relevant for the process and their follow-on documents (determined by the document flow set-up in the system)
- the base document change log
- the follow-on document change log

It was not possible to directly convert the lines into process instances because they were not ordered, the changes and document flows were in separate data sets, changes and documents were not grouped by process instances and the tables contained a lot of redundant information.

The duration of the process was determined by the amount of data possible to handle efficiently given the hardware at hand. The files contained respectively 5476, 8518, and 3529 lines. The period of analysis was one month for the sales document flow creation and four weeks for events related to follow-on document creation and base and follow-on document changes.

Preliminary data cleanup

The initial data cleaning effort focused on reducing the data redundancy. First, the lines which contained a document number, which elsewhere was stated as a follow-on document, were removed. Second, the columns which contained redundant data or data which did not contain information required by the MXML format were removed. At this stage, an extra step needed to be added to ensure data completeness in relation to process focus on manual tasks. The process was scoped to end with an invoice. However, 90% of invoicing was performed automatically by the system. The anticipated filtering of the systems tasks out of the process, while at the same time setting invoice creation as the ending event, would filter out 90% of interesting process instances. For that reason, all the invoices created by the system were assigned an artificial user ID to allow easy differentiation between automatic invoicing and automatic tasks in other areas.

Determining event granularity

In order to fit the SAP output to the requirements of process mining and ensure convergence of the logs, several decisions needed to be made. These decisions were highly dependent on the purpose of the mining and were found to influence the outcome of the analysis. They were:

- mapping user IDs to departments in which they were employed

- level of detail of the recorded document changes representing creation and update of documents
- recording changes on order rather than field level
- recording changes on document rather than line item level

Assigning events to instances

In order to recreate processes, every line, corresponding to an event, needed to be assigned to a particular process instance. In this case, process instances were represented by originating document numbers. In the cleaned up base flow table this was not a problem because every subsequent document was paired with the originating document, thus the number of the originating document could easily serve as process instance identifier. However, in change logs, SAP does not indicate the document flow and this needed to be recreated manually. In the originating document change log, the number of the changed document automatically became the process instance number. In the follow-on document change log, this required a series of lookups. First, the number of the changed document needed to be paired with the follow-on document in the document flow table. Then the number of the follow-on document needed to be paired with the number of the originating document. This number was then assigned to the change in the change log.

Converting the logs to the MXML format

The purpose of this step was to generate an XML text file out of spreadsheet tables. This was done using a custom-made macro application. In order to comply with the MXML format, all audit trail entries belonging to a particular process instance must be grouped together. The most efficient way to do this without the need to perform a high number of cross-table lookups was by using a sorting algorithm. First, document numbers were converted to the numerical format and all the lines from all three logs were loaded into one collection. This way it became possible to sort the objects in the collection by instance number. To perform the operation, the heap sort algorithm was used. In the final step, the instances were printed into an MXML file, adding process instance information every time an instance number change occurred. During the printing, lines within an instance were compared and duplicates were removed.

Analyzing the process log

After uploading into PROM, the log contained 350 event classes and 18 originators. The general log analysis focused on the statistics of the executed process. The overview of tasks by frequency revealed the frequently executed tasks and the long tail which pointed out changes to documents resulting from "special case" orders or error correction. Differentiating system tasks from manual tasks provided an overview of the degree of process automation.

Subsequently, an analysis of originators was performed. It revealed that the Logistics department carried out the most manual tasks, more than the Customer Service team. However, analyzing departments by task type showed that the former carried out 15 types of tasks, whereas the latter 110 types. This revealed that the work of Logistics was manual and labor-intensive but well-defined, whereas the Customer Service team was in fact tasked with trying to mediate between external process variability and the system.

Process discovery resulted in a process model which made it possible to determine the process complexity areas. In this case, a major area of concern turned out to be between order placement and shipment of products. Normally, the parts of the process related to inquiry and quotation should be the ones with the most variability, leading to a set of agreed terms and a fairly linear flow after a final order has been placed.

At this point there was a question whether deviations from the linear flow were a frequent occurrence or an exception, and how the deviations differ in frequency. The Heuristics plug-in provided some insight into this by displaying frequencies and dependencies between parts of the flow. However, a much more intuitive overview of the complexity was provided by animation of the flow. The Heuristics model was therefore converted to a Fuzzy model which could be animated. The animation highlighted the frequent flows vs. exceptions and showed their impact on the process execution speed. Each deviation from the standard flow was then reviewed and classified as an issue or not, taking into consideration both the nature of the deviation and its frequency.

The social network mining step was possible because SAP stores a user ID for each executed transaction and places it in the change log. As mentioned previously, in the MXML file each user ID was mapped to a corresponding department. In this sense, the functionality of the social network miner plug-in was used to determine relationships among group entities, rather than individuals.

The first type of organizational analysis executed on the log was handover of work. The analysis was carried out in two steps using the social network miner plug-in. In the first step, the plug-in was executed with default settings. The resulting graph revealed a complex structure of work handovers, which was not surprising and corresponded well with the complex process model discovered in the previous step. A ratio analysis revealed that all but one department was directly connected to the System, meaning that their work was automated. The Shipping department was found to have the highest potential for improving work automation.

The second type of organizational analysis was doing similar tasks based on the similarity coefficient calculation by the social network miner. The analysis revealed that similarities exist between the automatic ordering system and the sales personnel as well as the logistics and shipping department, which was not surprising given the nature of work done by these entities. The Customer Service department, however, was found to be doing tasks similar to almost all the other departments. This, again, revealed that it needed to deal with a lot of unstructured tasks and that the competencies were not clearly defined and distributed among the departments. The staff in the Customer Service department often acted as executors of tasks in the system requested by other members of the organization.

In order to analyze the performance of the process, the team used the Performance Sequence Diagram Analysis plug-in. It revealed that throughout the analyzed time span, the process was executed in 379 different ways. It also revealed that the top six patterns were used 1500 times. It was found that these patterns are the ones which represent the process instances which run as intended. This helped identify the tasks related to corrections and redundant work, which were targeted for elimination in the subsequent steps. The full diagram in the plug-in provided an indication of which tasks were related to process lag.

After the analysis was complete, the findings and recommendation for future steps were presented to the executive team. The presentation was a success; one member of the project team stated: *"I'd say they were blown away by the types of results they got. They'd never seen anything that was that type of analysis where they were showed the complexity of the orders, the timelines of some orders, the numbers of changes that were done to orders. That's exactly what they had in their gut feeling that was wrong, but they couldn't put their finger on why. This was ex-actly the type of data they were looking for. They got really energized".*

The mining study revealed that the process was very complex and pointed at the specific areas of complexity that the team needed to deal with. It identified the transactions which were the symptoms of underperformance. It also helped scope the process by determining which departments and tasks were involved in the execution and which presented the highest potential for automation. Since one of the study's findings was that the process was executed in 379 different ways during the analyzed time span of six weeks, the divisional president set the goal of having the process standardized. As the project team member recalled, *"they wanted to basically simplify the process then standardize it [...] and automate eve-rything we could automate. That was pretty much the goal that we were given."*

During the same meeting, the executive committee approved several recommen-dations made by the consultant on how to proceed. They included the scope of the process (stretching from customer inquiry to invoice, excluding manufactur-ing), the timing of the project (though the time span was shortened to 16 from the suggested 21 weeks), extension of the project team, appointment of a process owner, and approval of the overall approach. The company followed the consult-ant's prescription to employ a full-blown BPM initiative, as opposed to a process reengineering or systems improvement. The belief was that this would align the business processes and systems workflows, as well as help sustain the expected benefits.

4. THE KEY INNOVATIONS

4.1 Process

Despite having the IT system's side of the current state mapped by the process mining study, the core team decided to follow the consultant's advice and start with the as-is process mapping. The project team knew that process thinking was new to the division and involving participants in the mapping exercise would be a proper step towards establishing a process culture. After determining that the commonly used value stream mapping from the lean approach did not handle complex information processes well, the team decided to follow another method. *"We figured that using sticky notes would be the right way to go because we had a large room in one of the facilities with whiteboards. So the advantage was we could move them around. We had color-coded sticky notes for each of the areas. We start-ed to tell them three things we wanted to know: what's your standard process, what do you do that's a little of an exception but repetitive and what do you do that's really a one-off. Then we started with the standard process, then we added some small changes that were standard but not quite and the last thing we asked them to do were all the one-off's. As it turned out, the standard processes were fair-ly complex but when we added the other two areas we had lots and lots of com-plexity in the process."*

At that time the project team refrained from intervening in the inputs provided by the process participants, but focused on clarifying the technical issues, taking an advisory role to help the participants understand the hand-offs taking place through the system. After two full-day workshops devoted to mapping the current process, the team focused on creating formal documentation. Having evaluated several notations and software packages, they decided to go ahead with BPMN 2.0 and an office application with a stencil suitable for drawing the models. The final model of the documented process took about 50ft of paper on three walls.

Developing a future state of the process was the next step in the project. As the company did not have standard reference models which could be re-used locally, the team took the existing process as a starting point. The project manager's mantra consisted of the three words from the divisional president: simplify, standardize and automate. The team focused on all deviations from a standard flow of the process, figured out why they occurred and determined how they could be gotten rid of. Around half of the deviations were resolved by ensuring master data correctness. Other times, the team proposed solutions based on reducing 'red tape', e. g., implementing standardized rules and guidelines to replace involvement of management in day-to-day decision making.

One of the findings of the current state analysis was that across some parts of the organization the process had the same objectives but was executed in different ways. For instance, order-handling for standard products and spare parts was essentially the same, but the departments responsible for them carried it out in different ways and using different functionalities in the IT system. Similarly, shipping of products was done differently in different divisional locations. In those areas, the team worked to standardize the execution.

As the future state development progressed, the team realized that the redesign of the process was highly dependent on information technologies. First of all, having a technical background, the project manager was aware of the compatibility of the design propositions with the current and future systems landscape so he could advise the team on several key aspects. For example he knew that the division was planning to upgrade the enterprise system to a new version, which would imply different ways of executing certain procedures and had to be included in the redesign.

Second, the division was going through a global roll-out of new product configurator software. Since relatively little was known about the product in the US subsidiaries, the team contacted the project manager. It turned out that the part responsible for automating creation of configuration-based material documents in the system had an overlap with the project, but used a different methodology. The awareness of the ongoing IT projects in the division helped the team design a process that would be compatible with the to-be global solutions.

When dealing with improving the manual verification of taxability of customers purchasing goods across state borders, the project manager remembered that the company was using a tax system which had a feature automating that procedure. For some reason the feature was not used. The process could be simplified by enabling the feature and a little coding.

When the team worked with the shipping part of the process it turned out that the department did not use the functionalities of the system because master data were not always correct. They preferred to do a task manually rather than have the system do it and then have to check and correct the outcome. As one of the team members recalls, *"We found that in shipping we had a significant number of areas that were done manually. SAP was not providing what they needed because data wasn't correct. 10% of the data was incorrect so they did 100% of the forms manually."*

The team committed to ensuring master data correctness and the design of the new process assumed a high degree of shipping automation, including automatic and correct delivery of shipping labels, pro-forma invoices, NAFTA certificates and bills of lading. Along the way, the team found two other areas of improvement: automatic transfer of special shipping instructions from customer service to the shipping staff and automatic suggestion for the optimal shipping method, both of which led to significant manual work savings.

When the team redesigned the process according to the simplification, standardization and automation objective every change in the process diagram involved a change in the business. If the to-be process design got rid of a task related to master data verification, it required that the master data was correct. If it got rid of manual inquiry handling, it required that the customer used the web ordering system to request a quote. If it assumed that taxability is determined automatically, the tax system needed to be activated and configured. Following that path the team identified over 60 process rules that needed to be in place for the organization to be able to execute the to-be design. The rules were then grouped into 18 'concepts'. For each concept a business case was prepared, together with an implementation plan and metrics required to track the performance of the process in relation to the design.

In order to ensure that the process was followed, a governance method was put in place. If someone requested to change a part of the process, the process owner received the request and pulled in resources to form an advisory team and work out a technical and a business evaluation. The advisory team got either a small request or a business case, and then evaluated it and within 24 hours returned with a yes or no answer. If the requestor was not satisfied with the answer, they could make a more extensive business case and hand it in to the process owner again. The process owner then, together with the first decision, submitted it to the process committee for evaluation. As the project manager recalls, *"We've had that some of the first 3-6 months, but after that it seemed like they learned the rules, internalized them. We've had very few requests since then. In the beginning we had a lot of activity and now, close to a year later, we don't have many requests for changes."*

Having a clear set of rules made it possible to execute the process in a way which is compatible with the workflows in the system and, if need be, change the systems according to business requirements.

4.2 Organization

Upon the project's completion, a set of process governance concepts was implemented to support the process. It consisted of a process committee (that was transformed from the steering committee) with the responsibility for reviewing and managing the portfolio of the future process improvement projects. The process owner function was formally established to coordinate across the process, lead improvement initiatives, review performance indicators and advise on projects impacting the new process. One of the key areas of activity for the process owner is continuously ensuring proper maintenance of master data related to the process throughout the business. Furthermore, the process owner has the exclusive right to change the process and is therefore involved in parallel projects which might have an impact on her process.

4.3 Business

The main benefit of the project was materialized in the company's customer service area. By addressing challenges related to ensuring proper master data handling procedures, the project contributed to a more consistent and timely way of handling customer inquiries. First, as the company utilized a manufacture-to-order model based on complex internet configuration parameters, it was able to provide correct and timely information on what products and options are available and which will be available in the future. Furthermore, ensuring the use of the configurator across the entire company allowed the field sales staff and the internal customer service provide consistent availability information to the customers.

With a better managed process, the company became more predictable in terms of order processing. This resulted not only in improved delivery to promise, but also a set of clear-cut guidelines on the cancellation policy, i.e. stages at which an order could be withdrawn, when there was a fee involved and when cancellation was no longer possible as the product had shipped.

In addition, the company observed a range of internal benefits, such as lower stress and internal conflict between outside sales and internal staff. A clear and agreed on picture of the business process provided a cross-departmental learning opportunity, making employees realize their impact on their colleagues' work, as well as on the customer satisfaction. It resulted in a new, team-oriented culture aligned with the organization's value stream.

5. HURDLES OVERCOME

Management

The main challenge during the process mining endeavor was related to its cross-disciplinary nature. Retrieving data from the system and converting it to the desired format required highly technical skills such as writing database queries, coding data conversion algorithms and having an in-depth understanding of the data structures in the system. On the other hand, interpreting data transaction-based mining results so that they reflect the business process perspective required intimate knowledge of the business aspects of the organization. Process mining thus required inseparable blend of technical and business skills.

In order to fulfill the objective of ensuring situated, cross-disciplinary knowledge, the project core team was composed of four people. It was headed by the project manager, who was also a business systems manager in the division and as such had in-depth knowledge of the current and future state of the systems and other related IT projects. The process consultant brought in the process philosophy, methodologies, tools and standards. He educated the team, helped plan the project, facilitated workshops and presented results. Another person was dedicated to standards and documentation. His task was to maintain formalized project and process documentation and carry out the communication plan, which was particularly important to fulfill the learning objective of the project. Finally, the appointed future process owner was a member of the team in order to gather the cross-functional knowledge necessary to manage the process in the future.

Additionally, representatives from each department involved in the execution of the process were involved in the project: *"what we had in the project was a significant person from each of the areas that was involved. We had people from quotations, pricing, customer service, shipping, sales and invoicing on the project"*.

Finally, with erroneous master data being one of the problems identified in the initial study, the project included staff responsible for maintaining pricing, product and customer masters in the system.

Business

The main challenges faced by the project team on the business side were lack of process culture and lack of available BPM technology. In the former, the way the organization had worked before was characterized as a culture of heroes – one in which issues are solved only when they become problems. As this had been the approach the employees were used to, the project team needed to put extra effort in changing it. It did so by securing a strong support from the divisional executive team, who were present during each workshop and emphasized the importance and benefits of the process approach. The project was sponsored by the divisional steering committee which consisted of the top management in the US facilities. The key for selecting members was to find the highest local reports of the employees involved in the execution of the process. It ended up being composed of the entire executive team less a product development manager. In order to ensure that the process design was followed, the team established process metrics, one of which was based on process incompliance, meaning those situations that required manual master data correction. The establishment of process ownership accountability and authority was an important part of putting any particular instance back on track.

The second business hurdle, lack of available technology, was tackled by capitalizing on the data and software which already existed in the organization. The team utilized transactional data stored in the enterprise system, a standard office suite and a freeware application in order to carry out process discovery, analysis, design and execution monitoring. This helped avoid a holdup resulting from justifying an investment in a software platform in order to carry out a pilot project.

Organization Adoption

When the team presented recommendations on implementing the new project design to the steering committee, it included two scenarios: aggressive and moderate. In the aggressive scenario, the process was as slim and trim as possible and offered very few options to change. The moderate scenario was prepared in anticipation of organizational resistance in several areas. During the meeting, the steering committee instructed the team, *"in every case go for the most stringent, meaning the least complex, most simple, standardized [version, and] automate everything that's possible. Only change that to more moderate if somebody gives you feedback".*

That turned out to be good advice because the end the team only had two or three very small areas that they got a pushback on. In the areas of standardizing sales terms and conditions and freight methods, where the team proposed significant simplifications, the business units did not object.

Implementing the approved process required 18 focused change efforts, one for each concept. Apart from that, the team had to deal with establishing a process management organization and process metrics. To make matters even more difficult, the core team member responsible for standards and documentation left the company due to downsizing. The project team knew that handling this would be beyond the team's capacity and a suitable implementation concept had to be developed.

The team came up with an implementation concept based on work packages. The work, split into 18 work packages, was planned by the core team and delegated to 'owners'. The owners were employees knowledgeable in the areas addressed by their work packages. The work package owners reported to the project team, who coordinated the total effort. The idea was that the systems data clean-up effort, assignment of responsibilities, training workshops and technical developments would be finished around the same time for every work package, making the 'go-live' as brief a period as possible. Soon, the team found out it was not that easy.

Implementation of many of the work packages was dependent on changes in the IT systems. These changes took three forms: development of workflows, changes to the existing functionalities or adding new functionalities. At the company, the central IT unit has the sole authority to carry out such changes. Every time a business unit wants to implement a change, it is responsible for preparing technical specifications and sending them to central IT. In the central IT department the requests are assigned 'tickets', which are routed to technical experts in the area. When the work is complete, the local business unit receives an invoice.

The team was fortunate because the project manager was head of the Business Systems Department in the division. He was able to facilitate the development of technical specifications that were understandable from the IT perspective and corresponded closely to the requirements of the newly developed business process. In total, based on the business documentation of the concepts, the team submitted 12 tickets.

Soon it turned out that the central IT department had no capacity to handle the task. *"We didn't send them all at once but within a month we got all of the tickets in"*, recalls the project manager. *"They came back and said they were overflowed and the 12 tickets were too much"*.

This was a surprise to the team. Finishing the implementation of IT changes resulting from the process design took almost a full year.

BENEFITS

Nonetheless, after the implementation was complete, the organization noticed visible benefits from the project. Since this document describes a business process management case rather than a business process re-engineering case, apart from the immediate benefits to the organization it focuses on the less tangible, yet more far-reaching consequences of the implementation.

First, the project influenced the culture of the organization by introducing 'process thinking'. As a member of the project team states, *"It was an opportunity to take the people in the project who were mostly superusers and increase their SAP knowledge so that they had an overall process understanding from a technical standpoint. They knew what happened before them and after [in the workflow]. That was kind of a process mindset that was put into the organization."* After the project, the employees from the involved departments knew that *"they should not try and figure out a quick and dirty work around, but that there probably was a real method to use in SAP. They had a better understanding they could contact somebody if they had an issue rather than finding a workaround."*

By providing clear and simplified business rules, the project reduced complexity, especially in the customer service and pricing area. This positively affected customer service quality and reduced process errors. The organization also experienced significant savings in manual labor. Shipping saved about 30% of the time. Automation in invoicing went up to 95% from 50% before the project because of standardized shipping methods.

The main learning point for the local organization was that the BPM approach worked. A member of the management team concludes: *"We had no experience with that – so the process approach was key [...] That gave local IT some credibility that it can be a valuable player in those kinds of games [...] Before they had Supply Chain, Purchasing and Sales involved in some improvement projects but not much focused on business systems per se. That was probably the overall success."*

On a global scale, the project contributed to raising awareness of BPM and its benefits for the business. It demonstrated the types of value the organization could achieve from managing processes and outlined the required effort. The realized gaps concerned process competencies and availability of a BPM suite. Currently, the company plans a corporate-level adoption of BPM.

6. BEST PRACTICES, LEARNING POINTS AND PITFALLS

7.1 Best Practices and Learning Points

- ✓ Use existing technology to justify an investment in a more robust platform
- ✓ Capitalize on the existing data in order to diagnose the level of process maturity

✓ Facilitate process-centric IT/business partnerships in order to provide the applied, situated knowledge required by the process management activities

✓ Start small and scale up while accumulating expertise, BPM does not have to be a big bang

✓ Ensure top-level support to effectively introduce organizational change

7.2 Pitfalls

✗ Don't exclude any IT stakeholders early on, also those responsible for subsequent IT development

✗ Don't focus the management's attention only on the tangible, bottom-line benefits

✗ Don't rely solely on what the system tells you: a business process and systems process are both required to get a full understanding of the situation

✗ Do not exclude any members of the organization involved in the process; this goes for all the staff responsible for executing the process and for maintaining correct master data used therein

7. COMPETITIVE ADVANTAGES

The process supports the highly complex product configuration, allowing the company manufacturing its products to order. This provides customers with highly-tailored products, closely corresponding with their application requirements. The new process set-up, along with the underlying master data management, are key for an effective operation of the configurator, which is source of the company's unique value to their customers.

The learning approach utilized by the organization is a way to overcome the BPM adoption pitfall. Companies who have not invested in a full-blown BPM technology solution do not experience the benefit of managing their processes and thus find it more difficult to justify technology expenditures. This case showed that companies can do BPM with little cost and with the already utilized or readily available technology. While smoothing the adoption curve from a big bang to a small scale trial, the project shows how the observed benefits can serve as a justification for development of a BPM program, encompassing both, organizational and technological factors.

8. TECHNOLOGY

The project was based on four existing or free technology components:
- SAP R/3 to extract data for recreating the as-is and improve execution of the to-be process
- The ProM platform to carry out process mining, i.e. process discovery, performance analysis, social network analysis and organizational analysis
- MS Office Excel to pre-process and map data from SAP to ProM
- MS Office Visio to draw the as-is and to-be process diagrams

9. THE TECHNOLOGY AND SERVICE PROVIDERS

The project used internal resources and one external action-researcher from Aalborg University, Denmark (www.aau.dk), who acted as a business process consultant.

The software utilized in the project was supplied by:
- SAP (www.sap.com)
- Microsoft (office.microsoft.com/)
- ProM (promtools.org/prom5)

National Institute of Mental Health, USA

Finalist: Nominated by BP Logix, Inc., USA

1. EXECUTIVE SUMMARY / ABSTRACT

There is a critical need within the government to manage IT procurements in such a way as to ensure compliance with organizational and governmental standards, to secure the appropriate review and approvals for all such procurements, and to account for procurements and expenditures. To achieve this objective, the National Institute of Mental Health (NIMH), part of the National Institutes of Health (NIH), needed a more effective methodology and a more efficient business process for acquiring, tracking and managing IT equipment procurement. NIMH was able to accomplish this goal by designing a procurement process that supported compliance requirements, while also providing a comprehensive review and approval process for all procurements. To develop and implement that process, NIMH licensed business process management (BPM) software to automate and streamline its IT Procurement system.

2. OVERVIEW

IT procurement and investments for the Federal government are critical expenditures that must be closely managed and monitored. For NIMH, standardizing hardware and software procurements is a critical responsibility, as the Institute must concurrently manage its IT expenditures, improve support to its users and, at the same time, decrease overall (support) costs. This goal must be met while also addressing procurement requirements that are unique to the federal government. In addition, there are oversight and review process for all IT investments that are required by Capital Planning and Investment Control (CPIC). All Health and Human Services Operational Divisions, including NIH, must demonstrate compliance with the CPIC rules. To do so, a tiered review of every IT investment must take place. The goal of NIMH was two-fold: 1) To streamline the NIMH IT acquisition process and 2) Account for every expenditure and threshold. The Institute achieved this by developing a comprehensive, automated process that embraced the required workflow and signatures needed for each investment. Making that process consistent, accountable, timely, and efficient was essential to achieving the objective.

3. BUSINESS CONTEXT

IT procurements at NIMH were, at one time, decentralized to business areas within the Institute. This decentralization, however, made it difficult to support the various technologies that were procured, enforce IT procurement rules, or to address the ongoing government-wide requirement for IT services, software, and hardware. As a result, the decision was made to centralize the IT procurement process. This centralization was initiated within the Information Resource and Technology Management Branch, which provided IT support throughout the Institute. In order to centralize the procurement process itself, however, there was a need to change the procedures, particularly those that were still manual, as those processes were difficult to enforce, audit, and report on. When it was agreed that automating the IT procurement process would be of significant benefit to NIMH overall, an internal review was held to identify alternative approaches. After reviewing and evaluating potential solutions, NIMH IT ultimately identified the software solution and approach we believed would be the most effective way to standardize the IT procurement process.

4. THE KEY INNOVATIONS

4.2 Business Management and oversight of IT procurements at NIMH needed to be more effectively administered in terms of technology oversight, standardization, compliance with procurement regulations, and cost containment. This required centralization of IT management and oversight, as well as budgeting and control. However, expediency and accountability needed to be part of the centralization plan so that IT procurements could still be done expeditiously while maintaining compliance with standards and controls. The automation of this process was the key to achieving these objectives. Those processes and automations included:

- Centralized IT Procurements to one organization
- Automated Review of IT procurements to ensure compliance with technical standards, procurement process, management, and oversight
- Automated the procurement process based on business rules and required approvals for IT procurement requests
- Full accountability for review steps and timeliness

4.3 Process (See diagram following.)

The development of processes for managing IT procurements extended beyond the initial idea of 'just' automating current business processes. New processes were developed to address requirements and oversight of the IT procurements that were not in place previously. These included reviews for technology standards, review and approval of Requestor's management, compliance with Federal IT procurement rules, and custom review procedures based on either the type of technology being requested and/or dollar thresholds being requested. Specifically, those processes included:

- Contextual, dynamic routing of requests based on requestor organization, investment type, and expenditure thresholds
- Fully auditable review and approval process
- Ability to enforce required request information and approvals
- Embedded Capital Planning and Investment Control (CPIC) compliance requirements
- IT Purchase Request Workflow Diagram
- IT Purchase Request Workflow Diagram

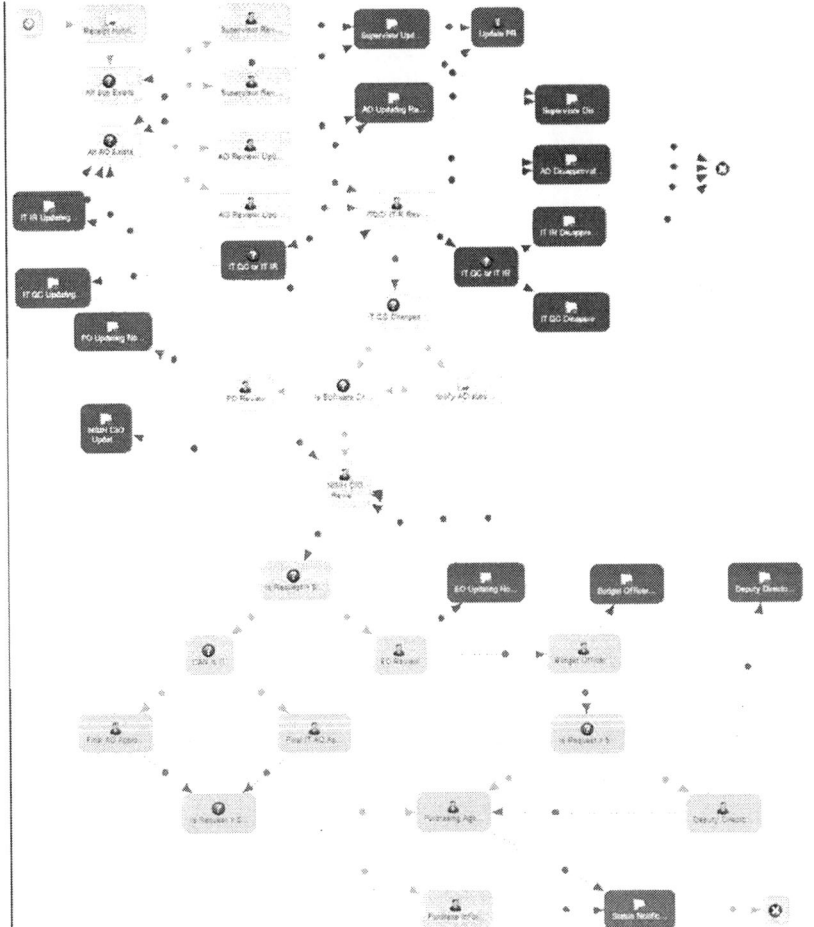

IT Purchase Request Workflow Diagram

4.4 Organization

The IT organization developed new roles and responsibilities to support this enhanced IT procurement process. These included technology review and approval, standards compliance, budget review, CPIC review, and procurement. The result was a consistent process with established roles and responsibilities, accountability of the organization in terms of following the process and expediency of request reviews, and documented compliance with the required reviews and approvals.

Specifically the organization gained:

- A centralized IT procurement review and approval process
- Documented compliance with IT procurement rules and requirements
- Streamlined IT procurement organization
- Improved support as a result of standardization

5. HURDLES OVERCOME

Management

The centralization and automation of the IT procurement processes presented numerous challenges in the management customer service, customer expectations, and organizational performance. NIMH IT has to present the case for centralization and automation to the business community to ensure that its needs would be met in a timely manner, while reducing costs in terms of support and standardization. The specific hurdles included:

- Business resistance to centralized IT procurement process
- Meeting Federal Government IT procurement requirements
- Accounting (auditability) for compliance with IT procurement requirements
- Acceptance of an automated procurement request process
- Standardization of IT procurement technologies

Business Centralization and automation of IT procurement presented challenges to the business community in terms of requiring review and approval of their purchases in advance, with the decision being based on existing standards and procurement rules. Their biggest concern was not being able to order what they wanted, and not having those orders processed in a timely manner. NIMH IT was able to help these requesters address their needs by standardizing the IT procurement process and implementing an automated, fully accountable business process.

- Adapting to standardized technology procurements
- Provision of business case requirements for new acquisitions
- Submission of requests through an automated process
- Development and adaptation of a consistent IT procurement process

Organization Adoption
- IT procurement and review standards and staffing
- Budgeting and management of centralized IT procurement

6. BENEFITS

The primary benefits revolved around cost accountability and savings, documented compliance with IT procurement rules, and increased productivity. This new approach to IT procurement enabled the IT organization to bring IT procurement into compliance with standards, reduce unnecessary purchases, and eliminate wasteful purchases overall. It also reduced the time required to account for IT purchases as well as the time required to process IT purchase requests. Specifics include:

6.1 Cost Savings ☐ Reduction of non-standard equipment and software procurements reduced expenditures by 95% ☐ Reductions of non-required equipment reduced costs by 20%

☐ Cost to account for IT procurements to support government reporting and data calls were reduced by 50%.

6.2 Time Reductions
- Time to review and process IT Procurement requests were reduced by 50% ☐ Time to report on procurements and compliance: 50%

6.4 Productivity Improvements
- Reduced effort to procure IT services, equipment, and software
- Ability to report on IT Procurement status and demonstrate compliance with procurement and CPIC rules is greatly enhanced
- Use of standardized equipment and software has resulted in lower service call volume in addition to documented higher customer satisfaction ratings for technical support organization

- Automation of these processes ensures compliance with standards and improves the overall compliance status of the Institute

7. BEST PRACTICES, LEARNING POINTS AND PITFALLS

7.1 Best Practices and Learning Points

- Conditional routing of requests based on request types and dollar thresholds were critical to the effectiveness of the application
- Broadening and expanding input to the form to include all aspects of procurement and property management substantially increased the impact of the application
- Extensive communication and training increased form utilization and compliance
- General user input during prototyping increased acceptance in the general usage community

7.2 Pitfalls

- Complex procurement and accounting considerations increased complexity of the workflows
- Changing procurement rules required changes to forms and workflow logic

8. COMPETITIVE ADVANTAGES

As a government agency, the advantages for NIMH reside in its ability to be compliant and accountable for all IT procurements initiated on behalf of the Federal Government and the American taxpayer. This form and workflow application (Process Director) has made a *substantive* contribution to NIMH's ability to review, approve, and account for IT procurements. Compliance with standards in terms of the technologies themselves, as well as procurement and property regulations is now very high, and the Institute can now demonstrate that it is in compliance, is fully accountable and auditable.

9. TECHNOLOGY

- BP Logix– Process Director (BPM software
- Microsoft SQL Server RDBMS
- Oracle RDBMS
- Windows Server
- VMWare

10. THE TECHNOLOGY AND SERVICE PROVIDERS

NIMH utilizes BP Logix Process Director business process management software (www.bplogix.com) to develop electronic forms (eForms) and workflows for the Institute, as well as to automate the review and approval process for its IT procurement requests. NIMH relies on the product's eForm, workflow, meta data, Knowledge Views (reporting), Custom Tasks (prebuilt functional models) and scripting (via APIs). By using APIs and web services, NIMH is able to integrate Process Director with other third party applications. We are also starting to deploy its Process Timeline functionality for our highly parallel, reproducible processes. The processes we currently have in place include both form-based (initiated by form submission) and workflow-based processes (or Knowledge View-based, which the workflow starts then attaches the form). The process functionalities we have utilized include sequential, parallel, parent-child, conditional, looping and customized.

Naval Special Warfare Group Four Government Purchase Card Program, USA

Silver Award: Nominated by HandySoft, USA

1. EXECUTIVE SUMMARY / ABSTRACT

Naval Special Warfare (NSW) is a division within the U.S. Navy that includes more than 2,400 active-duty Special Warfare Operators, known as SEALs. All of these personnel are divided among "groups". NSW Group 4 (NSWG4) consists of three Special Boat Teams (SBT) and one international training command—all working together towards the common goal of fighting the global war on terrorism. In the past, NSWG4 always had more than adequate numbers of craft, engines and spare parts. However, with today's current high demand for combat operations, security force assistance (SFA) and fiscal downsizing, NSWG4 had to develop a different business sustainment model to complete missions with less assets.

The solution expertly weaves Lean Six Sigma, Agile, and dynamic BPM into a system called SWIFT—which successfully met this challenge, and exceeded expectations. Within a 6 month time-frame, NSWG4 had an automated workflow solution in place that reduced procurement lead time, improved accuracy, visibility, and all around satisfaction and improved performance of the Government Purchase Card Program (GPCP) process. The automation for the GPCP using SWIFT provides visibility into the process, standardization, and forcing function for over 6,000 purchases and $5.2 million spent annually.

2. OVERVIEW

The Naval Special Warfare Group 4 (NSWG4) is responsible for development and testing of combatant craft and associated ordinance and equipment. NSWG4 monitors and certifies the Combat Readiness of assigned craft and SWCC (Special Warfare Combatant Craft Crewman).

In the past, NSWG4 has had more than adequate numbers of craft, engines and spare parts. However, with today's current demand for combat operations, security force assistance (SFA) and fiscal downsizing, NSWG4 had to develop a different business sustainment model to meet missions with less assets. This new model required speeding up the procurement process for craft repairs and spare parts. By decreasing the ordering cycle time for repairs and parts, less craft and assets are required to meet continued customer requirements.

Prior to April 2011, the purchasing of boat requirements involved customers manually filling out purchasing paperwork and routing packages consisting of printed paper forms and substantiating documentation. The manual flow of information increased inaccurate purchasing information and there was no visibility into the process. Customers were often unaware of the procurement status, including delays on parts and services, which could ultimately force mission-critical boats and equipment out of commission.

NSWG4 customers and logistics support personnel developed a solution to streamline purchasing process workflows, using Toyota Production System (TPS) process improvement methodology. TPS is based upon deck plate employees driving process improvements while senior leadership serves as coaches and mentors.

To help establish priorities for which processes needed to be improved first, employees first targeted the Government Purchase Card Program (GPCP) process, which is for procurements less than $3000 ($2500 for services). The team agreed on implementing workflow automation with three specific goals of providing process (1) visibility, (2) standardization to reduce errors, and (3) accountability.

In October 2010, NSWG4 hosted a two-day off-site meeting and invited the daily owners and users of the GPCP process to participate and provide their input on how to improve this process. Using Shingo value stream mapping techniques, which separates the process steps from the operational steps, the 25-person team defined how to standardize the process, by removing excess steps and identifying over 40 different points of automation. The standardization removes errors by providing a "turbo tax" menu of choices including requirement samples. The team called the project SWIFT - Special Warfare Information Fast Tracker.

Within a six-month time-frame, NSWG4 had an automated workflow solution in place which was successfully up and running, reducing procurement lead time, improving accuracy, visibility, and all around satisfaction and performance of the GPCP process.

RF Logistics LLC (RFL), in concert with HandySoft, designed, developed and delivered into production the SWIFT solution. This was definitely a team effort, with strong leadership from NSWG4 keeping the project focused, providing the resources and empowering employees to drive the change across NSWG4. Built upon BizFlow, HandySoft's automated business process workflow software application, and guided by input and active participation from the SWIFT team, this solution streamlines, provides visibility and forcing function for the NSWG4 GPCP. For the first time, customers now have visibility into the Government Purchase Card Program (GPCP). Through automation, users can track the status of an order, while the process moves faster and easier, and management is able to measure the process. On 450 requests/month, the average lead-time is now 3.2 days from request to completion—before the implementation of this new workflow automation, the process traditionally took several weeks, with considerable process time variation and major inconsistencies. The automation for the GPCP using SWIFT provides visibility into the process, standardization, and forcing function for over 6,000 purchases and $5.2 million spent annually. NSWG4 can now measure cycle times, and capture other valuable financial data. So successful was the implementation at NSWG4 (echelon III command), there are now plans to implement the software throughout NSW (echelon II). SWIFT is now the success model for future process improvement initiatives.

3. BUSINESS CONTEXT

Previously, the NSWG4 relied on antiquated and manual driven processes for their government credit card purchases. The process was entirely paper driven, relying on hand written approvals and signatures and often required tracking down those with appropriate approval credentials. Without a standardized government card purchase and approval system, products and supplies could not be tracked; the process was cumbersome and hit or miss, delaying the procurement, approval, and delivery of critical equipment.

The SWIFT project established a model that works within the Naval Special Warfare culture. This program delivered immediate and significant increases in productivity, efficiency, and accuracy for NSWG4, and has opened the door for other workflow automation implementations including all contracts, to continue the improvement in delivery of service to support the SEALs in their mission.

4. THE KEY INNOVATIONS

4.2 Business

NSWG4's new government purchase card program, SWIFT, now standardizes the credit purchase and approval process across all boat teams, while providing visibility, control and an audit trail for all purchases. Stakeholders throughout the approval chain can now track and monitor purchases and buyers know exactly which step they are at in the process. The SWIFT program is accessible from anywhere with Internet access around the world.

There were several key elements that led to success with this program:

- Incremental change led by employees: NSWG4 used TPS (Toyota Production System Model) to implement incremental change to drive organizational increases in productivity and efficiency. The model from Toyota (called the Toyota Production System (TPS) model) uses small rapid improvements events (Kaizen) led by the employees and mentored by senior leaders to drive projects. NSWG4 is using this methodology rather than the traditional activity based model, which mandates meetings, tollgates, excessive charts and measurements. NSWG4 didn't try to 'boil the ocean;' it focused on solving specific problems.
- Speed: From defining the process specifications to going live with SWIFT was only six months. Securing buy-in from the stakeholders and end users encouraged active participation as the work progressed, and BizFlow, the COTS solution used as the basis of the implementation, was easy to use and needed minimal customization, delivering most of the requirements out of the box.
- Cost: Using superior commercial off-the-shelf software that required minimal customization kept development costs down. And because the requirements were clearly defined upfront through the offsite, and leadership really listened to the stakeholders and kept them engaged, the process went smoothly and everyone involved was in agreement regarding what the final product should deliver.

The end result: an immediate increase in productivity, faster, more accurate purchasing and ordering, standardization, transparency, and an easy to use adhoc reporting mechanism that provides management with complete process oversight.

4.3 Process

Prior to April 2011, the purchasing of boat requirements involved customers manually filling out purchasing paperwork and routing packages consisting of printed paper forms and substantiating documentation. The manual flow of information increased inaccurate purchasing information and there was no visibility into the process. Customers were often unaware of the procurement status, including delays on parts and services, which could ultimately force mission-critical boats and equipment out of commission.

Now, for the first time, customers have visibility into the Government Purchase Card Program. Through automation, users can track the status of an order, while the process moves faster and easier, and management is able to measure the process. Currently, processing approximately 450 requests per month, the average lead-time has been reduced to 3.2 days from initial request through to completion—before the implementation of this new workflow automation, the process traditionally took several weeks, with considerable process time variation with major inconsistencies.

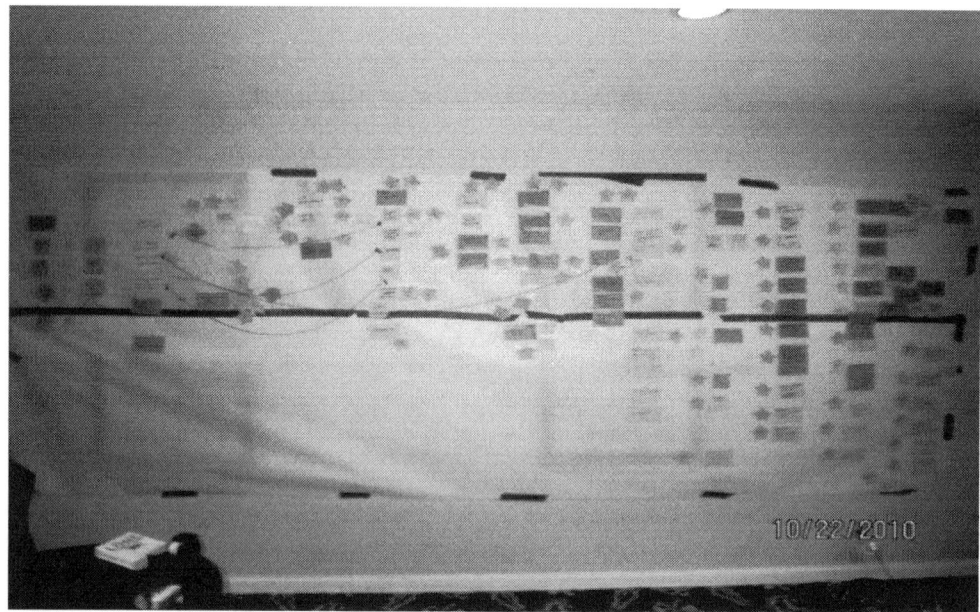

Picture of the GPCP Value Stream Map from the Kaizen event, which was led by the credit card holders, approving officials and agency program coordinator.

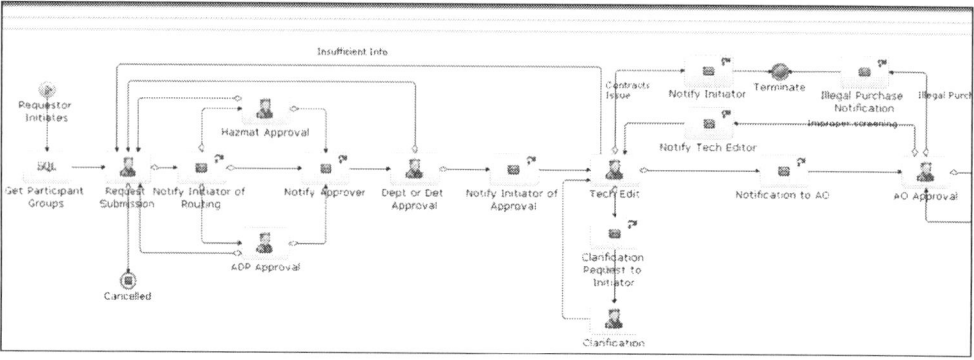

BizFlow by HandySoft Computer Screen Status: Workflow automation not only shows the latest status of each purchase request but has the capability to send emails to personnel at each step of the process. E-mails remind employees of needed actions or provide the latest status to customer.

4.4 Organization

The impact of this program on the employees was significant; SWIFT not only improved the time required for processing orders and requests, but also significantly improved accountability, transparency, and visibility into the process. No longer does an order sit on someone's desk waiting for action; if no action takes place within the set time parameters, the request is automatically forwarded to that person's supervisor, ensuring the workflow continues.

A key element was the involvement of those individuals who actually use the program, ensuring that the workflow process was accurate, and that there was buy-in from those most impacted by the procedures. This integration of Toyota Production System (TPS) process improvement methodology took a bit more time up-front, but ensured the system accurately reflects the pain points and priorities of those actually using this system every day.

5. HURDLES OVERCOME

Management

When the project was first initiated, management took the time to think through how to ensure they got buy-in from the employees who would use the system, and how to determine accurately what the actual problem areas were. The approach was defined to ensure input from those most impacted—and that approach is a major reason why this effort was so successful. At the beginning of the project, NSWG4 asked customers at the deck plates the specific challenges related to the GPCP. Using Shingo value stream mapping techniques which separate the process steps from the operational steps, the team, consisting of 25 personnel, standardized the process by removing waste (excess steps) and indentifying over 40 different points of automation. The common theme was a lack of defined process, contract status visibility and timeliness.

NSWG4 used "Voice of the Customer" workshops to identify the Team (who), Goals, Scope, Pain, Requirements, Impact, and Schedule.

- Primary Customer—SEALs & SWCCs
- Secondary Customer—Logistics & Support Personnel
- Tertiary Customer—Finance & Audit

Business

Based upon inputs from the teams, NSWG4 awarded a contract to implement a workflow software tool. This approach was chosen because it enables the customer to enter his requirements electronically and track the progress of the purchase. The focus was to support the users, make the process easier and more user-friendly, and increase transparency and accountability. BizFlow by HandySoft, a robust BPM solution, was chosen as the foundation, to ensure the new system could be built quickly and would be intuitive and easy to use.

Organization Adoption

Because research indicates over 60% of all major transformations fail to achieve established goals, NSWG4 introduced the new software incrementally by first automating the GPCP process. The GPCP is used for purchases below $3,000 for supplies and $2,500 for services. At NSWG4, the command averages over 6,000 purchases a year, with $5.2 million spent annually.

And to ensure that the system addressed the users' pain points, at the beginning of the process, NSWG4 hosted an off-site meeting and invited the daily owners and users of the credit card process. Using Shingo value stream mapping techniques which separate the process steps from the operational steps, the team, consisting of 25 personnel, standardized the process by removing waste (excess steps) and indentifying over 40 different points of automation. The team called the project SWIFT (Special Warfare Information Fast Tracking). Because the team who would use the system literally created the points of automation, there was immediate acceptance and adoption of the system as soon as it was up and running.

6. BENEFITS

6.1 Cost Savings

Implementation of SWIFT secured significant cost savings, time reductions, and transparency in the Government Purchase Card Program process. The implementation of this system is part of an overall lean strategy to reduce inventory by more than $7 Million over the next three years. The first part of the strategy was to move NSWG4 contracting closer to the customer, which reduced overall ordering cycle time by implementing ordering agreements with vendors. The second part of continuous process improvement was to use workflow automation (e.g. BizFlow) to further speed up the ordering process.

More important than money is the increase in operational readiness by repairing combat craft and training faster and with fewer defects. In addition, the lessons learned from decreasing contracting ordering cycle time enables NSW to purchase fewer craft and engines without compromising effectiveness

6.2 Time Reductions

This system reduced the credit card ordering cycle time to 3.2 days (56%). An estimated 4.6 man-years was gained because of the increased efficiency of the system: customers now have purchasing visibility including email status notifications instead of wasting time manually tracking requirements. The continuous workflow improvement program is being replicated at NSW. NSW targets are an additional 20 man-years in productivity gains in the next year, producing a 400% ROI.

6.3 Increased Revenues

As this is a government organization, the goal was not to increase revenues, but to capture significant cost savings, improve efficiency and transparency. All of these goals were realized.

6.4 Productivity Improvements

Four contracts are now issued to supply Navy SEALs around the world (80% of Goal). There is a 30% decrease in contract defects. This system also reduced the average boat repair contract time by 20 days (78%) and parts contract time by 55 days (70%).

Overall productivity improvements and organizational improvements include:
- Decreased Cycle Time
- Improved process cycle efficiency
- Embraced by Management
- 100% end-to-end visibility
- Zero defect rate and audit compliance
- Across the board accountability

7. BEST PRACTICES, LEARNING POINTS AND PITFALLS

7.1 Best Practices and Learning Points

✓ The GPCP process leveraged a unique combination of methodologies to ensure success, combining Lean Six Sigma, Agile, and BPM. The project's foundation was built on Lean Six Sigma principles combined with Kaizen events to model and improve the process.

✓ A best of breed BPM technology, BizFlow by HandySoft, was then able to deliver on those process requirements through Rapid Application Development (RAD) session and Agile development methodology to quickly turn the requirements into a production, web-based acquisition management system in support of the SEALs and SWCCs.

✓ SWIFT is now the success model for future process improvement initiatives. The SWIFT project established a model that works within the Naval Special Warfare culture. The model is based on 5 key principles that drive process improvement:

- o Lean is a journey: design the system in segments and show rapid results to build momentum;
- o Management must be willing to empower their team to make decisions starting at the evaluation stage;
- o Design a process which reduces errors on the front end and reduces extra steps;
- o Identify the right stakeholders and leverage Kaizen events to speed the process improvement effort;
- o Lean + Agile + BPM (BizFlow) = success.

7.2 Pitfalls (Things to avoid)

✗ Make sure you get buy-in from the users of the system and the true stakeholders at the beginning of the process.

✗ Keep stakeholders involved, engaged, and active participants throughout the process—this will help ensure the system actually does what is needed to solve the problems identified.

✗ Don't try to 'boil the ocean'; focus on solvable problems and reasonable goals.

8. COMPETITIVE ADVANTAGES

The competitive advantages from this implementation are significant—by improving efficiencies and streamlining ordering processes, SWIFT helps NSWG4 focus on what they do best—fighting the war on terror—rather than spending so much time on paperwork to ensure they have the tools and supplies needed.

Specifically, this program provides:

- Total acquisition process **visibility** from purchase request to asset receipt through online monitoring, providing the system users FedEx like capabilities through the system. Real-time visibility into where the process is at any given time.
- Email notifications result in **accountability** by triggering required approval and action steps by approver.
- Real-time Purchase Requisition reports listing out costs, vendor data, and approvals **saves time and ensures accuracy**.
- Significant **efficiencies** in Order Cycle times for purchase requests.
- Eliminated paperwork through **electronic request forms** with product and vendor attachments.
- E-Signatures with date/time stamps for each process approval is **compliant** with audit requirements.
- Bottom line: SWIFT allows for SEALs and SWCCs "to do what they do best" instead of tracking down paperwork and material.

9. TECHNOLOGY

NSWG4 worked with RF Logistics and HandySoft to develop the specification and then customize BizFlow by HandySoft into the solution defined and desired by the SWIFT team. The GPCP process leveraged a unique combination of methodologies to ensure success, combining Lean, Agile, and BPM. The project's foundation was built on Lean Six Sigma principles combined with Kaizen events to model and improve the process. A best of breed BPM technology, BizFlow by HandySoft, was then able to deliver on those process requirements through Rapid Application Development (RAD) session and Agile development methodology to quickly turn the requirements into a production, web-based acquisition management system in support of the SEALs and SWCCs.

The BPM solution, BizFlow by HandySoft, provides enterprise users with capabilities that improve their success, efficiency and self-reliance when dealing with ad-hoc business challenges, such as those faced by the SWIFT team in the GPCP process. BizFlow provides structure and traceability to dynamic business and structured business processes and web applications, increasing the transparency of ad-hoc tasking, and allowing users to clearly visualize and track "work in progress."

In addition to the use of BPM technology as the foundation for this implementation, NSWG4 applied Six Sigma principles to help them move from disparate paper processes to a single, streamlined, unified process for GPCP procurement. NSWG4 conducted several Lean Six Sigma Kaizen events that included all the SWIFT team stakeholders involved in the GPCP request process to get a clear understanding of the end-to-end process, and to ensure that the new solution would address the approval and processing requirements of each respective contributor. The end result was SWIFT - a Lean Six endeavor of constant process improvement, which addressed and solved the following challenges indentified by the stakeholders:

- visibility with a credit card purchase request
- standardization and adherence to checklists
- forcing function to require appropriate action within an allotted amount of time
- process scheduler and established metrics
- accountability during the approval and sign-off activities
- specific guidelines or processes for 'special' requests that fall into ADP or HAZMAT categories

SWIFT makes use of the BizFlow monitor where graphic icons display all of the approvers in the purchase request approval path. As the request is routed through the various approvals, the user initiating the request can look online and see at what stage (i.e. reviewer) the purchase request is in the process. This visibility can be monitored through either the graphic icons that represent the approvers or via an activity table depicting the date and time stamp of the submission for approval and the date and time stamp of the actual approval.

The introduction of the BizFlow tool required the standardization of workflow processes, activities and forms used by the former paper based system. Standardizing the GPCP request processes and activities eliminated the inconsistencies experienced with the paper process, and greatly improved process cycle times while also creating an on-demand auditing system.

BizFlow also has a "forcing-function" where once a purchase request is created and submitted, an email notification is sent to the next reviewer in the process path for approval and a scheduler or clock is triggered for the allotted time established for the next activity. The email directs the reviewers to log into BizFlow, review their "work list" and review the purchase request(s) that require action. In the event that the next-in-line reviewer is out of the office, another approver can be delegated to act upon the purchase request. As the NSWG4 users became more comfortable and knowledgeable with the process, the approval process times decreased considerably.

Oversight and accountability is provided throughout SWIFT from the tracking number to the other monitor features. The electronic mail notification and scheduler functionality is directed to the specific user(s), requiring that they act upon the purchase request within a given time-frame or the request is elevated to that user's supervisor. Additionally, those "special" item purchase requests that fall into required ADP or HAZMAT approval categories now have specific approval paths for routing. There is also the ability to view the defined set of reviewers and approvers that are identified beside each activity. Also, if a purchase request lacks the appropriate justification and/or documents at the beginning of the process, the next-in-line reviewer can return the request immediately to the requestor with comments detailing why the request is incomplete and what actions are necessary to secure approval. This accountability relieves the "downstream" pressure for short-turnaround reviews and approvals previously experienced on the back-end of the purchase request process.

All of this accountability contributes towards getting the process "right" at the beginning stages by eliminating the defects to ensure the reviews and approvals are moving through the approval path towards a successful purchase.

10. THE TECHNOLOGY AND SERVICE PROVIDERS

HandySoft provided business process management (BPM) software (BizFlow), application development, and customer support for this program. HandySoft is a leading global provider of Business Process Management (BPM), Tasking and Compliance software and solutions for government and business organizations. BizFlow® is the first and only BPM Suite on the market to seamlessly integrate and automate dynamic tasks, case management, content collaboration, and structured processes along with Process Intelligence and RIA capabilities to drive visibility, control and productivity across all work that happens within an organization. For more information, visit www.handysoft.com.

RF Logistics provided consulting and integration expertise for this project. The firm played a prominent role in facilitating the Kaizen event, gathering the business requirements, developing the workflow application and conducting end user training. Founded in 2003, RF Logistics, LLC is a veteran owned small business dedicated to bringing process improvement to the workplace. They focus on business process reengineering and automated data operations for logistics & warehouse management, business & office management, or asset visibility at all levels of an enterprise. For more information, visit www.rflogistics.com.

County of San Joaquin, USA

Gold Award: Nominated by Oracle USA

1. EXECUTIVE SUMMARY / ABSTRACT

County of San Joaquin Information Systems Division Modernizes and Integrates Law and Justice Systems

The modernization of San Joaquin County's Integrated Justice Information System (IJIS) was a strategic initiative that started with setting our visions and goals to modernize interfaces and functions that continue to support the law and justice duties of the residents of San Joaquin County, Sheriff's Office, Public Defender, District Attorney and Probation Department, as well as the needs of other local, state and national law enforcement entities. We focused on reducing unnecessary redundancy and consolidating like functions to decrease costs and improve overall system performance. Additionally, new nationwide standards, such as National Information Exchange Model (NIEM) would allow us to collaborate more effectively with state and national law enforcement. This modernization is critical to San Joaquin's support of law enforcement and the public safety of over 650,000 residents. Our choice to modernize IJIS using Business Process Management (BPM) and Service Oriented Architecture (SOA) technologies aligned with our strategic vision of lowering our business risks by providing agility with phased modernization:

During the period 2009-2011 the San Joaquin County Information Systems Division was faced by a huge challenge. With the decreasing funds and staff in San Joaquin County it became critical that Information Systems Division provides support in development of new Case Management Systems so the functionality provided by these systems can fill in the gap made by the decreasing manpower in Law and Justice Departments. The CIO of Information Systems Division devised a strategy to deal with this challenge and assigned this task to its BPM Center of Excellence team. The BPM COE team involved highly in workflow management, service integration and business process development with the use of Business Process Analysis suite, Service Oriented Architecture and Business Analysis Monitoring tools. In the three years mentioned County of San Joaquin gained the maximum ROI from the investment it had made in Service Oriented Architecture, Business Process Modeling and Business Activity Monitoring. It has fully established Governance models developed by its Center of Excellence for BPM. Following major Case Management Systems and Business processes were developed during this period:

- Online Citation Inquiry and Payment System.
- District Attorney Case Management System.
- JCAD (Application for Mobile Police Units)
- Online Assessment System
- Adult Probation Case Management System.

The County spent around 20,000 man-hours to complete this effort and deliver systems successfully for its customers including San Joaquin Courts, District Attorney and Adult Probation.

Think Big: We chose a BPM and SOA for our long-term EA modernization. It had to be robust, scalable, secure, standards-based, and open to last and meet our long term vision

Start Small: Our first production system on was the Local Area Warrant System (LAWS) which was completed in less than 6 months.

Move Fast: 4 additional systems (On-line Citation Inquiry-Payment Systems, Probation Web- based Criminal Conviction Assessments System, JCAD (mobile CAD interface), District Attorney CiberLaw Case Management System and Adult Probation CMS) were deployed from 2010-2011.

With the tightening budgets we have had to move from a waterfall methodology to Agile development model. Our investment in modernizing our Enterprise Architecture (EA) with SOA and BPM technology has allowed us to make this transition, integrate with state and national justice systems, and improve service to our County.

2. OVERVIEW

IJIS provides a Web-based system to link over 650,000 residents, 6,600 users internal users, 18 agencies countywide and other law enforcement systems nationwide. Prior to our modernization effort processes were integrated in a point-to-point tightly coupled approach. This proved to be a high Total Cost of Ownership and High Risk approach to running our business. Many activities, especially in reporting and the transfer of information ended up being manual and inefficient.

Our modernization initiative focused on these three aspects: Replace an outdated and difficult to maintain warrant system to improve the county's ability to manage making arrests, issuing warrants, and maintaining histories, and to transition to the new state court system; Implement service-oriented architecture (SOA) to simplify integration between several county law and justice systems with diverse architectures and transfer law enforcement data to court system's mainframe; Ensure the highest level of security for sensitive data .

Our original processes used a lot of legacy systems with tightly coupled integration processes that were unsustainable from both a cost and risk perspective. With our BPM and SOA modernization processes are now implemented with both the Orchestration and Service Bus Layers. This allows for better agility, re-use, and scalability. We've evolved from a Monolithic Legacy based EA to a Service Oriented EA. This then allows us the flexibility of migrating our business logic out of proprietary environments. Our end state objective is to abstract our EA capabilities into the appropriate layers to allow us more agility and flexibility to meet our future requirements. We combine BPM, Service Bus, BAM, Application Development scaled onto Application Server and implemented Security and Governance SOA and Security Management technologies.

Essential was a Center of Excellence sponsored by the CIO and led by our Project Manager/EA leader. The project team consisted of core IT staff and Subject Matter Experts matrixed based on the project requirements. Key members also sit on the Governance Board that manages change management, project scoping, budgeting, and service level agreements from both a business and IT perspective.

Our stakeholders span the residents of San Joaquin County, Sheriff's Office, Public Defender, District Attorney and Probation Department, as well as other local, state and national law enforcement entities. The new systems now supporting them are Local Area Warrant System (LAWS), On-line Citation Inquiry-Payment Systems, Probation Web- based Criminal Conviction Assessments System, District Attorney CiberLaw Case Management System; and the Adult Probation Case Management System (Mainframe replacement) implemented in Aug, 2011

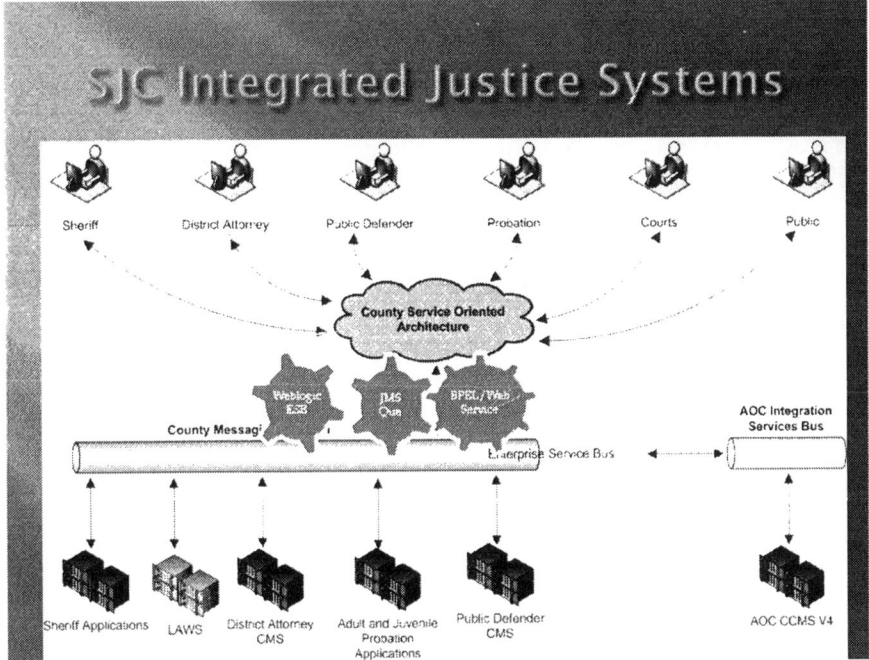

Figure 1: IJIS includes integration of many County Systems and with the California Administrative Office of the Courts (AOC) California Law Enforcement Telecommunications System (CLETS)

The most difficult phase was when we first started implementing BPM and SOA, both from a technology experience and organizational culture standpoint. We had to adjust to a different agile approach to our EA. In the long run this change proved essential to our success.

3. BUSINESS CONTEXT

The County is continually assessing its current business and computing environment, searching for opportunities to increase operational efficiency and improve the service it delivers. During this assessment, a number of issues ("Business Challenges") were identified. A summary of the Business Challenges are listed below:

Decreasing Budgets: Government budgets in California are being stretched and will continue to be stretched into the foreseeable future. San Joaquin County will have limited dollars available to invest in technology; those dollars must be invested for the greatest overall good to the County.

Growing County Population: San Joaquin County is one of the fastest growing counties in the nation. As the County's population grows, the demand for County services and the cost of delivering County services will grow correspondingly.

Changing Demographics: As the population in San Joaquin County changes, so do the County's demographics. The number of households in San Joaquin County that have and use a computer is growing. County government faces the challenge of delivering cost effective solutions to constituents that will likely expect government services to be commensurate with the services they receive from private businesses – namely services that are available when it is convenient for the customer and available via their home computer.

Service Constrained by Organizational Structure / Process : In many cases today, it is very difficult for citizens and businesses to know who within County government provides the services they seek. In certain instances, multiple departments are involved in delivery of the service, requiring a citizen to travel around San Joaquin County, going from department to department, in order to complete the entire transaction.

Aging Criminal Justice Information System: The County's Criminal Justice Information System (CJIS) was developed in 1986. The system is used on a daily basis by nearly every law enforcement entity within the County. The system faced two challenges. First, the Administrative Office of the Courts required a modernization of California's systems. Second, the County's existing Criminal Justice Information System reached a point where the technologies it utilizes have become obsolete and difficult to maintain. A system outage caused by a failure of one of these older technologies would have a tremendous impact on the daily law enforcement operation in the County.

Selection and Use of Technology

San Joaquin County spends millions of dollars annually on technology. The County's technology investments are often made with a departmental focus rather than with a broader countywide perspective. The inconsistent selection and use of technology can result in duplication and excess cost to the County as a whole. The inconsistent use of technology can also create barriers to data sharing and technology use that lead to higher cost of ownership and lower benefits from the technology investment.

4. THE KEY INNOVATIONS

The modernization of our Integrated Justice Information System is a strategic initiative that started with setting our visions and goals in 2005 and laid out our road map for the future. We set forth to develop interfaces and functions that continue to support the law and justice duties of the Sheriff's Office, Public Defender, District Attorney and Probation Department, as well as the needs of other local law enforcement entities. During the redevelopment effort, the County will focus on reducing unnecessary redundancy and consolidate like functions to decrease costs and improve overall system performance. The key innovations in systems implemented during 2009-2011 period were the following:

- Architecture and setup of County Cloud services for online Citation Inquiry and Payment system. This innovation involved setup of encryption, proxy and service invocation in the County DMZ environment. The Citation system serves over 1000 inquires and payments for County Citizens each day and has helped save time and revenue for Residents and County.
- Design of workflow, Integration and Governance processes for Booking, Warrants, Courts systems with District Attorney system. This interface serves 200 Bookings each day with 70-100 Complaints filed with Courts, 100 Court Calendars served each day.
- Development of Assessments interfaces with Probation Mainframe and new CMS. The System transmits and exchange of information for over 15,000 active probations and 400,000 Court Cases online.
- Design and Development of workflow for intake of Probationers in new Probation Caseload CMS. The interface transmits Offender information for over 200 offenders daily with details of Court Minute Orders, Arrest

Charges, Personal Information and Conditions sent across the interface online.

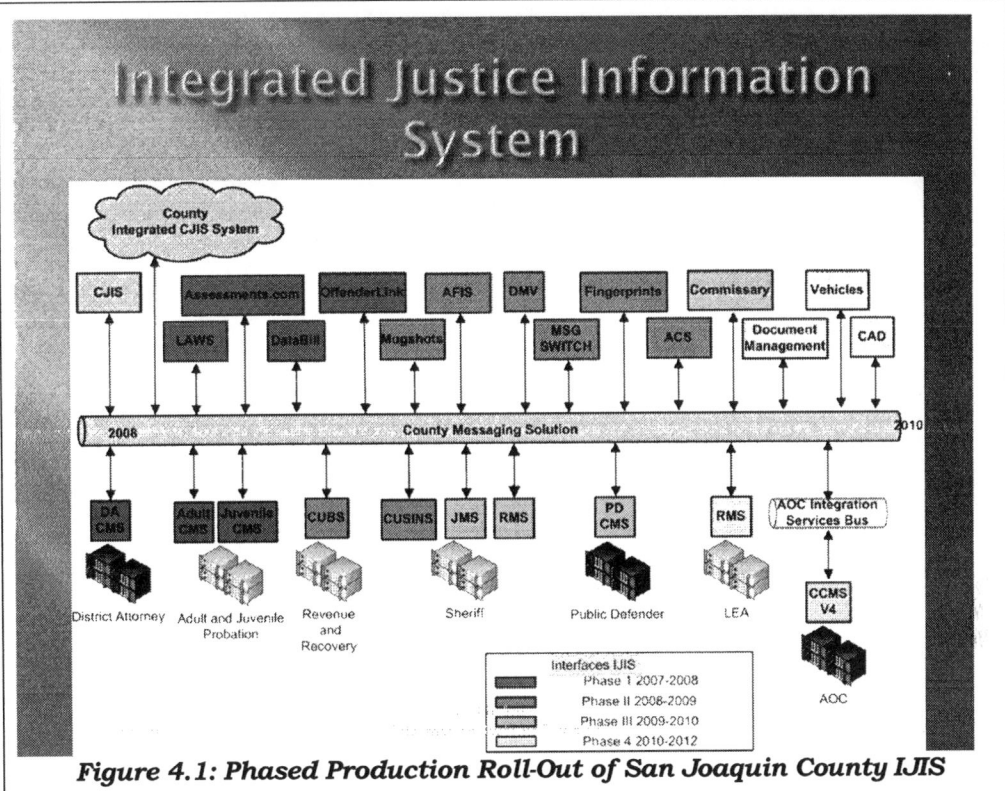

Figure 4.1: Phased Production Roll-Out of San Joaquin County IJIS

Our choice to modernize IJIS using SOA and BPM technologies is both aligned with our strategic vision and met to lower our business risks by providing agility and a phased implementation roll-out:

Think Big: We chose a BPM and SOA for our long-term EA modernization. It had to be robust, scalable, secure, standards-based, and open to last and meet our long term vision

Start Small: Our first production system on was the Local Area Warrant System (LAWS) which was completed in less than 6 months.

Move Fast: 4 additional systems (On-line Citation Inquiry-Payment Systems, Probation Web- based Criminal Conviction Assessments System, JCAD (mobile CAD interface), District Attorney CiberLaw Case Management System and Adult Probation CMS) were deployed from 2010-2011.

With the tightening budgets we have had to move from a waterfall methodology to Agile development model. Our investment in modernizing our Enterprise Architecture (EA) with SOA and BPM technology has allowed us to make this transition, integrate with state and national justice systems, and improve service to our County. San Joaquin has been recognized for this on-going innovation with numerous industry awards (e.g. CIO 100, Government Computer News).

4.2 Business

During the time from May 2009 to Oct 2011 County of San Joaquin has successfully implemented the following Case Management Systems and On-Line applications using Business Process Flow and Service Oriented Architecture. San Joaquin County has invested highly in developing the business model workflow as well as utilizing SOA to integrate desperate systems and thus successfully achieving the goal of unified Case Management System.

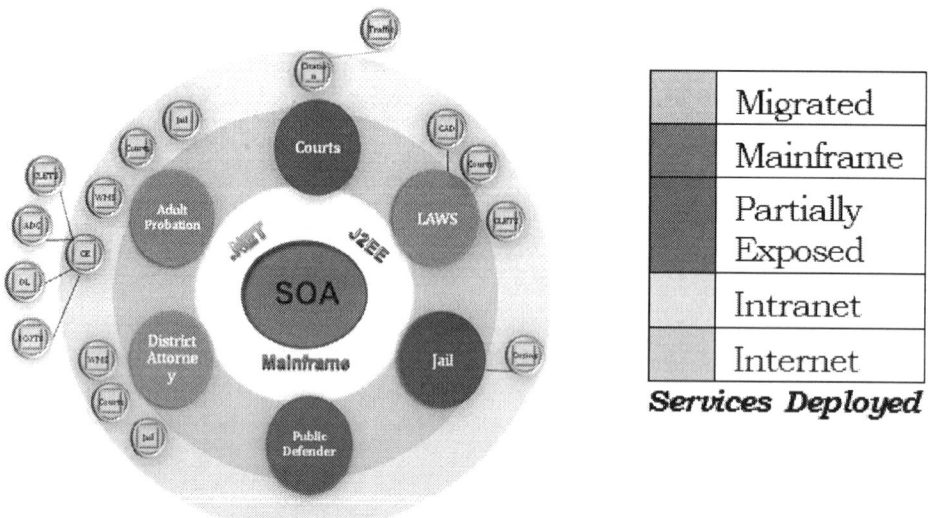

	Migrated
	Mainframe
	Partially Exposed
	Intranet
	Internet

Services Deployed

Fig: Law and Justice Modernization 2010-2011

Following are the major System Implementation from 2009-2011

On-line Citation System for Citizens of San Joaquin County. This system serves over 650,000 citizens and processes over 1000 online inquiries for traffic tickets and accepts payments online thus saving time and cost and increasing efficiency for the County.

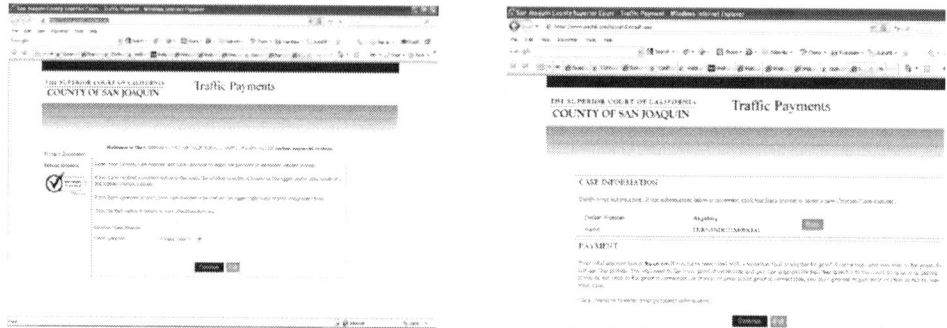

Web based online Citation Inquiry and Payment System

On-Line Assessments System was implemented for County Probation Department in Sep 2010. The online Assessments system provides data for over 15,000 active probationers with details of 400,000 court cases. There are 15-20 assessments performed daily and it has helped save time, paperwork and effort to manually evaluate the risk level. With the Assessment tool the Probation Officers are able to evaluate the risk in minutes where it used to take 4-8 hours for the manual process.

District Attorney Case Management System was implemented and went live in May, 2011. The Interfaces are created between Mainframe, Oracle and .Net systems to transfer highly sensitive data for Booking, Complaints, Court, Filing and Offenses and involves over 13 interfaces. BAM dashboards are created to actively monitor the activity on data transfer and look at live data.

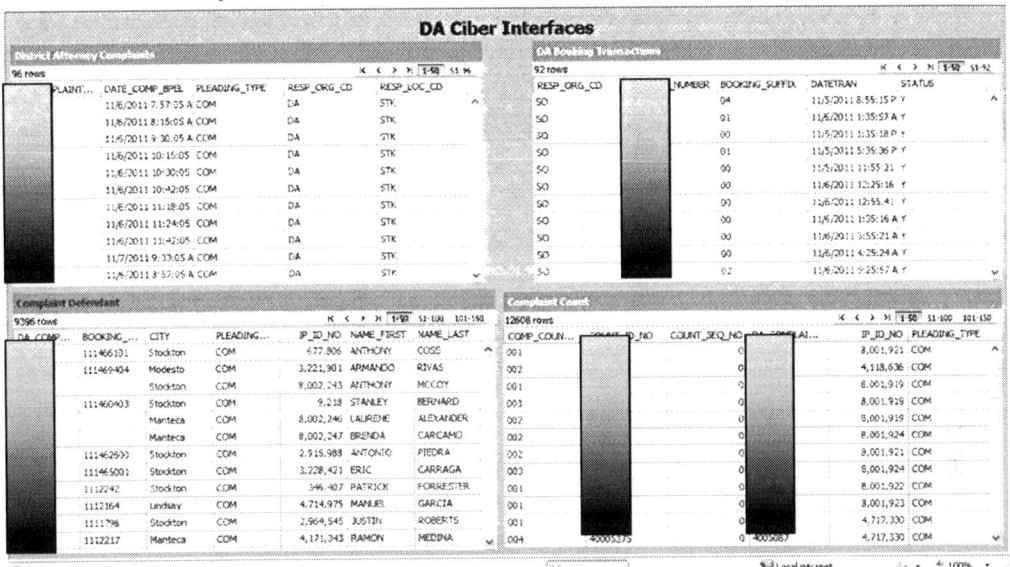

Adult Probation Case Management System was implemented from Jan-2010 to Aug-2011 and went live in Aug 2011. The County serves approx 15,000 active probationers and maintains data for approx 250,000 Court Cases for Probationers. Comments by Probation Lead "Benefits of Caseload Explorer- We have never had so much information integrated from other systems. Included are Offenderlink, Assessments.com, Laws, CUSINS, CJIS (booking from the jail, DA's office info.) This is a huge benefit because much of this information would have to be entered manually in the past. Also the minute orders coming across from the court automatically was new, these would also have to be manually processed previously. Within Caseload Explorer, many of our other systems and information we need to access if only a click away. We have never had systems before in this Probation department that communicated back and forth automatically, some numerous times a day. We are able to highly customize screens and permissions and have been able to share this system with many of our outside partners because of this ability. This system is EXTREMELY user friendly and we are able to extract information and run reports we would have to ask ISD to query in the past. Number of Probationers we now serve- we provide services to over 15,000 defendants in some form or fashion."

The Implementation of new Adult Probation System has facilitated the workflow of servicing to the probationers as well as tracking different information related to a probationer. This has resulted in saving a lot of time and effort to collect information or send information to relevant system.

Features of Caseload Explorer System

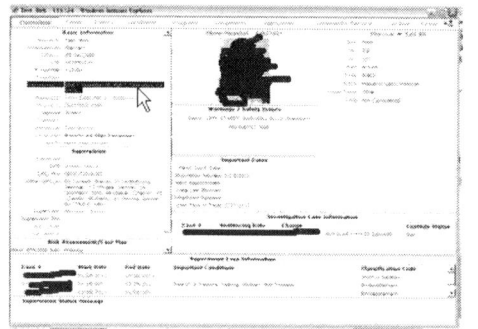 

Display of information and ease of navigation

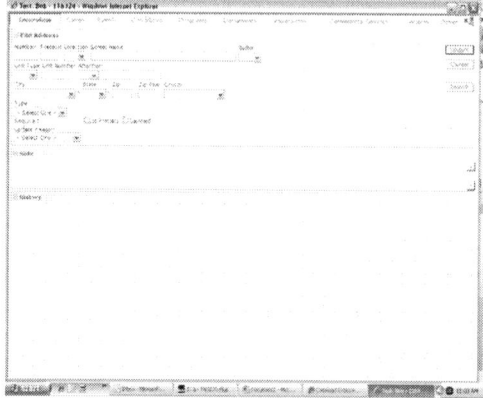

Personal Information (Collection and inquiry)

To enter Chrono , it used to take a lot of effort and navigation was not easy

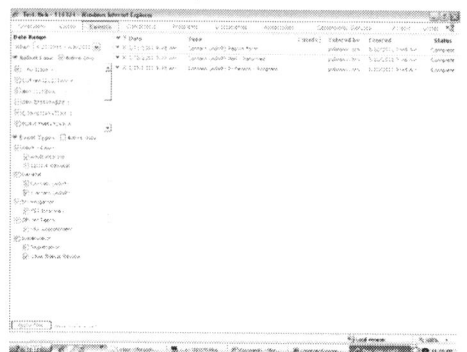 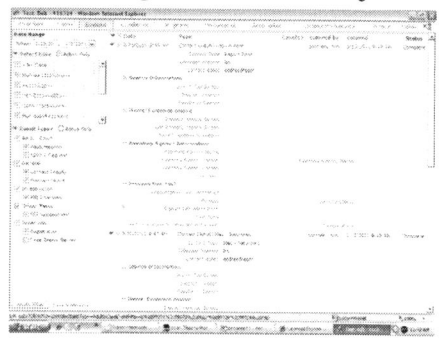

Entry and navigation of Chrono

Ease of Navigation

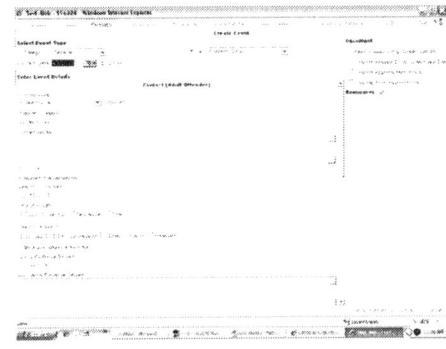

Workflow of Intake from Courts Referrals and BAM Dashboards

One of the biggest challenges faced during implementation of the new Case Management System was to develop a workflow for the intake of new Probation cases from CJIS mainframe to the new Caseload Explorer system. The Caseload Explorer is a .net system running on sql Server 2008. To overcome this huge challenge the County Interface development team worked with the Automon development team to create a workflow where the information is sent from Mainframe to Oracle and Sql Server staging databases. The Caseload Explorer creates a view for the records that need to be processed and so the Probation User can perform the intake of Probationers, Conditions, Charges and Personal information using the developed workflow.

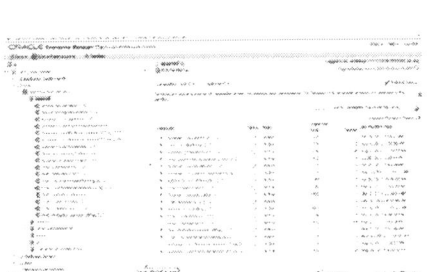

20 Interfaces transfer data from mainframe to sql server database

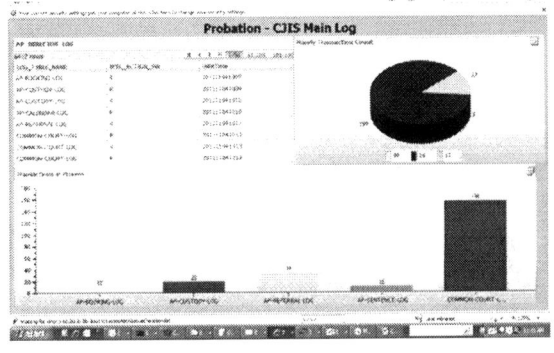

Probation Dashboard shows realtime view of transactions

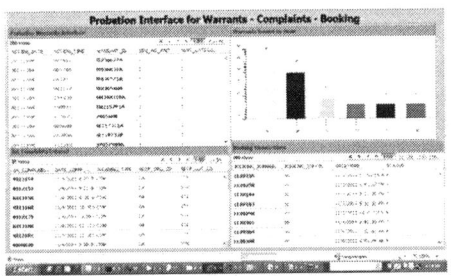

Probation Interface for Warrant, Complaint, Booking, Custody

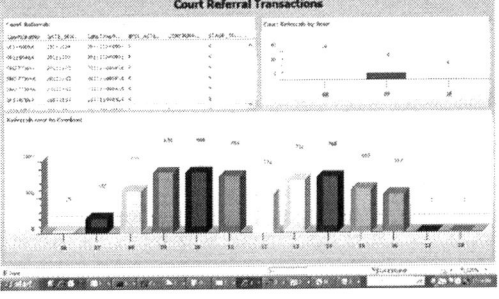

Court Referral Transactions

Interface with Exchange

Caseload Explorer also interfaces with San Joaquin County Exchange server. This function provides updates on local outlook appointments as soon as an appointment is created on the Caseload Explorer. The Interface team and San Joaquin Exchange Lead worked on the interface development and have been able to successfully develop and deploy this in production environment.

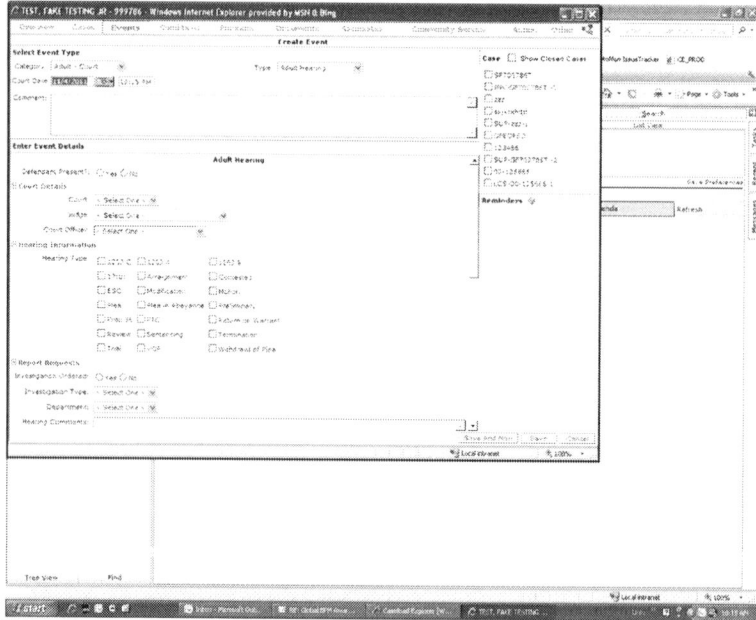

Creation of appointment in Caseload Explorer and interface with Exchange 2007.

Assessments Interface

Doing an assessment on an offender is now a click away where as it used to take more than four hours.

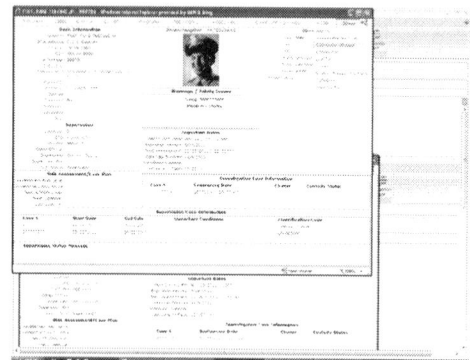

Online Assessment from Caseload Explorer

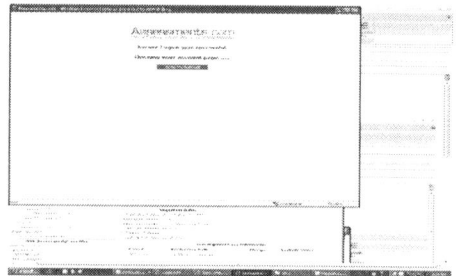

ADC application

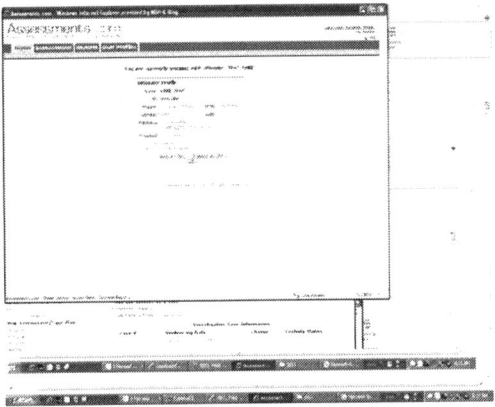

Assessment of an Offender

Offenderlink Interface

This interface provides link between County Adult Probation Application and online reporting application. The Probation users enter the TRS as a new program and the next day the person appears in Offenderlink.

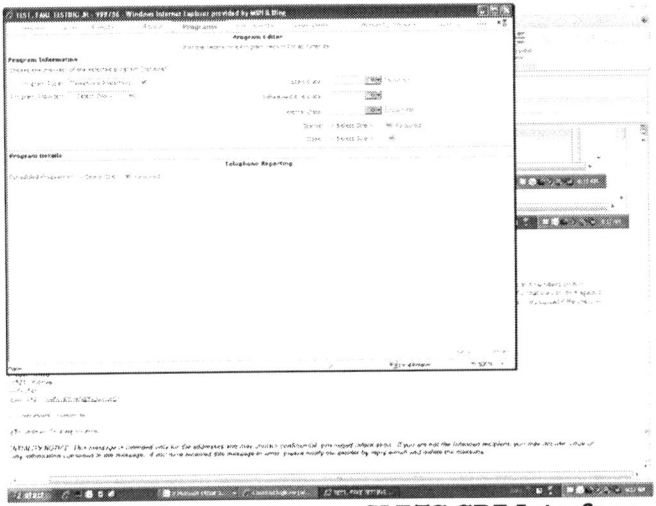

CLETS SRF Interface

The California Law Enforcement Telecommunication System Interface with Supervised Release File is developed in new Adult Probation Caseload Explorer and transfer offender data to state system as a batch process.

The County is continually assessing its current business and computing environment, searching for opportunities to increase operational efficiency and improve the service it delivers.

4.3 Process

With our BPM and SOA modernization processes are now implemented with Case Management, Business Orchestration and Service Bus Layers. This allows for better agility, re-use, and scalability.

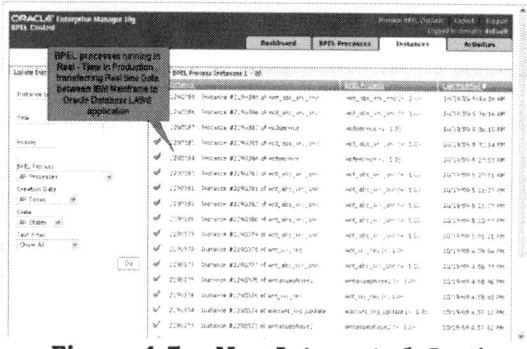

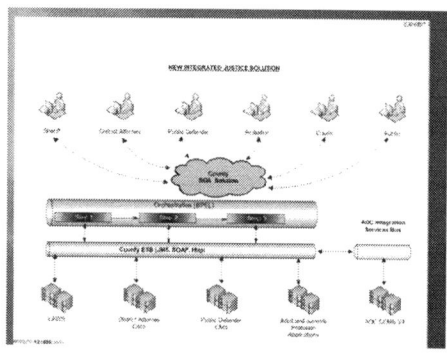

Figure 4.5a: New Integrated Justice Solution Process

Figure 4.5b: Process Monitoring of the Processes

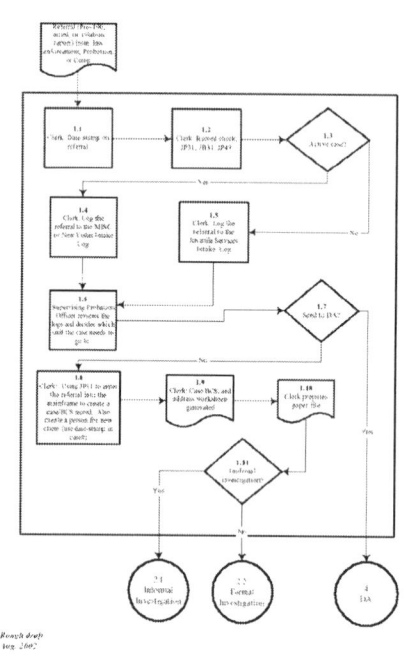

Caseload Explorer was designed "by Probation Officers for Probation Officers," but the development team always includes members who focus on process and workflow across the Probation Department, and in its dealings with external stakeholders such as the Courts, District Attorney, and Law Enforcement. During the process analysis, attention was especially paid to those processes that could be improved through the use of the features of the new case management system.

Left: Example Intake Process

Caseload Explorer records many different types of "events" in a case. Events are configured as appropriate to each task, but a good example is the Contact Event. In this event the officer's workflow includes the steps of scheduling a future or current contact (as needed), recording data when the contact occurs, completing documents using the data entered, and calendaring

reminders for follow up. The data collected then is used to produce statistical reports, court documents, and the like. However, for the officer this is a seamless and efficient process.

Officers need to see a variety of information presented in ways that answer questions that come up in the course of offender supervision. In the previous example we spoke of events. An offender can accumulate hundreds of events in their record over the course of a five year probation. In order to turn this glob of data into useful information, robust filtering tools are provided to the user. Making data easy to get it into the system is a good thing, but isn't too valuable if that data can't be efficiently extracted as useful information.

The following example is of how event filters have been used to display only the contact events on an offender. The events are "collapsed" in this view, but are easily expanded to display the underlying data.

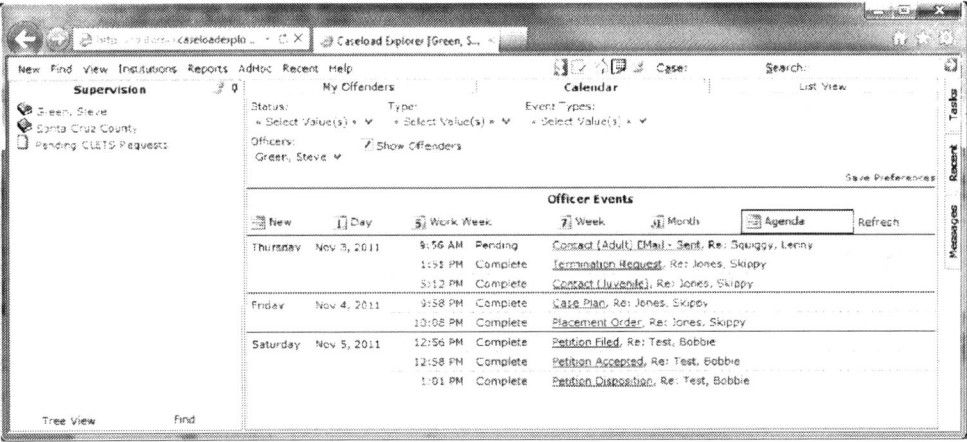

The focus on the work performed by Probation staff is evident when the application is first opened. They are presented with tabs, menu choices, and views that help them get started on their work with a minimum of navigation of the system. Multiple views, wizards, and input screens are no more than one or two clicks deep to begin and complete a large number of tasks and workflows.

Example Interfaces for Case Load (example mug shot for illustration purpose only)

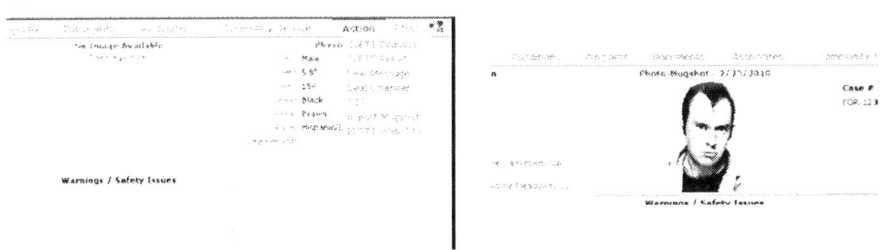

The core principal behind our modernization is a phased approach to leveraging SOA Adaptation. We are evolving from a Monolithic Legacy based EA to a Service Oriented EA.

As you can see in Figure 4.6 our use of SOA allows us to move from a high risk, tightly coupled legacy environment to Step 1 which abstracts our services and process layers. This then allows us the flexibility of then migrating our business logic out of the proprietary environments.

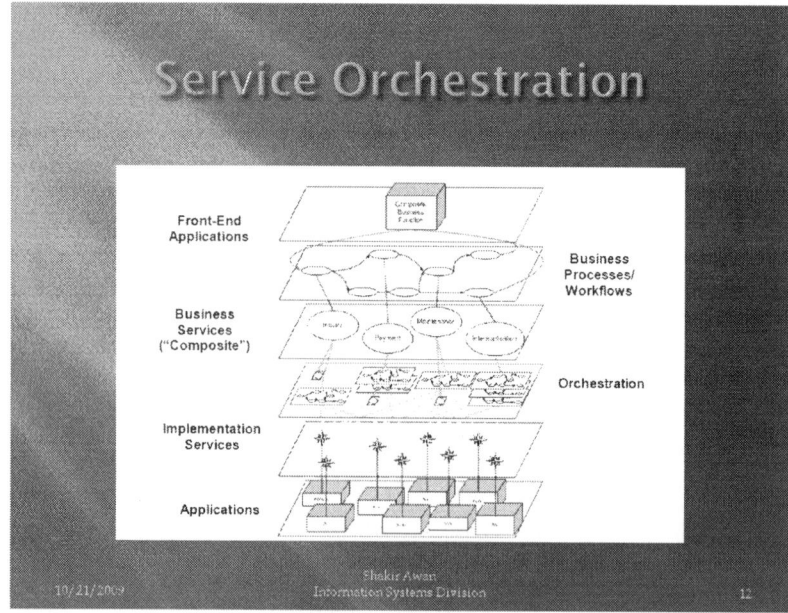

Figure 4.7: IJIS Using BPM and Workflows as key part of SOA Modernization

Our end state objective is to abstract our EA capabilities into the appropriate layers to allow us more agility and flexibility to meet our future requirements.

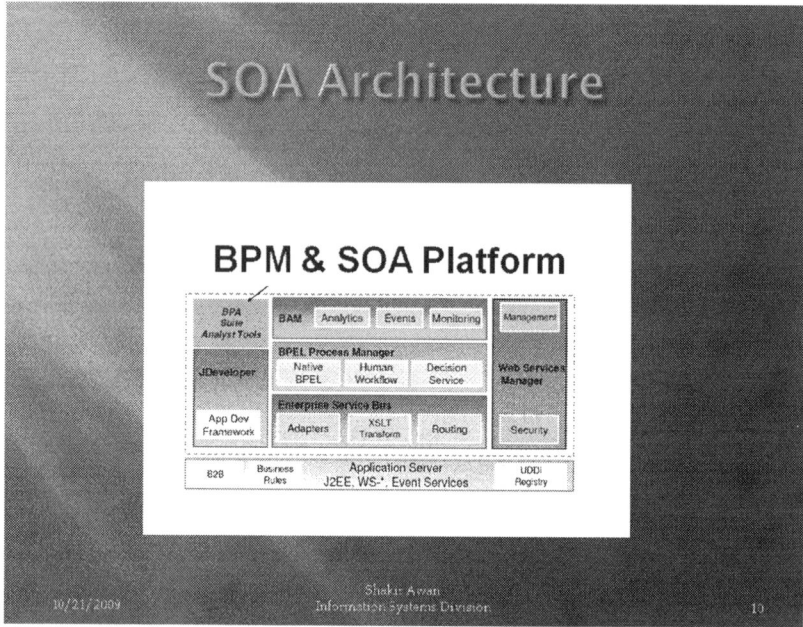

Figure 4.8: Specific BPM and SOA Components Used

Specific BPM and SOA components we took advantage of spanned the gambit. As you can see in Figure 4.8 we combine BPM, Service Bus, BAM, Application Development and scaled it with deployment onto Application Server and implemented Security and Governance SOA and Security Management technologies as well. We truly took a holistic approach to BPM and SOA and truly believe that the sum of the parts working together provides more value than just adding together each single component.

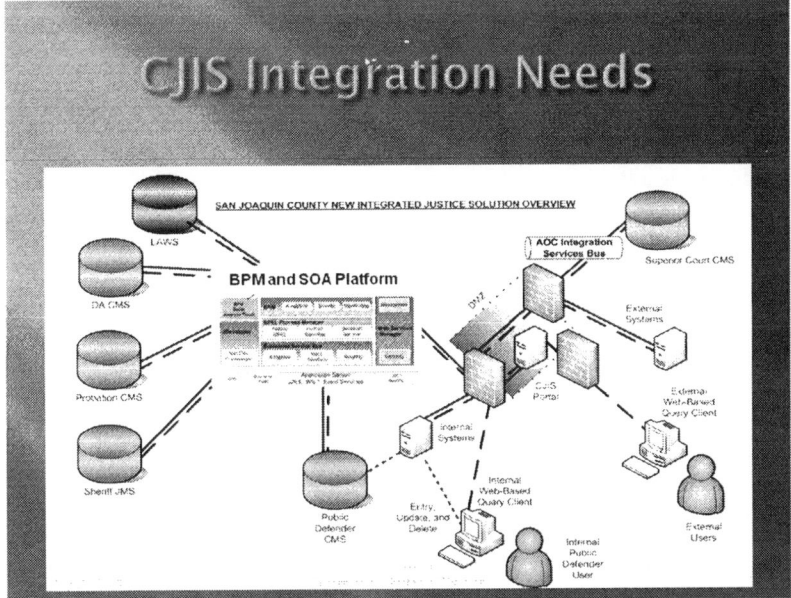

Figure 4.9: BPM and SOA as enabler of San Joaquin's new IJIS

This BPM and SOA Platform enabled us to modernize into a robust, scalable, secure, and agile Enterprise Architecture (see Figure 4.9 above).

4.4 Organization

A critical part our success has been the proper alignment of our Strategic Vision to the way our organization was enabled to plan and execute (and continues to execute) our modernization project.

We first established key project benchmarks to ensure our modernization effort met our key objectives:

- Dedicate resources for SOA. (2006)
- Enhance County SOA maturity. (2006-2007)
- Development on DA-Courts-LAWS interfaces.(2007-2008)
- Develop County SOA Hub (2008-2009)
- Implementation of new Probation CMS (2010-2011)
- Development for Probation-Courts-DA-LAWS interfaces (2008-2011)
- Preparation and Development for AOC-County V4 Integration (2009-2011)
- AOC-County V4 Integration Projects (2011-2014)

Communication of our Strategic Vision was critical in keeping our organization aligned and ensured we were executing to standard.

Our Best Practice Strategy:

- San Joaquin County seeks to maximize the investment of each dollar spent on technology in order to improve overall business operation and service to the public. To accomplish this, the County will make appropriate investments in technology in order to:
  - Improve County Service Delivery
  - Expand County Services
  - Realize Efficiencies

To accomplish these goals the County will, with guidance from the County's Chief Information Officer (Director, Information Systems Division), focus on four strategies:

STRATEGY #1 The County will sponsor projects that provide secure public access to government services.

- Wherever possible, the County will provide on-line public access to appropriate government information
- The County will seek public input on what County services or information they would like available on-line
- The County will promote electronic commerce as an alternative form of delivery of government services and transactions
- The County will ensure security and confidentiality of information and electronic transactions, giving special attention to compliance with the Health Insurance Portability and Accountability Act.

STRATEGY #2 The County will provide standards, guidelines and training to facilitate innovation and a cohesive business operation.

The County will:

- Develop and actively maintain a comprehensive IT Disaster Recovery Plan
- Develop, maintain and actively enforce comprehensive Information Security policy and procedure
- Establish a coordinated approach to automating shared business processes
- Continue to support an Information Technology Management Committee responsible for the review of all major IT efforts in the County
- Adopt and implement the Federal Enterprise Architecture (FEA) model for technology
- Apply project management techniques to all IT projects
- Establish, promote and enforce countywide IT standards
- Establish tools, methods and policy that facilitate the concept of collecting information once and sharing the information with those individuals who have the right to use it

STRATEGY #3 The County will develop and implement a robust, interoperable information technology (IT) environment.

The technologies and practices implemented by the County will:

- Manage data to satisfy the needs of a diverse customer base
- Support the collection, storage, and utilization of multi-media, including text, audio, images, maps, and video
- Consolidate (where appropriate) like technologies to reduce costs, eliminate unnecessary redundancies and free up limited technology staff
- Reduce the need to store paper documents
- Provide flexibility and ease of access to County services and information
- Foster greater collaboration and data sharing
- Focus on selecting proven, "off-the-shelf" solutions wherever possible
- Improve the reliability and responsiveness of the technology being used

STRATEGY #4 The County will utilize technology to control operational costs.

The County's operational costs are likely to grow as the County strives to serve the needs of a rapidly growing population. The County will consider the following as a means of controlling costs:

- The County will investigate software solutions as a means of reducing on-going software maintenance costs
- Where feasible and prudent, the County will seek to establish public / private partnerships for the implementation and support of technology
- The County will review the replacement of computer hardware to determine if its useful life can be extended
  - Adopt SOA as the integration standard
  - Identified highly talented staff within our team
  - Chose a product as integration software
  - Selected a manageable project for proof of concept (Think Big, Start Small, Move Fast)
- To make our organization aligned with our Vision and Strategy meant we had to invest in re-aligning and training our organization.

A core competency of Our Strategic Vision: Technology Skills and Training of Workforce

The County's reliance on technology increases each year. The County has made significant investments in enterprise wide systems that are now used daily for a variety of essential administrative and program functions. For the County to be effective and efficient, its workforce must be adequately trained in the use of technology. When we first started our Modernization Project in 2005, there was not a comprehensive technology training program in the County, and the technology skills of the County workforce varied greatly from department to department. One of the key benchmarks we set ourselves early on was to dedicate resources for SOA, which we met in 2006. We then established a structured project team directly supported and sponsored by the CIO. We also trained our team on SOA, BPM, Database, and JDeveloper technologies and maintained core staff on these technologies. Additionally, we used an Agile Development methodology which required a broader education process to ensure all stakeholders new what to expect as well rolled-out capabilities.

As we focused on our first effort, the modernization of Local Area Warrant System (LAWS), we stood up a Center of Excellence (CoE) sponsored by the CIO and led by a Project Manager and Systems Analyst V. The project team consisted of core IT staff and Subject Matter Experts (SMEs) matrixed into the project team throughout the project. This team expands and contracts based on the project development cycle. Key members of this team are also sit in the Governance Board that manages change management, project scoping, budgeting, and service level agreements from both a business and IT perspective. For our Change Management Process any change to the system or process is requested by the Business Users and Information Systems Change Management compiles a formal request to Change Management Board for approval.

For the technical change management IT uses Version Control for Change Management. This tool is being used by SOA and J2EE development team.

Overall, End Users, LAWS and SOA Technical and Functional teams, Managers and the Change Control Boards are part of our CoE.

All of these facets are essential teams within our CoE and ensure not only our continued success, but also our alignment with the Counties Strategic Vision.

5. HURDLES OVERCOME

There were a lot of cultural challenges that we faced; the information exchange between legacy systems and new Case Management Systems was required so it provides ease of workflow use for presentation of intake data. To accommodate this huge challenge the County relied on its BPM & SOA Centre of Excellence for development of workflow and services for Law Enforcement, District Attorney, Courts, Adult Probation and Public Defender Users. The critical information exchange is monitored by the use of BAM dashboards and alerts. In case of interface exchange not following the business rules an alert is send to the concerned User to correct the information. LAWS Users receive daily Warrants from Courts and process these warrants with updates, abstracts, worksheets and Bookings.

The critical information is submitted back to Courts Legacy systems. The new Booking is submitted daily to District Attorney CMS where Complaints are created and submitted from the SOA interface to Courts to create Court Cases. The courts create case and submit information back to District Attorney in case a review is needed or a Calendar appointment is set. New referrals are sent each day from Courts to new Adult Probation Automon Caseload CMS.

At an average around 100 Probation cases are referred and handled through the BPM workflow and SOA interface. Eight different systems communicate with Probation CMS to update and exchange information in real time and batch mode. Probation Users make daily Assessments on offenders. This has helped enormously in saving time, effort and cost and increasing county efficiency to process probation information. Our End users were not accustomed to a mouse and we had to provide both hot keys and mouse usage but slowly the Users found out the usefulness of mouse. Also the Users had to move to different screens on mainframe vs one page on LAWS showing all consolidated information including CLETS, CAD, NCIC and Local Warrants.

This huge advantage was very quickly realized by the whole community. The development time for interfaces in SOA setup has a turn-around time of 4 weeks vs 24 weeks in the mainframe system. Another huge benefit of SOA is that the SOA development team is able to change the business logic very quickly due to Jdeveloper and development environment.

6. BENEFITS

San Joaquin County seeks to maximize the investment of each dollar spent on technology in order to improve overall business operation and service to the public. To accomplish this, the County will make appropriate investments in technology in order to:
- Improve County Service Delivery
- Expand County Services
- Realize Efficiencies

This modernization effort lead to 4 new systems going into production: JCAD – LAWS Interface (November 2009); On-line Citation Inquiry-Payment Systems (Feb 2010); Probation Web- based Criminal Conviction Assessments System (September 2010); District Attorney CiberLaw Case Management System (May 2011), Adult Probation Caseload Case Management System (Aug 2011).

After implementing the BPM & SOA Architecture, San Joaquin County realized the following overall benefits:
- Adult Probation Manages 15,000 Active Probationers and links to 7 Separate systems online through 24 active Interfaces. Management of 240,000 approx Court Cases and related information for the Probation Department.

- One Police department saved $20,000 annually in license fees due to re-useable integration and other Police departments can potentially do the same.
- New Interfaces built in 1/6 the time compared to Mainframe. Saving 20 weeks per Interface
- 25% less officer time spent on non-productive activities * 200 = 40 FTEs time being utilized more efficiently.
- 500 daily citation payments on-line benefiting residents (>$500K annually)
- 100 daily probation assessments now automated (4000 average records accessed daily)
- Sharing of the data now average over 30 million transaction annually
- Collaboration available with state and national systems with webservice interfaces (now >800 transactions daily)
- Development cycles from 12 to 6 months initially; now 3 month cycles (saving over 12 Full Time Equivalent developers)
- Going Green cutting printing by an estimated 1 million pages per month
- End to end access for field personnel (e.g. mobile access to officers) coupled with the efficiency gains from all end-users versus old mainframe access points
- Average access times reduced to < 3 seconds from hours
- Secure and Trustworthy Solution with new On-site/Field Access
- Single view of the operation versus Mainframe multi-application access
- Reduce or Eliminate Risk of Wide Systematic Failure

Figure 6.1 (a-c): LAWS system allows warrant tracking across all Justice stakeholders and real-time access to state and national systems (AOC and CLETS)

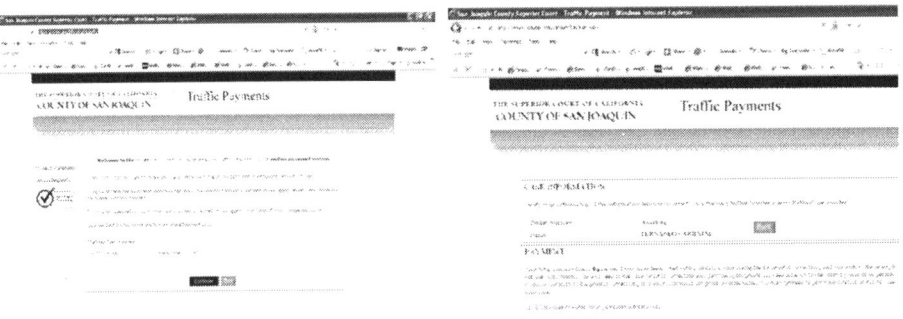

Figure 6.2 (a & b): On-line Citation Inquiry-Payment Systems also provides the public with secure, better, faster, and more convenient self-service.

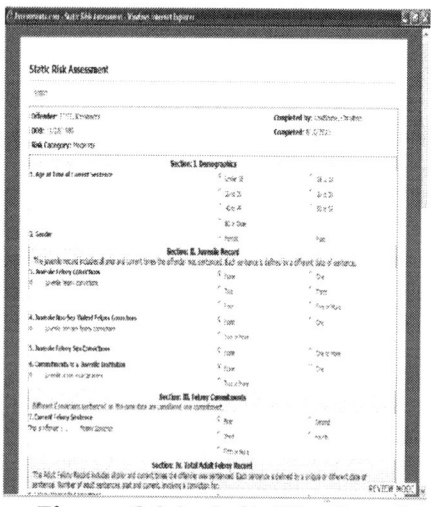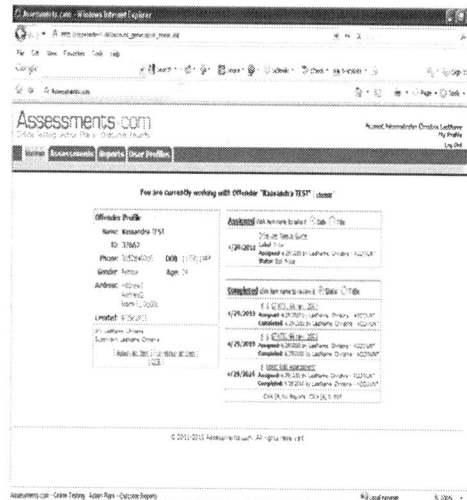

Figure 6.3 (a & b): The San Joaquin Probation Assessments system provides a web-based Assessment system for Criminal Conviction and Sentencing record.

7. BEST PRACTICES, LEARNING POINTS AND PITFALLS

7.1 Best Practices and Learning Points

- ✓ *Think Big, Start Small, Move Fast*
- ✓ *Don't assume customer and/or partners will modernize at the same pace as you*
- ✓ *Develop and configure mainframe adapter in SOA environment. You need to look at what jdbc gateway solutions are available to connect to mainframe, then configure these libraries in SOA.*
- ✓ *Learn the mainframe transaction environment, is it data&time based transaction sequence or event based sequence of transactions, what it means is that if it is date&time no matter what order you send to mainframe these would be sorted correctly. In the other case if it is event based then make sure the SOA takes care of the sequence of transactions needed to be send to mainframe otherwise the system will not work properly.*
- ✓ *Maturity Level in SOA is extremely important. The local IT resources should be well versed with the technology. Choose a manageable project.*
- ✓ *Governance in SOA and transparency in transactions across systems is a must.*
- ✓ *Establish a clear Chain-of-Command, with appropriate sponsorship levels*
- ✓ *Establish a Center of Excellence (CoE) with a core team that includes SMEs from the customer(s) when possible*
- ✓ *Governance across the project and services is essential*
- ✓ *Processes (that matter) usually span and require interfaces with external partners or customers*
- ✓ *Include your external partners in project communication*
- ✓ *Know your "As is"*
- ✓ *Knowledge of legacy environment*
- ✓ *Skill sets, including SOA*
- ✓ *Get Buy-In (IT & Business & Leadership – Executive)*
- ✓ *Foster Business Desire for Change*
- ✓ *Push for the upfront investment – "not your father's system"*
- ✓ *Constant marketing*

✓ Adhere to a Reference Architecture
✓ Take a phased approach to its implementation
✓ Phase I – Build Reference Architecture with initial business components
✓ Phase II – Technology pilot at select sites
✓ Phase III – Build out enterprise SOA services aligned with strategic plan and shareholder feedback and use metrics
✓ Maintain project management discipline

7.2 Pitfalls

✗ "Turning-off" legacy systems without understanding the business logic that connects it to other systems
✗ Scalability is not a given in mainframe, you have to send transactions in sequence. In other words you have to throttle the transactions send to mainframe.
✗ Re-publishing capability is a must
✗ Don't have a build and they will come philosophy
✗ Don't underestimate challenge of changing thoughts from IT infrastructure to providing Business Services

8. COMPETITIVE ADVANTAGES

The Enterprise Integration Gateway solution using BPM and SOA suites are a key component in San Joaquin County modernization initiative. By adopting the BPM & SOA technology the County was not only able to integrate internal and external systems but also use the newly developed frame work for future application development. This also keeps us in alignment with the Counties Strategic Vision and Directives from the California AOC.

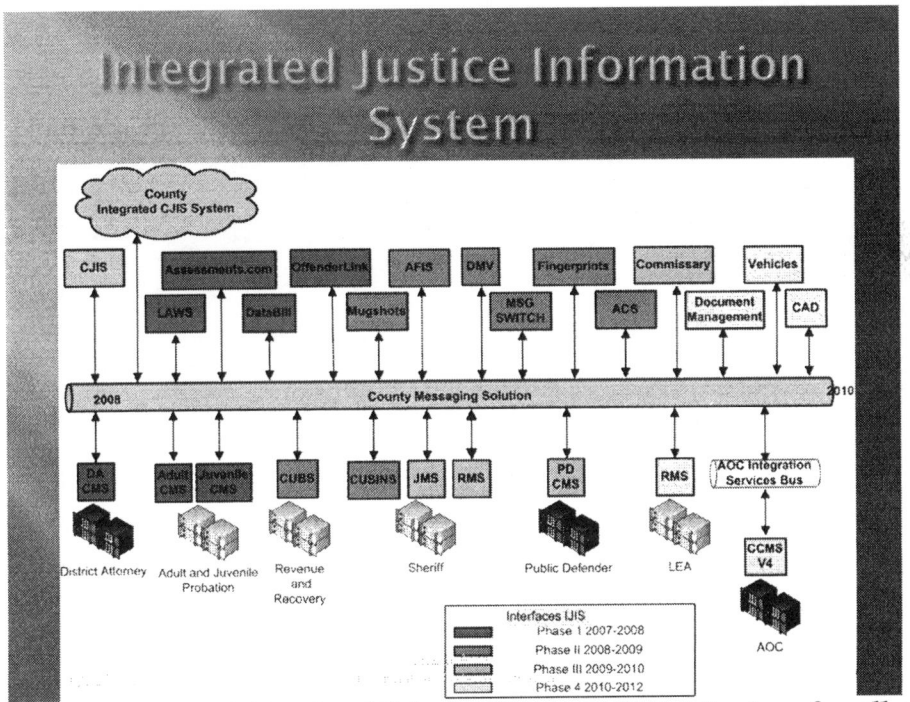

Figure 8.1: BPM and SOA Established a Successful Architecture for all our Future Modernization and Enables Agility

"With tools like Application Development Framework and BPM & SOA Suite, we have greatly reduced the complexities of our previous system, thus enabling development staff to focus on business logic and flow, and thereby saving time."– Jerry Becker, Chief Information Officer, County of San Joaquin Information Systems Division

- With the move to BPM and SOA we can now make interfaces in 4 weeks, when it took us 24 weeks on the mainframe. And these new interfaces are also much more productive for the end-users. After the LAWS went into production, we are continuing to build out capabilities with 4.5 FTEs augmented by SMEs when required.

- The San Joaquin County modernization initiative has been recognized by the California AOC as a Best Practice Implementation that not only provides continued value to San Joaquin County, but also a potential roadmap for success State-wide. This project has also been awarded CIO 100 and Government Computer News Awards among other awards.

9. TECHNOLOGY

Our modernization objective was to abstract our EA capabilities into the appropriate layers to allow us more agility and flexibility to meet our future requirements. And have this aligned with our Strategic Vision.

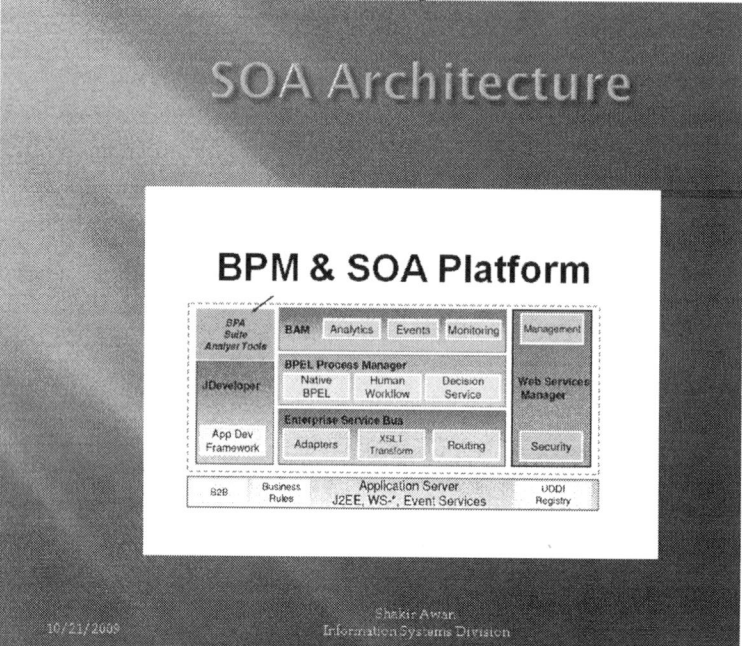

Figure 9.1: Specific BPM and SOA Components Used

Specific BPM and SOA components that we took advantage of spanned the gambit. As you can see in Figure 9.1 we combine BPM, Service Bus, BAM, Application Development and scaled it with deployment onto Application Server and implemented Security and Governance SOA and Security Management technologies as well. We truly took a holistic approach to BPM and SOA and truly believe that the sum of the parts are worth more than any single component.

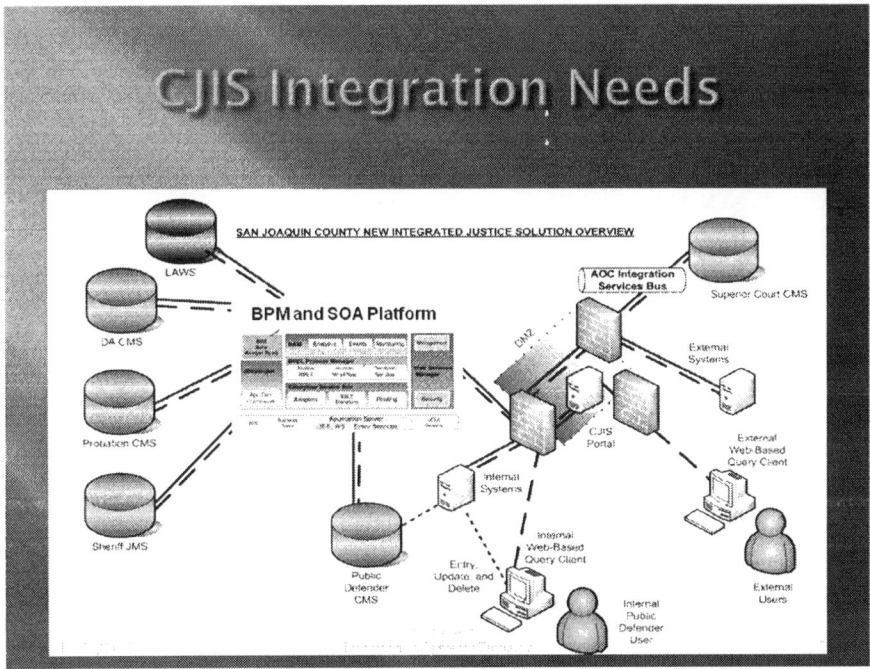

Figure 9.2: BPM and SOA as enabler of San Joaquin's new IJIS

This BPM and SOA Platform enabled us to modernize into a robust, scalable, secure, and agile Enterprise Architecture (see Figure 9.2 above).

10. THE TECHNOLOGY AND SERVICE PROVIDERS

Products Used:

- Oracle BPM / BPEL / BAM
- Oracle Application Development Framework
- Oracle SOA Suite
- Oracle Application Server
- Oracle Database
- Oracle RAC
- Oracle JDeveloper
- Oracle Internet Directory
- AutoMon Caseload Explorer
- www.oracle.com and www.automon.com

Audi Japan KK, Japan

Gold Award: Nominated by Bizagi, UK

1. EXECUTIVE SUMMARY / ABSTRACT

At a certain point of business maturity, companies find it necessary to increase productivity and efficiency in order to stay ahead of industry standards. Audi Japan KK, importer of Audi vehicles and subsidiary of Audi AG, discovered that to reach operational efficiency it was necessary to gain more control and visibility over its core management and administrative processes. To fulfill this objective, the financial department decided to develop a BPM initiative within the organization that would revolutionize the operations of Audi Japan KK.

A year ago, Audi Japan KK decided to begin the automation of several of their core back-end administrative processes within the financial department; processes that were found to be too manual and paper-based, which made them inefficient and difficult to manage.

Audi Japan KK has a SAP system put in place to manage their financial operations and Bizagi was selected as the complementary BPM solution for process automation. They were also clear about getting a solution that was easy-to use, painless to implement and would automate everyday processes. The objective was to increase transparency and quality, and reducing reliance on paper-based trails and processes. This solution also needed to be replicable in other company departments and Audi subsidiaries around the world.

2. OVERVIEW

The BPM initiative at Audi Japan KK was conceived in the financial department, where processes were paper-based, executed manually and inefficiently managed. Processes included delicate and high level Requests for Approvals for a certain activity or spending purpose. Processes like this one would need to be approved by the President of the company whose availability is limited, and certainly, manual processes are not the best option to act quickly and flexibly.

The Request for Approval (RFA) process was the first one to be automated at Audi Japan KK. The process covers the requests of almost 20 departments and divisions within the organization which are frequently requesting funds for different purposes and initiatives. A single request could often need more than 5 approvals from other supporting divisions and even from the sales department. Depending on the amount requested, the process needs different levels of approval. For smaller quantities it goes through the involved departments and divisions and finalizes with the approval of the Financial Controller. For larger quantities the request needs to be additionally approved by the Financial Director and the President of the company.

There is a short version of the Request for Approval process (Management RFA) which has also been automated, this is similar to the previous process but between top management and controller only (no departments involved).

Between these two processes the system is used by almost 100 users, however this number will certainly increase as the company is now launching to production 6 more processes this month: Overseas Trip approval, Domestic Trip approval, Personnel change approval, Purchase Order creation, Request for Payment (equivalent to accounts payable) and Budget Control Administration.

Tangible results and benefits were noticed immediately after the automated RFA processes were set to production. Implementation was very quick and Audi Japan KK was impressed by the ease-of-use of the selected BPM tool. They were able to experience significant results such as increased transparency and quality of the RFA process, reduction in process cycle times, increased operational efficiency, better workload distribution and improved budget control.

One of the major challenges was to really understand what BPM was all about, and to start moving the BPM initiative from the financial department towards senior management in order to be adopted as a new organizational culture and innovative best practice across the organization.

3. BUSINESS CONTEXT

For Audi Japan KK the whole idea of automating processes was an innovation. Audi Japan KK started with the evaluation of BPM tools and found Bizagi BPM Suite to be an appropriate option for its ease-of-use, flexibility and self-training options. Finding out that with Bizagi it was very easy to model and diagram processes and then easily move them to execution, was a motivation for initiating the change program.

On the other hand, believing and seeing that fast results could actually be achieved was also a key motivator to start acting and showing others the benefits and results obtained in a very short period of time. Audi Japan KK was impressed by the capabilities, features and flexibility of the software. It was definitely a good practice to start with a quick win process while learning more about BPM and Bizagi. Starting small but with a good example of how to achieve faster results was an efficient way to get the interest of potential stakeholders within the organization and to trigger more activities around the BPM initiative.

Audi Japan KK also wanted to ensure that they could have a roadmap to further their support for business processes across departments and the business itself.

4. THE KEY INNOVATIONS

4.2 Business

The automated processes are all internal processes engaging many other departments and divisions within the organization. For anyone involved in a RFA process, whether a requester or an approver, the workflow of the process is now clearer, people are much more prepared in advance with the necessary documentation before the process even starts and approvals can easily be done through a web page. This is an important achievement in terms of efficiency and process quality and transparency.

Depending on the information entered by the requester through a simple web interface the process itself decides the path that needs to be followed and the level of approval needed. Managers and executives at Audi Japan KK are constantly on business travel, so it was important to create a way in which they could do approvals via an internet application, avoiding the delays and miscommunication that could arise from approvals over the phone or email. Approvals are done on time now as approvers receive a notification from the sys-tem and they are able take an action anywhere, anytime, all they need is an internet connection. For the financial department, this traduces to increased control and visibility over the process, and optimized management of tasks and activities related to budget control, archiving and filing.

Audi Japan KK believes that this BPM initiative has changed their fundamental business structure and put them in a position where it will not limit their growth and will certainly revolutionize the operations of Audi Japan KK. It is important for companies to understand the value that business process management can bring in terms of clarity of processes, efficiency and reducing the volume of paperwork.

4.3 Process

The RFA process was a manual and paper-based process which relied on approvals made over the phone or email. Approvals were not easily done due to approvers business traveling and it was more of a "people chasing the people" process which leads to lack of quality and inefficiency. Approvals over the phone or email can be easily back dated affecting people's jobs and activity performance. Inefficiencies were experienced within the financial department where it was not possible to manage budget and transactions with the sufficient level of control and visibility.

After the RFA automation the scenario changed for all stakeholders, including requesters, approvers and employees from the financial department. New requests are done in a much easier manner and through a web portal, the system then activates the approval processes and sub processes. The system can decide by itself whether to involve or not certain approvers or pre-approval sub processes depending on the type and amount of the request. Notifications are sent to sales people and managers for required approvals and notifications are sent to requesters when their request is denied. Requests are then flagged and processed immediately; allowing requests to be handled on time as they arise.

The system now also allows maintaining additional information like annotations and attached documentation that can be used by requesters to support their request or by approvers to make a decision on the approval. When requests are approved, a PDF is generated with the approval in local language (Japanese) for easier classification and archiving. This complements the activities performed by their ERP (SAP) system.

The process architecture was defined by the financial department at Audi Japan KK, acting as the principal stakeholder of the processes to be automated, and according to their requirements for process compliance. It involved the creation of forms and documents, assigning roles, creating rules and mapping individual processes, all done with ease and speed. Process models were reviewed by Bizagi consultants for better quality models and advice on best practices for potential reutilization of the system in other Audi departments and subsidiaries worldwide.

The automated RFA process at Audi Japan KK could be easily reproduced or adapted as needed by other organizations, even in other industries. Audi Japan KK has recently included to the system another 6 processes (Overseas Trip approval, Domestic Trip approval, Personnel change approval, Purchase Order creation, Request for Payment (equivalent to accounts payable) and Budget Control Administration) and will potentially include processes with dealers and retail in the near future reaching approximately 400 users nation-wide.

4.4 Organization

At an organizational level, the key innovation was to actually start speaking the BPM language. The financial department is now a model to follow by other departments within Audi Japan KK. All levels of the organization are now aware of what they have done and can testify on the benefits and positive impact that process automation and BPM brings for the business and the employees.

Employees at the financial department are now more efficient and productive, they need to handle less paperwork, approvals are archived in a more organized manner and they have more control and visibility over their operation, which also leads to increased compliance with company and auditory policies. The RFA process is more transparent and people are also making a lot more effort to follow and meet the process standards.

Due to the improved budget management and control (which is now done almost in real time), the financial department was able to save time on administrative tasks and reallocate headcounts into more valuable jobs and distribute workload more efficiently.

As with any other new initiative that involves organizational change, it has taken a little time for people to adopt the new way of working, however, as the implementation and set to production of the first processes was done very quickly and results were observed immediately, it was much easier to engage other actors and stakeholders. Audi Japan KK knows that growth is inevitable, and with it, new ways to increase efficiency and to stay ahead of the business need to be implemented.

5. HURDLES OVERCOME

There weren´t too many hurdles to overcome in this project. As mentioned before, the major challenge was to begin a BPM initiative from cero, without any profound knowledge about process automation and BPM within the organization. However, this challenge was overcome with the selection of a BPM tool that was easy to use, very user friendly, with the option of self-training courses, guides, resources and documentation which made the whole BPM experience very satisfactory.

Implementation of the first processes was really quick and flexible and positive results were observed almost immediately. This was used as a strategy to expand the project, including more processes and increasing organizational adoption.

6. BENEFITS

The main focus of the automation of the RFA process was achieving transparency and quality. For this reason, other associated benefits have been obtained too, but quantitative metrics are not available at this moment.

Most of the benefits observed are related to faster decision making, improved process control and visibility, better budget control and efficiency within the financial department at Audi Japan KK.

6.1 Cost Savings

For certain, there have been cost savings as a result of the automation of the RFA process. These are related to the reduction of paper-work and administrative tasks, the reallocation of headcounts into more valued jobs and the better distribution of resources and time.

6.2 Time Reductions

The RFA process experienced a significant reduction in average cycle time during the first months in production. After Japan´s earthquake in March it has been really hard to measure real cycle times as the business was affected by external and out of control factors. However, as business in the country has become more stabilized, these new average cycle times will for certain be achieved again.

Also with the implementation of the Management RFA process (the short version of the RFA process) unnecessary approvals and waiting times have been avoided for certain requests, resulting in reduced cycle times for high level requests.

6.3 Increased Revenues

Audi Japan KK has probably observed indirect increases in revenue due to the reduction of manual activities, improved efficiency and the reallocation of work and resources in the financial department. However, it is not really measurable, due to the type and focus of the project.

6.4 Productivity Improvements

Productivity and efficiency rates have increased among employees in the financial department. The reduction of paperwork, manual-based processes and unnecessary delays for approval requests have contributed to a much better performance and control of their operation. They have also been able to save time in administrative tasks such as archiving and filing which lead to optimized distribution of workload and responsibilities.

Documentation is better classified and organized, making it easier to find and track past records and approvals when required by auditors or senior management.

7. BEST PRACTICES, LEARNING POINTS AND PITFALLS

7.1 Best Practices and Learning Points

✓ It was definitely a good practice to start with a quick win process which sets the base for faster results and easier replication

✓ Really important to evaluate BPM solutions and select the one which makes you feel more confident due to ease of use, flexibility and transparent implementation.

✓ Change the organizational structure and culture smoothly, without crashing with existing ways of doing things and showing the real benefits and positive impact of the change.

7.2 Pitfalls

✗ It is recommended to get a third opinion on the work done. After Audi Japan KK got Bizagi to review their process models, some best practices and tips for process modeling were given which could have saved time in the modeling phase.

8. COMPETITIVE ADVANTAGES

The key for competitive advantage is to act fast. With Bizagi, Audi Japan KK was able to do this. As soon as the necessity to improve transparency, quality and efficiency of their processes was detected, the financial department was able to learn about process modeling and BPM very quickly, automating their first processes and obtaining positive and demonstrable results in a short period of time.

The BPM project changed Audi Japan KK fundamental business structure and put them in a position where they are ready and prepared to support any other business process with agility, allowing short and long term growth and sustainable competitive advantage.

9. TECHNOLOGY

Audi Japan KK selected Bizagi BPM solution to model and automate their business processes.

The first step was to download the free Bizagi Process Modeler from Bizagi´s website to start diagramming and modeling the RFA process. Bizagi Process Modeler is a drag and drop application which is very easy to use and it can also be used to generate process documentation. Audi Japan KK then used Bizagi BPM Suite to automate their processes, this means, to turn their process models into executable applications. With Bizagi it is very easy to move from process modeling to execution, without the need for technical knowledge.

Bizagi BPM was able to offer a complete solution which included activities and functionalities such as design and implementation of the process workflow and automation of processes. As Bizagi is an integrated BPM Suite, Audi Japan KK was able to manage the complete process life cycle without any other additional or external tools. Bizagi is flexible and capable of integrating and automating several processes at the same time, creating a robust system that can be easily adapted to business growth as more and more processes are automated.

Bizagi is also a good complement to other systems, such as SAP ERP in this case, and in a near future they can be seamlessly integrated when the system grows.

From a technological point of view, the project was launched without any critical issues, making it possible to achieve production in a few weeks. The technological platform consists of a very basic installation with a single server and SQL database.

10. THE TECHNOLOGY AND SERVICE PROVIDERS

Audi Japan KK selected Bizagi BPM (http://www.bizagi.com) for the implementation of their first BPM initiative. Bizagi is a leading BPM solution capable of empowering businesses of all types and industries around the world, providing them with unprecedented adaptability to changing business and market conditions through optimal business process automation (execution) and continuous improvement. Bizagi is a business productivity tool for faster process automation. Bizagi´s built-in functionalities, ease of use and flexibility makes it the ideal BPM solution to obtain faster results. In Bizagi, most of the common and reoccurring requirements in process automation have been pre-built. These refer to:

- Control and visibility
- Alarms and notifications
- Performance analysis and reporting
- Auditing and traceability
- Workload routing and balancing
- Quality
- Mobility
- Robustness
- Integration
- Corporate features (multi-tenancy, BPMN process engine, multiple language support, time-zones, long lasting process transactions, enterprise data model, among others)

Bizagi is available in multiple editions to support the varying needs of organizations. The corporate editions are appropriate for mission critical and core business processes, satisfying the most demanding needs in larger organizations. Corporate editions (Enterprise .NET and Enterprise JEE) are similar in functionality, the only difference is the platform where they execute.

Viteos Capital Market Services Ltd., India

Silver Award: Nominated by EMC, United States

1. EXECUTIVE SUMMARY / ABSTRACT

Viteos Capital Market Services Ltd. (Viteos) is a hedge fund administrator and operations service provider for financial services companies. As a small, but quickly growing company, Viteos began to outgrow its systems and sought a solution that could automate manual processes, reduce paperwork, help the company meet compliance standards, scale up or down to meet changing demands, and remain cost-effective.

The company arrived at a solution that combined an element of its existing system—Microsoft SharePoint—with a more robust business process management (BPM) and document-management solution—EMC Documentum xCelerated Composition Platform (xCP)—as well as virtualization with VMware. This combination enabled the company to meet its increasing document processing needs while maintaining familiarity for its users.

2. OVERVIEW

Viteos Capital Market Services Ltd. (Viteos) is a hedge fund administrator and back-office service provider offering tailored solutions to hedge funds and institutional investors around the world. Headquartered in the United States, with offices in the United Kingdom, the Cayman Islands, and India, its global delivery model combines cutting-edge technology with 24×7 support from highly qualified professional staff across the globe.

As a small firm within its industry, Viteos encountered challenges faced by the industry as a whole as well as those that reflected the company's need to compete with larger firms. One industry-wide challenge was the necessity of **automating manual processes** and **reducing paperwork** to save time, increase efficiency, and decrease errors. K. B. Venkataramanan, senior vice president and chief information officer at Viteos, describes the team's philosophy behind automation: "Any process that is repeatable is automatable." The team wanted to build the new processes to be as "straight-through" as possible, with minimal human interruption. However, they recognized that they must also bring human interaction into play when subjective decision-making, understanding, or judgment was needed.

Another industry-wide challenge was to more **consistently meet compliance, regulatory, and legal requirements** in each country in which the company operates. Finally, **achieving secure, 24×7 uptime** was critical, because, as a global service provider, the company deals with markets and customers in every time zone.

One challenge related to being a smaller firm was **the need to pay as little as possible for infrastructure** to help keep profit margins high. The other challenge was to **ensure scalability**; the company foresaw growth and required a platform that could grow with it.

The new solution consists of Microsoft SharePoint (already in use by Viteos) on the front end and EMC Documentum xCelerated Composition Platform (xCP) on the back end. This solution helped Viteos meet all of the challenges mentioned earlier.

The new system retained SharePoint as a user interface (UI), making the transition largely transparent to end-users. Documentum xCP provided additional benefits, including process simplification, a decreased need for additional IT specialists when work increases, increased capacity, a reduction in audit time, a reduction in time to onboard clients, and productivity improvements.

3. BUSINESS CONTEXT

To drive success, Viteos needed to make improvements in several areas of its operation.

Once trading commences, Viteos electronically captures all trade information, determines the profit and loss (P&L) for each trading day, and calculates the P&L of the fund, which determines investor returns. The faster and more reliably these processes can be run, the more clients the company can service.

At least six pieces of paperwork are associated with each client transaction, including a background check, a money-laundering check, citizenship verification, and bank communications and processes. When multiplied by many transactions and clients, there are numerous opportunities for error when these documents are handled manually. Fewer errors result in more efficient processes, happier clients, and greater compliance with regulatory requirements.

Another area needing improvement was Viteos' profit margin. High returns for the company's high–net worth clients are critical to the company's success, so every expenditure must be reduced as much as possible. The company wanted to reduce its investment in computer hardware, data center rentals, and the need for additional IT staff.

Viteos also needed to refine its process with regard to audits—an expected part of operations within the heavily regulated financial services industry. There were two ways to do this: (1) become more capable of retaining documents to meet compliance, regulatory, and legal requirements, and (2) have a fast way to provide documents to regulatory agencies when audits did occur. The company needed features to help it accomplish these two goals. In addition, Viteos needed to improve its uptime to better serve global clients in world markets on a 24×7 basis. Finally, as a company growing at 15 percent year over year, Viteos required a solution that can accommodate everything from a small team to thousands of users.

Viteos sought a solution that would improve all these elements of its operations.

4. THE KEY INNOVATIONS

4.1 Business

Viteos caters to a large number of clients spread across the world and across multiple time zones. These clients need to be able to access information about their assets at any time of day or night. The new solution included the development of a web portal that allows clients to securely access the information they need when they need it. The portal helps Viteos reach out to clients as well as the investors, brokers, and fund managers who interact with them.

4.2 Process

Previously, the company's processes were well documented in the form of standard operating procedure (SOP) documents. Each SOP defines a process and the controls associated with it. The goal was to determine which of these processes were automatable, using the guideline, "Any process that is repeatable is automatable."

The result is a fully paperless system. As an example, the company's trade-confirmation process was converted from paper to electronic format. When a trade is complete, a confirmation is generated that describes the trade. Historically, the confirmation was a paper-based system that used fax. Now, the process involves efax, instead. Fund managers can view "confirms" onscreen rather than on paper. When they need to communicate with clients, they can log in to a portal and check how many confirms are open as well as the value and volume of each.

The know-your-customer/anti-money-laundering (KYC/AML) cycle has also been automated. This cycle confirms for regulatory agencies that records related to investors are kept, including verification of investors' existence, credentials, and where investment funds originate.

Similar processes have been converted throughout each phase of the trade life cycle:

- Trade capture
- Pricing
- Corporate actions
- Content management system and over-the-counter processing
- Reconciliation and control
- Accounting
- Investor services

4.3 Organization

The major impact on employees is the way training is delivered upon hiring. Training time has been reduced considerably now that it is delivered via a categorized knowledge repository consisting of videos, product documentation, and process maps. Because of this change, hands-on training is no longer needed.

5. HURDLES OVERCOME

5.1 Business

The IT team took a unique approach to developing the end solution. They wanted to pair Documentum xCP as a back end with SharePoint (which they were already using) as a front end. They were unable to find system integrators who understood what they were trying to do, so the team of five learned the tools and built out the solution themselves. To serve their internal customers, the system needed to meet the following requirements:

- Processes needed to run
- Processes needed to be repeatable, with no tolerance for error
- The requirement for end-users to learn new technology needed to be reduced as much as possible
- Back-end technology needed to be transparent to end-users

Mr. Venkataramanan notes, "Once we understood the goals, implementation was simple."

5.2 Organization Adoption

Because end-users were already employing SharePoint, its continued use was critical to adoption of the new solution. With uninterrupted use of SharePoint, the company was able to realize pronounced benefits, with no training or implementation of new software required. As a result, the IT team attempted and achieved

100 percent adoption with virtually no learning curve; user adoption was instantaneous and straightforward.

6. BENEFITS

6.1 Cost Savings

Cost savings have been realized because of IT virtualization, compliance, and a reduced need to hire additional employees:

- Virtualization (the ability to run more applications on fewer servers) has reduced the need to purchase additional physical servers by 30 percent.
- Compliance has been increased to 100 percent, considerably reducing auditing and legal fees.
- The previous solution, consisting of SharePoint only, required a good deal of support and infrastructure to maintain. The new solution, which incorporates Documentum xCP, is designed for the enterprise environment and therefore requires less administration and maintenance. So, there has been no need to hire additional IT staff, even as the business has grown.

6. 2 Time Reductions

Time savings can be measured in full-time resources, audit time, and the time it takes to onboard a new client:

- Continuation with the previous system would have required hiring approximately 15 full-time employees; the new system avoided this costly increase.
- Previously, a first-time audit took 45 working days; Viteos is now able to perform the same function in fewer than seven days.
- Using the previous system, new clients were onboarded in about one quarter (three months). Now, they go through the same process in about one month.

6.3 Increased Revenues

As a result of the new system, Viteos' capacity has increased by 35 percent. As a result of this increased efficiency, the company is able to grow its business by 15 percent year over year.

6.4 Productivity Improvements

Mr. Venkataramanan describes productivity improvements in terms of the number of defects and the speed with which information is turned around to clients: "I am happy to state that defects have come down to a negligible number, and we are now able to turn information around in under 45 minutes." Productivity has been seen in these areas, as well:

- Ease of use
- Effective management of volumes of data and their quick retrievals
- Ability to be flexible as the market changes its processes
- Organizational consistency
- Simplified processes

6.5 Greater Compliance

Every process that Viteos performs must have a maker and checker. By automating the process, the workflow auto-routes the data to the checker for verification and captures the date/time stamp of when the data was verified before delivery to the client.

In addition, auditors are given access to the system to check the transaction flow. Because all the documents generated are available, time spent by the process heads has been reduced to a minimum.

7. BEST PRACTICES, LEARNING POINTS, AND PITFALLS

7.1 Best Practices and Learning Points

✓ *It is important to be aware of all customer touch points—that is, always think about the customer. Business process can often seem like a back-end thing that is automated, and people are not involved. But, if you don't think about customer touch points, your efforts will not be successful.*

✓ *The company's success in this transition was driven by user requests rather than "the IT team's imagination." Every process was defined from a business perspective in terms of the corresponding benefit.*

✓ *It is important to have goals for what you are trying to achieve rather than simply adopting the latest trends.*

✓ *For best results, view the situation as an enterprise-wide initiative rather than a single problem initiative. When evaluating a solution, ask how it will benefit the enterprise.*

✓ *Anything that can be done to automate information makes operations run faster and better. E-forms are useful for this process.*

7.2 Pitfalls

✗ *Security must be considered from the beginning, as it is much more difficult to build in after the fact.*

✗ *It is critical to ensure a certain level of "process maturity." That is, any processes being considered for automation should already be set. If you try to convert processes that will continue to change or evolve, you will not get the kinds of benefits you expect.*

8. COMPETITIVE ADVANTAGES

Although many companies dabble in business process management (BPM) or automate one part of their business, other parts may be technologically behind. Viteos has standardized on a platform with a broad feature set that lets the company address applications and processes in every area of business. Efficiencies in each area contribute to those in other areas, creating a fully optimized system.

Having created a thorough, reliable system, the company can focus on fund trading and wealth management rather than its IT services. By eliminating paper-based processes, Viteos has greatly improved the speed and accuracy of interactions with consumers, governments, and businesses, thereby creating a significant competitive advantage.

This ability to operate at full effectiveness also brings down the costs associated with broken or antiquated systems, keeping margins at competitive levels. If not for these cost savings, the company could not sustain its success.

9. TECHNOLOGY

Viteos' previous system ran on an outsourced model. Applications were hosted outside the organization by various service providers. These services were scattered, and there were too many applications to manage. The goals were (1) to consolidate all services under one roof and (2) create the ability to expand and contract to meet seasonal demands. The team sought a system flexible enough to meet these goals and inexpensive enough to keep costs down.

The new system incorporates Documentum xCP as the back-end document repository and SharePoint as the front-end UI. Viteos was already using SharePoint, but SharePoint lacked the ability to grow with the company and meet its demands. So, the team sought out a solution that would pair well with SharePoint and meet its challenges—now and into the future. The great benefit of this pairing is that users did not have to learn a new interface, saving time and money that would have been spent on training.

After researching other solutions, the team settled on Documentum xCP. The solution was not the least expensive and required learning Java, but Viteos has been happy with the results. In particular, the company values the agile nature of the software, which can change along with procedures and laws. IT does not have to shut the entire system down to upgrade. And the system can support users running different versions.

The new system also incorporates VMware for virtualization. With this solution, the number of physical servers needed has been reduced considerably. The new solution allows the company to maintain servers at two separate locations (Mumbai and Bangalore) that are replicated and seamlessly communicate with each other. So, no matter where in the world clients are, data are always ready for delivery to them.

10. THE TECHNOLOGY AND SERVICE PROVIDERS

EMC Corporation is a global leader in enabling businesses and service providers to transform their operations and deliver IT as a service. Fundamental to this transformation is cloud computing. Through innovative products and services, EMC accelerates the journey to cloud computing, helping IT departments to store, manage, protect and analyze their most valuable asset—information—in a more agile, trusted and cost-efficient way.

EMC products and services leveraged in this solution include:
- EMC Documentum xCP (http://www.emc.com/xcp)
- EMC Documentum Consulting

Carbones de Cerrejón, Colombia.

Finalist: Nominated by Bizagi, United Kingdom

1. EXECUTIVE SUMMARY / ABSTRACT

Cerrejon is the largest open-pit coal mine in the world, with 30 years in the market, and an integrated operation which involves a thermal coalmine, a railroad of 150 kilometers and a seaport able to receive ships of up to 180 thousand tons of capacity. Cerrejon was looking to improve the coordination and orchestration between several areas – the commercialization offices (Dublin and Atlanta), Foreign Trade and Logistics, Financial Accounting, Accounts Payable and Treasury (Colombia) – from the moment a client placed an order until the coal was received.

For this, Cerrejon required a collaborative solution that besides bringing agility to the business, offered flexibility and would allow satisfying the requirements of local regulations. Cerrejon selected Bizagi BPM Suite to automate the coal sales process, which integrated to its ERP, would enable the management of all the transactions derived from the commercialization of the coal, consolidating a robust platform for the conciliation of payments and collections.

2. OVERVIEW

Cerrejon is the largest open-pit coal mine in the world with an income of US$ 2,300 million, 10 thousand employees, and an annual production of 32 million tons exported through its own port. With a huge tradition and expertise in the market, Cerrejon found it imperative to improve the coordination and orchestration between all the areas involved in the coal sales process. Cerrejon relies on two commercialization offices located in Dublin (Ireland) and Atlanta (United States) for their coal sale process. Cerrejon´s integrated operation also involves a thermal coalmine, a railroad of 150 kilometers and a seaport able to receive ships of up to 180 thousand tons of capacity. Whenever a customer places a purchase order, several activities and tasks are activated around the different departments and divisions involved, such as the commercialization offices (Dublin and Atlanta), Foreign Trade and Logistics, Financial Accounting, Accounts Payable and Treasury (Colombia).

Interaction between the areas involved in the coal sales process were manual and took too long to be executed; therefore, the necessity to make the business more agile and gather more control of the business operation was evident. Cerrejon decided to undergo a BPM project to automate the complete coal sales process. This was the first project at Cerrejon based on the BPM principle and aligned with the process management corporate strategy implemented in the company.

Cerrejon has an ERP system in place used to manage all the transactions derived from the commercialization of the coal. Cerrejon needed to select a flexible and collaborative BPM tool capable of transparently integrate to this ERP in order to build a solid and robust platform to support orders, payments and conciliation processes. After an extensive evaluation of tools and an open bidding process, Bizagi was selected as the BPM solution for process automation. Bizagi was chosen for its vast experience in the implementation of BPM projects, the support levels offered and its international presence. Cerrejon also needed to guarantee that the chosen BPM tool would allow satisfying the requirements of local regulations in an efficient manner.

After the implementation of the BPM project, Cerrejon was able to increase business process agility, improve integration and visibility, reduce the invoicing cycle time and consolidate information and processes. As customer orders are now processed faster, time to market has also improved satisfying both internal and external customers.

The major challenge faced was dealing with the complexity of the coal sales process, due to the geographical location of the different stakeholders and the sensibility of the information handled. In a technical perspective the BPM system had to integrate the information from diverse sources, such as the ERP Ellipse, Minetrak (a system used in Puerto Bolívar, Colombia, to control the information of loading and boarding), and Aramis (an invoicing control system used in the commercialization offices).

3. BUSINESS CONTEXT

The coal sales process at Cerrejon is complex due to the geographical location of the different stakeholders and the sensibility of the information that it handles. Tasks and activities to cover the coal sales process were done manually and there wasn´t a central repository for documents and information. This affected the integration between the involved departments and divisions making it harder to gain control and visibility over their operations. This also had an impact on process and invoicing cycle times.

Cerrejon found that there was a huge opportunity to improve their business agility by automating the coal sales process with a BPM tool that would also allow seamlessly integration to their existing ERP system and other legacy applications. The key motivation for Cerrejon is their mission itself: "Make the maximum possible, not the minimum required". Driven by this statement, Cerrejon decided to implement a business process management system to increase the agility, control and visibility of the coal sales process, as well as to integrate the different areas involved to reach a proper consolidation of information and processes.

4. THE KEY INNOVATIONS

4.2 Business

This was the first project at Cerrejon based on the BPM principle and aligned with the process management corporate strategy implemented in the company. This new way of doing things certainly changed the business. Purchase orders are now placed, registered, processed and delivered much quicker than before, increasing the time to market while having more internal and external customers satisfied.

Tracking and visibility over the process has also allowed avoiding bottlenecks, complying with delivery times and satisfying local and industry regulations. This has made the business more agile while increasing efficiency and productivity.

With the flexibility and robustness of the BPM system that was implemented, Cerrejon is now sure that they count with a solid business structure to overcome future growth and potential changes in market and business conditions.

4.3 Process

As mentioned before, the coal sales process is complex as it involves several departments located in different places around the world, and tasks and activities which need to be done in sequence or in parallel by people interacting with systems and applications. Tasks and activities were manual, giving space to an important opportunity to improve and increase efficiency.

The BPM solution implemented by Cerrejon includes all the sub-processes and the corresponding documentation of all the areas involved, from the commercial to the operative area. It is a system in its maximum expression, where the people, the technology and other aspects are integrated, such as: legislation, companies, legal vehicles, currencies, among others. The BPM coordinates and orchestrates all these players and concepts from when the client orders the coal until it is received.

The new BPM system also integrated information from diverse legacy applications and systems, such as the ERP Ellipse, Minetrak (a system used in Puerto Bolívar, Colombia, to control the information of loading and boarding), and Aramis (an invoicing control system used in the commercialization offices).

All the financial and process reports can be accessed via a very simple interface. Also, the system sends alerts to inform the actors in the process which of the activities they own are close to expire. This brings additional support to the user in order to satisfy the time control that the law dictates for the presentation of documents, reducing the risk of non compliance of the current norms.

After the implementation of the BPM system, Cerrejon is able to centralize and consolidate information to be visible and available for all process stakeholders. It is also possible to integrate the work done by several offices such as the commercialization offices at Dublin and Atlanta, the Foreign Trade and Logistics office in Colombia and the Financial Accounting, Accounts Payable and Treasury departments.

Bizagi delivered the consulting services to help Cerrejon and all the process stakeholders to build the process architecture according to roles and responsibilities. This was done through a planning and design phase where the process was initially mapped and defined while detecting opportunities for process improvement. Cerrejon used Bizagi Process Modeler to apply the general process design principles.

Although the implemented BPM system was developed specifically for Cerrejon´s complex coal sales process, it can certainly be used as a model for processes including several offices in different locations which need to interact and work together for a single purpose: a sale, an approval, etc.

4.4 Organization

For the organization it was a real innovation to start thinking about BPM and to value the benefits and positive impact that it could bring to the business. The principal stakeholders made all the organization believe in the project and were able to gain the necessary compromise from the people and senior management for the successful development and completion of the implementation.

Bizagi delivered training and support services for the implementation of Bizagi BPM Suite at Cerrejon. With the On Target methodology for project management, and with the support of the different areas involved, the work was done in Bogotá, Puerto Bolívar, Dublin and Atlanta.

The BPM system caused a positive impact on employees. Most manual activities were eliminated and replaced by automatic tasks which can be managed, processed and completed using the BPM system. This made the business more agile and efficient and employees more productive.

The solution was implemented in only 6 months, reaching the production stage with all areas integrated, achieving visibility of the whole process, and with a centralized parameterization of the business conditions through the Business Rules Engine (BRE). This is the system layer which contains the business rules and conditions that govern the process execution. The rapid and successful implementation also increased the motivation of everyone at the organization, especially those involved in the coal sales process.

5. HURDLES OVERCOME

The biggest challenge was to deal with the complexity of the coal sales process due to the geographical location of the actors and the sensitivity of the information it handles. However, with a careful and detailed process mapping, design and planning phase, with the help of Bizagi´s consultants, it was possible to overcome this challenge.

The second challenge was to integrate Bizagi BPM with the existing ERP and legacy applications. The flexibility and ease of use of Bizagi BPM Suite helped to overcome this challenge together with the consulting, training and support services offered by Bizagi.

6. BENEFITS

6.1 Cost Savings

More than cost savings, the project justification was based on reducing the risk of penalties due to errors in the registration and reporting of transactions to the government entities, to delays in such reporting, and to errors in the calculation of taxes and loyalties.

6.2 Time Reductions

Cerrejon was able to significantly reduce the cycle time of the coal sales process, making it possible to handle purchase order registration, processing and invoicing much faster than before.

As a result, Cerrejon also gained a reduction in time to market, being able to satisfy customer requirements regarding delivery times and to comply with local and industry regulations.

6.3 Increased Revenues

Not applicable for this project.

6.4 Productivity Improvements

With the consolidation of information and processes the coal sales process is managed in a more efficient manner, reaching a better business productivity and agile performance. The reduction of manual activities also increases employee productivity. Improved control and visibility makes tracking easier and enhances process traceability.

7. BEST PRACTICES, LEARNING POINTS AND PITFALLS

7.1 Best Practices and Learning Points

✓ *Spend enough time in the planning, definition and design phase to minimize risks and errors in the implementation.*

✓ *Involve consulting, training and support services in the project to guarantee a higher level of success.*

✓ *Involve the correct and necessary stakeholders and actors to increase compromise and organizational adoption.*

7.2 Pitfalls

Based on Cerrejon's experience in this and other similar projects developed, these are common pitfalls in the use of the BPM system technology:

✗ *Not planning and allocating enough resources for the testing of the solution built.*

✗ *Handling process exceptions in the BPM system.*

✗ *Developing the BPM system based on the as-is process without analyzing non-technology related improvement opportunities first (using tools such as LEAN, Theory of Constrains, etc).*

✗ *Developing the BPM System with a 'build-to-last' concept instead of a 'build-to-change' concept.*

✗ *Not using the BPM system as a continuous process improvement tool.*

8. COMPETITIVE ADVANTAGES

Thanks to the implementation of Bizagi BPM, Cerrejon increased the integration between the people and the sub-processes which are part of the coal sales operation. In this way, the mine completes the sales cycle, from the mine to the client, with the security that the required information in each step is correct and opportune, and satisfies the current regulations. At the moment, the coal sales registration and control process managed through the BPM platform, tracks and controls the sale of 32 million tons of coal a year. Due to this volume of annual sales, the benefit of having a clean process and without errors constitutes a competitive advantage for Cerrejon.

Cerrejon is now able to make sure it has all the necessary certificates in each ship, according to the laws of the receiving countries and relating to specifications such as amount of coal, calorific power, humidity, ash, etc. The documentary handling of the characteristics of the coal is supported by the BPM system, grouping in this platform all the relevant documents for the process.

9. TECHNOLOGY

After an extensive evaluation of tools and an open bidding process, Cerrejon selected Bizagi for the automation of the coal sales process. Bizagi BPM Suite was chosen for its vast experience in the implementation of BPM projects, the support levels offered and its international presence. Bizagi is a complete BPM Suite which offers an enterprise-class platform for complex, mission critical and high availability business processes in any type of organization.

With Bizagi BPM Suite it is possible to model/diagram processes and then convert them into running applications (execution). Bizagi Process Modeler is an easy to use drag and drop application for process modeling and documentation. After processes are modeled, it is very easy to move to process execution, where Bizagi creates a web application used by end users to interact with the system.

The solution was implemented in only 6 months, confirming Bizagi´s compromise of achieving faster results.

10. THE TECHNOLOGY AND SERVICE PROVIDERS

Cerrejon selected Bizagi BPM (http://www.bizagi.com) for the implementation of their first BPM initiative. Bizagi is a leading BPM solution capable of empowering businesses of all types and industries around the world, providing them with unprecedented adaptability to changing business and market conditions through optimal business process automation (execution) and continuous improvement.

Bizagi is a business productivity tool for faster process automation. Bizagi´s built-in functionalities, ease of use and flexibility makes it the ideal BPM solution to obtain faster results. In Bizagi, most of the common and reoccurring requirements in process automation have been pre-built. These refer to:

- Control and visibility
- Alarms and notifications
- Performance analysis and reporting
- Auditing and traceability
- Workload routing and balancing
- Quality
- Mobility
- Robustness
- Integration
- Corporate features (multi-tenancy, BPMN process engine, multiple language support, time-zones, long lasting process transactions, enterprise data model, among others)

Bizagi is available in multiple editions to support the varying needs of organizations. The corporate editions are appropriate for mission critical and core business processes, satisfying the most demanding needs in larger organizations. Corporate editions (Enterprise .NET and Enterprise JEE) are similar in functionality, the only difference is the platform where they execute.

CONAGUA: Comisión Nacional del Agua, Mexico

Gold Award: Nominated by PECTRA Technology, USA

1. EXECUTIVE SUMMARY / ABSTRACT

As a result of regulations and initiatives of the Government of Mexico in 2004, the *Subdirección General de Infraestructura Hidroagrícola*[1] of CONAGUA –*Comisión Nacional del Agua*[2] decided to start a BPM project in order to standardize, organize and control the management processes of budgetary resources for public works and procurement services (more than one thousand million dollars each year), through an online system of information available for public consultation by citizens.

With over seven years of implementing BPM, the CONAGUA *Subdirección General de Infraestructura Hidroagrícola* reports multiple benefits: greater adoption of BPM (from 1 to 18 processes in place, with 700% growth in number of users and the incorporation 23 new states, 13 regions and 15 cities to the project), a recovery of the total investment in the first 18 months and savings in materials / supplies of USD340,000 a year and current expenditure of USD238,000, greater employee satisfaction (50 and 76%) due to a 67% reduction in administrative and manual activities -mostly reporting; improved citizen perception and credibility due to availability of information about the public works for hydro-agricultural infrastructure development; numerous awards received: Honorable Mention in the 2005 Annual Award of Transparency, Innova acknowledgement for considering that the system has a favorable impact on the six good governance strategies; among others. It is important to mention that although the processes were targeted to public works, now they also serve to manage both the substantive associated products and services or investment, and current expenditure.

2. OVERVIEW

Prior to the BPM implementation, there was no concept of process for technical and administrative activities. In fact, the activities connected to the Administration and Development of Hydro-agricultural Infrastructure were performed manually and through written documents, which resulted in indirect capture, validation, and delivery of information costs. It was impossible to monitor and evaluate investments in public works and services.

Since 2004, the CONAGUA *Subdirección General de Infraestructura Hidroagrícola* optimized the macro process called "Administration

---

[1] The *Subdirección General de Infraestructura Hidroagrícola* (General Sub-directorate of Hydro Agricultural Infrastructure) is an infrastructure agency of CONAGUA whose mission is to 'Manage and develop hydro-agricultural, with the involvement of the community, to attain sustainable water use. "

[2] The *Comisión Nacional del Agua* ((National Water Commission) is an autonomous division of the *Secretaría del Medio Ambiente y Recursos Naturales* -Department of Environment and Natural Re-sources of Mexico. Its mission is to manage and preserve national waters, with the involvement of the community to attain sustainable use of resources.

and Development Hydro-agricultural Infrastructure", automating programming, budgeting, procurement, monitoring the implementation, and closing of the investment projects for development of federal hydro-agricultural infrastructure (drainage, roads, levee protection, water control structures such as culverts and fords, and crossing structures such as bridges, etc.) being carried out by the 22 Distritos de Temporal Tecnificado (DTT)[3] in the country.

Implementing BPM allowed CONAGUA to improve its image and provide access to all of society to information relevant to assessing and monitoring the performance of public administration, through the transparency portal: http://sgh. CONAGUA.gob.mx- thus complying with the, and with the *Ley de Obras Públicas y Servicios Relacionados* -Act of Public Works and Related Services- and with the *Ley Federal de Transparencia y Acceso a la Información Pública Gubernamental* - Federal Act of Transparency and Access to Public Government Information. In addition, the *Subdirección General de Infraestructura Hidroagrícola* accomplished an outstanding improvement of resource management efficiency, achieving:

- Reduction of costs: USD 340,000 per year in materials / supplies and USD 238,000 a year for current expenditure.
- Recovery of the investment in the first 18 months
- Time optimization, reducing reporting tasks from 50% to 5%
- Elimination of inefficiencies resulting from the high workloads of the technical and operational staff.
- Decentralization and expansion of regional and local level processes, overcoming the obstacle of geographic dispersion.
- Optimization Public Works Investment Programming, Procurement and Implementation process.

In the words of Major CONAGUA IT:

"The implementation of a BPM project meant a superb achievement for the institution, taking into consideration the demands of the Mexican community to governmental entities and organisms, favoring greater control of tasks, processes and actions carried out by their officers and employees," highlights Mr. Juan Carlos Garcés del Ángel, Operating Coordinator of Hydro-agricultural Management System belonging to CONAGUA.

"An honest and effective administration that provides more and better services to citizens is the goal of governments. The implementation of BPM allowed us to design a system to digitally administer operations, ensuring citizens full access to information and a better control of the tasks performed by govern-mental entities, their officers and employees", says Mr. Isidro Gaytán Arvizu, System Director of TSDs, CONAGUA.

3. BUSINESS CONTEXT

As many other Latin-American countries, Mexico lacks transparency in the actions and services that the Government provides its citizens with. The national annual survey on citizen's perceptions and attitudes, prepared by the Department

---

[3] The *Distritos de Temporal Tecnificado* (Distritos de Temporal Tecnificado) are areas responsible for generating and developing investment projects that establish the characteristics of the work to be per-formed, each taking into account the particularities of the geographical area where it is located. These activities are carried out through public works contracts and related services. In addition, in the DTT machinery and equipment are purchased to hand over to users as a means to maintain and operate the infrastructure built. These DTT are located in 9 states, covering an area of 2.7 million hectares and 115,000 users.

of Internal Affairs confirms that 94% of Mexicans believe that citizens ought to participate to combat such lack of transparency, and 75% considers that existing lack of governmental transparency is a shared responsibility[4]. In keeping with that idea, the management of federal resources for public works is a critical process susceptible to deviations.

For that reason, the Mexican Government enacted two laws that motivated the Subdirección General de Infraestructura Hidroagrícola of the Comisión Nacional del Agua to implement a BPM solution:

- *Ley de Obras Públicas y Servicios Relacionados* (Act of Public Works and Related Services). The purpose of this act is to regulate actions involving planning, scheduling, budgeting, procurement, expenditure, performance, and control of public works as well as of their related services.

- *Ley Federal de Transparencia y Acceso a la Información Pública Gubernamental* (Act of Transparency and Access to Governmental Public information). This act establishes a number of duties to sort and preserve documentation included in files belonging to entities and departments of the Federal Public Administration (FPA), with the aim to foster transparency in public management, accountability, and access by individuals to information held by the State. The latter Act is considered an important step in the process of government transparency, given that it allows users to view information that is of interest through the Internet portals of government agencies.

After both laws were decreed, the BPM project was born within the frame-work of good governance policies implemented between 2000 and 2006, to improve management and technical control processes of the public administration in the Subdirección General de Infraestructura Hidroagrícola operational tasks.

The first process was to decide to automate "Administration and Development of Hydro-agricultural Infrastructure", specifically monitoring Procurement and Execution of Public Works. Its implementation is reinforced by the strategies adopted by the administration of President Felipe Calderon in the program "Management Improvement" through the systems: Efficient Processes and Digital Government", which aims to increase the efficiency of the institutions through the overall improvement of their processes from their standardization and use of appropriate communication and information technologies to improve processes by implementing integrated systems and automated applications, institutional and interinstitutional.

As a result of new regulations and initiatives of the Government of Mexico, the Subdirección General de Infraestructura Hidroagrícola decided to start a BPM project to transform the management methods; to overcome the obstacle of geographical dispersion; and to manage the diversity of media and, mainly, to achieve:

- National standardization of activities, eliminating tasks that do not add value.
- Monitoring and control of public works resources using a technological platform.
- Availability of work resources – through Internet-, opens to public consultation.

---

[4] "Survey on Corruption and Citizens Attitudes"; Department of Internal Affairs; Mexico; 2004.

4. The Key Innovations

4.1 Business

The adoption of BPM enabled the *Subdirección General de Infraestructura Hidroagrícola* to positively impact on their mission of 'Administering and developing hydro-agricultural infrastructure with the involvement of the com-munity to achieve sustainable water use. Furthermore, the implementation of an approach based on processes directly synchronized with the 6 attributes of Good Governance:

- **An Honest and Transparent Government**: opening information to public consultation to achieve transparent governance and help restore the confidence of society in their government.
- **A quality Government**: improvement cycles applied to processes optimize the delivery of services that government provides to society.
- **A Digital Government**: use of new information technologies and tele-communications allowed automation of management related to public works and provided citizenship access.
- **A Government that costs less:** more efficient processes by reducing non-value activities and administrative costs of public works operations, and by optimizing the allocation of resources to areas that offer more and better benefits to the population.
- **A Professional Government:** attracting and retaining women and men best trained in public service.
- **A Government with better regulatory capacity**: eliminating red tape and ensuring the public safety and agility of activities, as a factor that boosts overall competitiveness.

With respect to compliance with these regulations, Juan Carlos Garcés Ángel says: "The standardization of activities and reduction of non-value tasks, cou-pled with process control, modernized government management in an env*ironment of efficiency and effectiveness, within a framework of transparency, thus strengthening the confidence of society in the system"*.

Externally, Federal Public Service entities that are engaged in Public Works try to replicate the processes that make up the BPM project, while internally there was a significant transformation in the way the organization operates and the attitude of the people who work there. According to Mr. Sergio So-to Priante, Assistant Director General of Hydro-agricultural Infrastructure CONAGUA: *"Implementing a BPM solution has resulted in a radical transfor-mation of the tracking methods for the uses of federal budget resources"*.

On the other hand, the decentralized implementation of the solution has overcome the obstacle of geographical dispersion, allowing the operations to extend beyond the boundaries of Headquarters, connecting Regional and State Management Offices , and operational staff in 22 *Distritos de Temporal Tecnificado* (DTT), located in nine states across the country, covering 2.7 million hectares. All simply connected via the internet.

Thus, the following was accomplished:

- Full knowledge of all activities carried out in each *Distrito de Temporal Tecnificado*.
- National standardization of activities, eliminating tasks that do not add value.

- Monitoring and precise control of public works resources using a technological platform. During 2003-2007, investment resources worth USD 35 million were administered jointly with the federal government and user organizations.
- The availability of work resources - online and via the Internet - open to public consultation.

Other important achievements and effects of the BPM project are described in the following sections of this case.

4.2 Process

4.2.1 - Before the BPM Project

Before the implementation of the BPM project the *"Administration and Development of Hydro-agricultural Infrastructure"* process was performed manually and through written documents, which resulted in indirect capture, validation and delivery of information costs.

"The process was carried out using paper documents, and reports about the progress of the activities were also in paper format. The way in which information was processed was like craftwork, given that everyone processed information as they wished, in the format they wished, using the media they could (by phone, fax, mail or email). Concentrating and decoding this information was a task too costly in time, resources and money", explains Gaytán Arvizu.

There was no concept of process for technical and administrative activities. Everything was understood as watertight compartments, with a strong vertical structure, which made operation difficult as each district fulfilled its functions in a different way. Coordinating and managing the different activities carried out represented a great challenge.

In turn, Gaytán expresses that "the use of non-standardized formats and methodologies and, above all, the lack of knowledge about relevant aspects of processes and procedures did not allow making an efficient public work execution follow-up. Neither was it considered the means to keep the Districts' users informed, nor the citizens in general". That meant management delays and less control, with the added difficulty that the information provided to citizens was limited and not always reliable.

On the other hand, the importance of the staff's functions was left aside due to the magnitude of tasks related to documents and reports, thus significantly discouraging human resources specialized in technical tasks. Spending half of the working day with a secondary activity such as producing reports summarizes the problem faced by CONAGUA. The agricultural producers' dissatisfaction with the institution's staff, which carried out more and more office and less fieldwork, was constant. The existence of said problems was due to:

- Reports based on estimated data, thus being difficult to articulate due to their partiality and diversity.
- Incongruity in the physical and financial progress of works, without reports on the destination of resources.
- Inaccurate information transmission, which increased the administration costs.

Also, the agricultural producers had a general lack of information regarding the annual investment amount in each District, the programmed and developed activities, the moment when works were started, the service-provider companies that were awarded the biddings and the progress and conclusion of activities, among others.

Thus, "the General Sub-directorate of Hydro-agricultural Infrastructure of the Water National Commission decided to implement the System of Hydro-agricultural Infra-structure Processes Management, with a BPM suite", Gaytán Arvizu declares.

4.2.2 - The BPM Project

As a result of improved processes at the *Subdirección General de Infraestructura Hidroagrícola* (SGIH), in 2004 the Hydro-agricultural Management System was launched (BPM Project internal name) that contains a macro process called Administration and Development of Hydro-agriculture Infrastructure in order to standardize, organize and control the processes of budget resources management, procurement, monitoring and closure of public works, services and procurement, through a system of online information available for public consultation.

The above macro process includes several support processes:

- Programming and budgeting;
- Tender and contract;
- Monitor and close contracts; and
- Process evaluation through indicators.

The system also has an integrated process called *"Decentralized Administration of Hydro-agricultural Infrastructure"*, which are used by the boards of directors of the 33 Civil Users' Associations in the *Distritos de Temporal Tecnificado* to carry out the integration of its program of infrastructure preservation; the inventory and diagnostic of the public works and machinery transferred by the *Comisión Nacional del Agua* (CONAGUA), as well as capturing and updating the list of beneficiaries and monitoring the program of collection of contributions for the preservation of public works and maintenance of machinery that benefit them.

Figure 1. Macro processes, Support Processes and BPM Project Programs undertaken by the Conagua Subdirección General de Infraestructura Hidroagrícola.

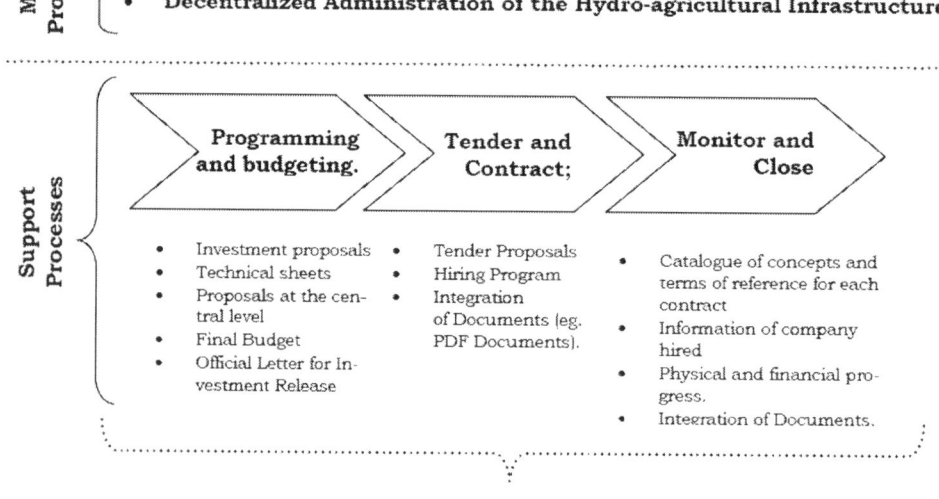

Process evaluation through indicators

The main operational processes of the *Subdirección General de Infraestructura Hidroagrícola* are closely related to the budget program structure established by the *Secretaría de Hacienda y Crédito Público* -Ministry of Finance and Public Credit- and distributed in budget chapters, and also by the decentralized activities of CONAGUA to the Civil Users' Associations.

Before the implementation of the BPM project, it was impossible to monitor and evaluate investments in public works and services. Today, the information presented to public and open consultation, through the Transparency Portal, is organized around three sub-processes: Programming and Budgeting, Tendering and Contract, and Execute and Monitor. Next, as an example, the diagram of the first sub-process is presented, with its main activities and displays.

Figure 2. Diagram of one of the subprocesses "Programming and Budgeting" and of the activity "Develop regional proposals".

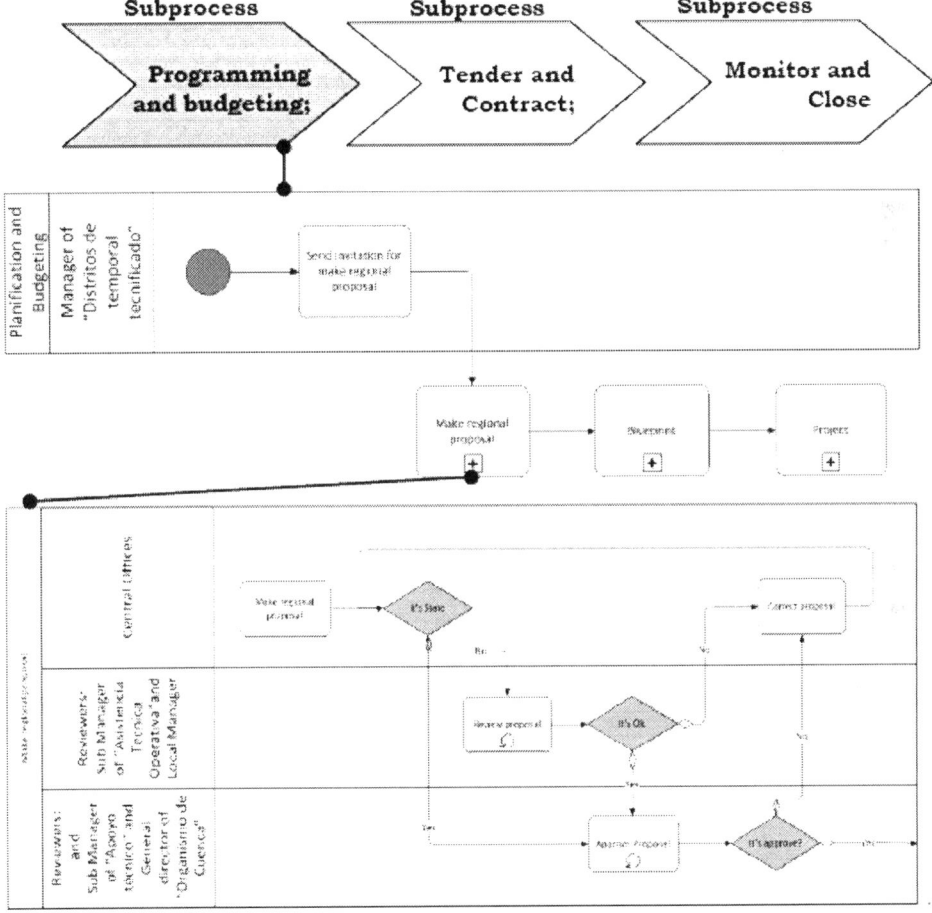

Access: Transparency Web Portal

The Transparency Web Portal is the access point – via Internet – in which users can make consultations by selecting the fiscal period or year they refer to. The information is classified according to the Administrative Hydro-agricultural Region it belongs to.

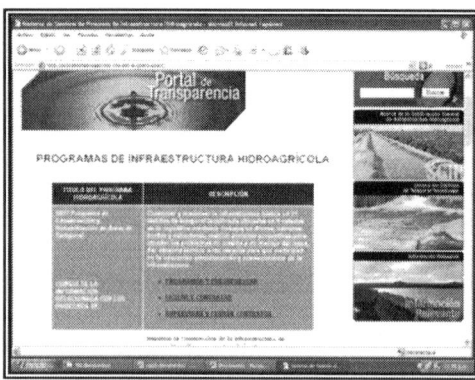 

Programming and Budgeting

The information of these sub-programs refers to the budget allocated to invest-ment. In addition, there is a sub-program called *"indirects"* and is assigned for current expenses. Investment programs come up from local needs, ending in the issue of the Investment Release Letter. Through the portal, it is possible to have access to information about budgets. Details of the regional proposal or project portfolio can be obtained by clicking in the underlined sub-program. The following screen will then be seen:

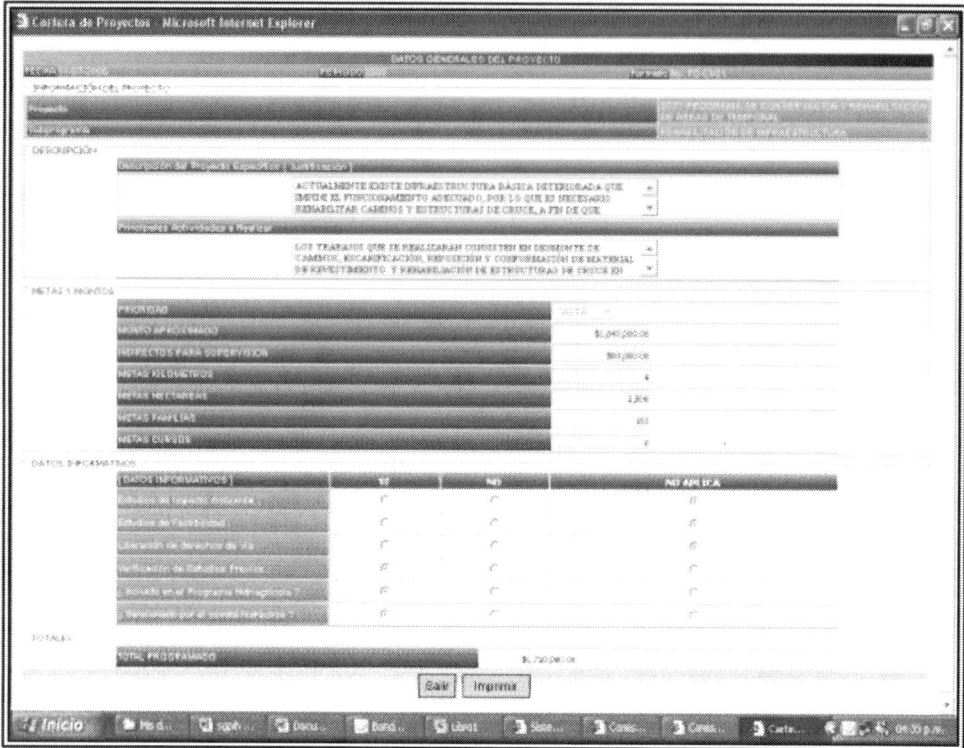

It shows the project justification and major activities to be performed, it´s priority, the requested amount budgeted for both the subprogram and for the supervision of the work, and the total. Besides there are the established goals and comple-mentary information data are described.

Tender and Contract

This sub-process starts with the amounts authorized in the OLI and starts the bidding program, which is carried out in a parallel and complementary way to the process developed through Compranet Web Page, (http://compranet.gob.mx) for all the public administration entities. This sub-process finishes with the contract signed between CONAGUA and a contractor company to carry out the tasks requested by the institution. Every contract has a technical-economic proposal for the tasks and is monthly scheduled.

In this sub-process, the system makes the information transparent according to the contract or order number, and the bidding number. On these grounds, the bidding procedure is stated and the bidding scheduled and real dates are established.

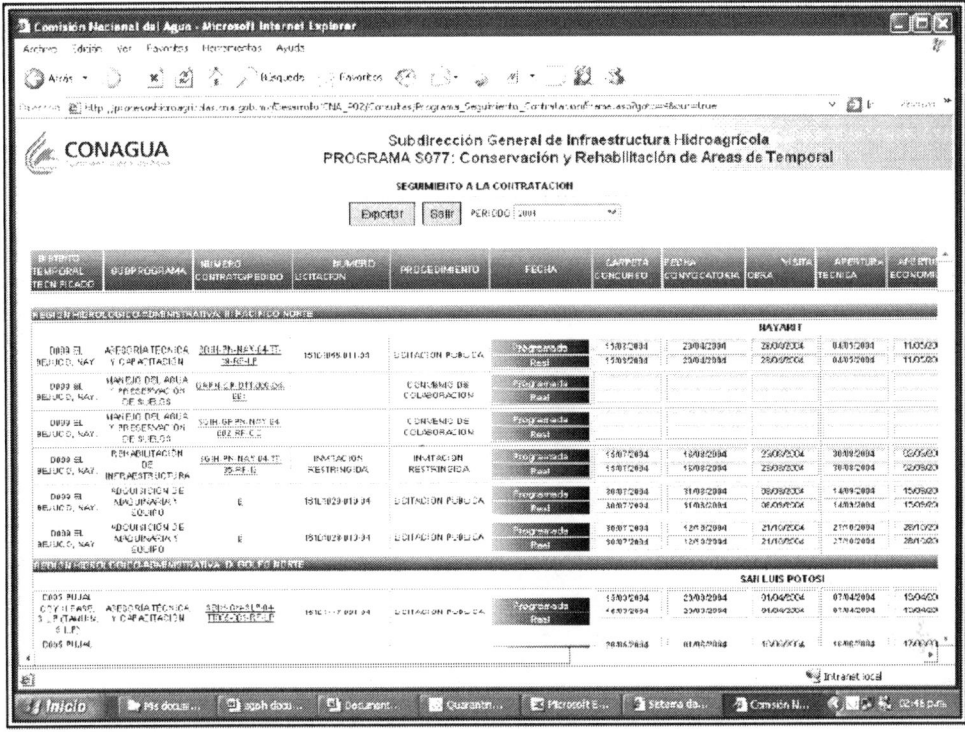

Monitor and Close

The process starts when the economic proposal is uploaded in the system and the institution representative supervises the carrying out of the works, and finishes with the acts of handing over, settlement, and termination of rights and duties, associated to each contract.

Just like the other sub-processes, this one can be visualized in the following way:

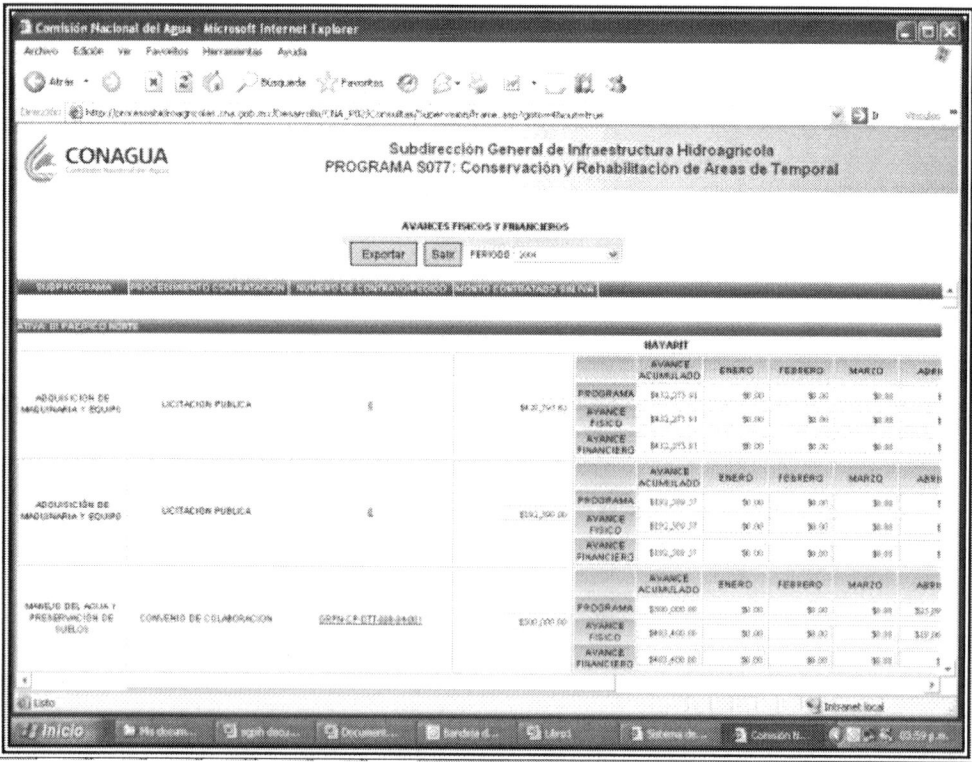

For each contract, the screen shows the bidding method, the order or contract number, a summary of the budgetary resources measured in Mexican pesos, monthly scheduled and based on the technical-economic proposal of the procured company, and the corresponding space to show the physical and financial progresses.

In this way, the user, according to his/her profile, carries out the activity, captures data from the physical and financial progress as they are generated, and immediately become transparent in the transparency portal.

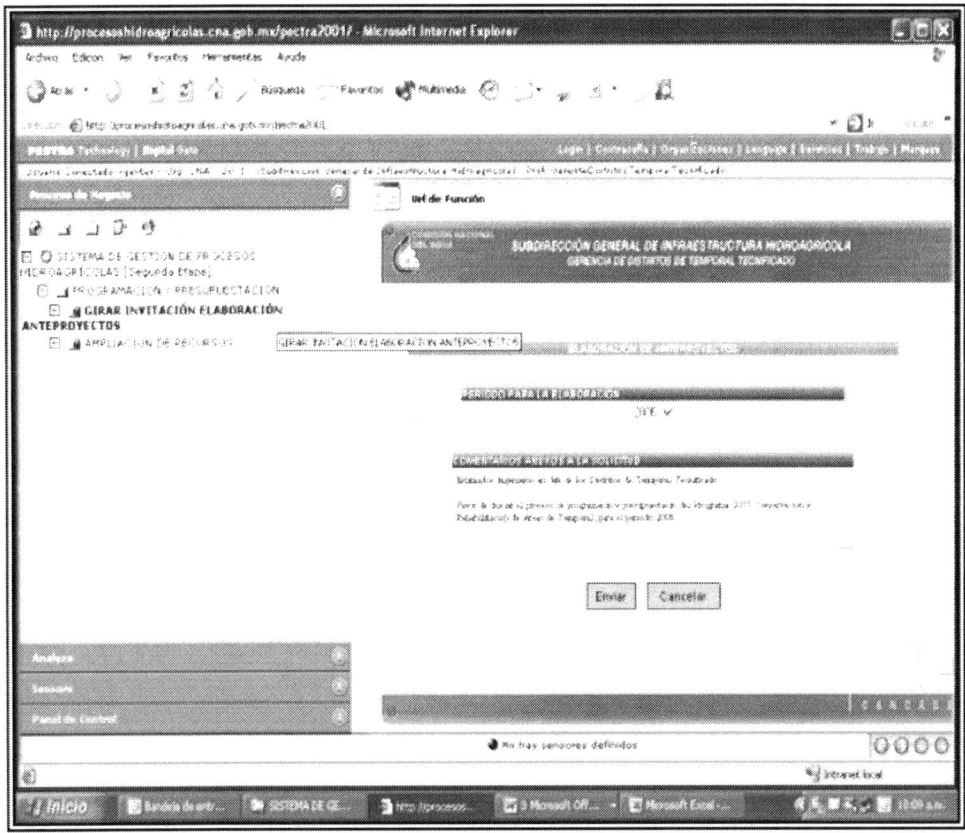

Here it is the screen to start capturing information. The process name and stages it is going through are on the left. In the same left column, downwards, there is an information multi-factor analyzer, a system control panel and there are also monitoring censors. The first capture screen is on the right. Every process is organized in a group of activities that give rise to a product. With the automation, the activities communicate among them through the instance that is a kind of baton. In this way, the user, according to his/her profile, carries out the activity, captures data and then *"releases the instance"* or passes the baton for the second activity.

For example, this screen corresponds to the District Authority's profile. The profile, on the left column, has the detail of the process' different stages in which he/she takes part. Notice the fact that his/ her activities within the process are different from the ones seen before and that belong to the profile of the Manager of TSDs. In this case, the District Authority has already passed the stage of elaborating the portfolio and continues with the stage of elaborating tender packages and programs.

The system also has a screen for the users who have profile and capture license to be able to express their comments and suggestions regarding the system's efficiency. Those opinions are the base to carry out improvement actions.

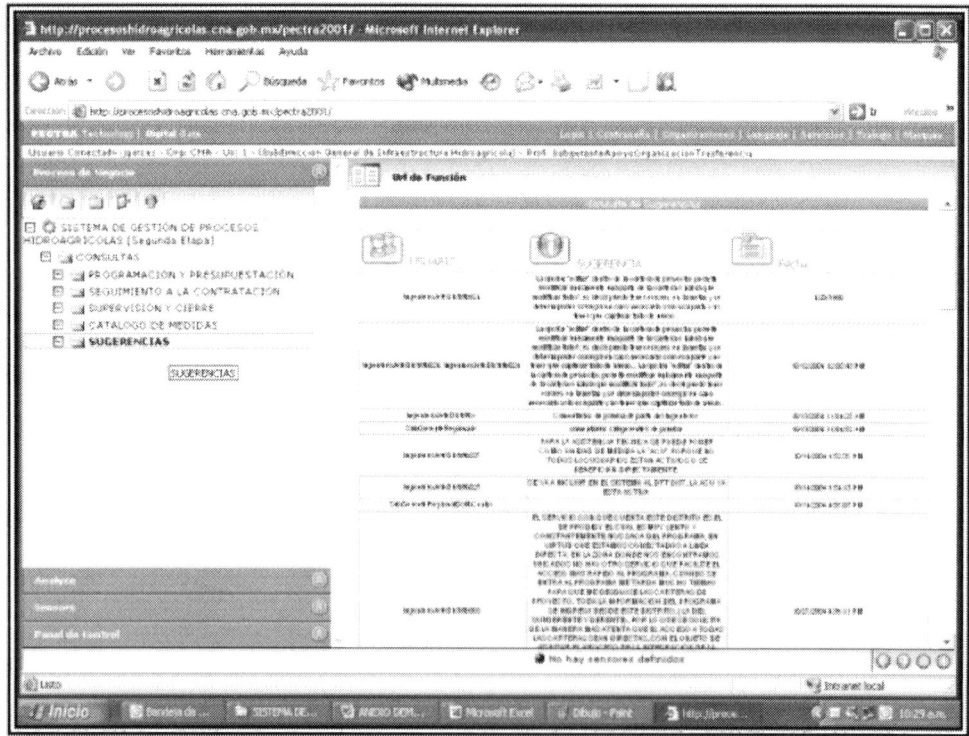

The following figure describes the architecture of the solution used by the *Subdirección General de Infraestructura Hidroagrícola* CONAGUA.

Figure 3. Architecture of the Hydro-agricultural Management System (*).

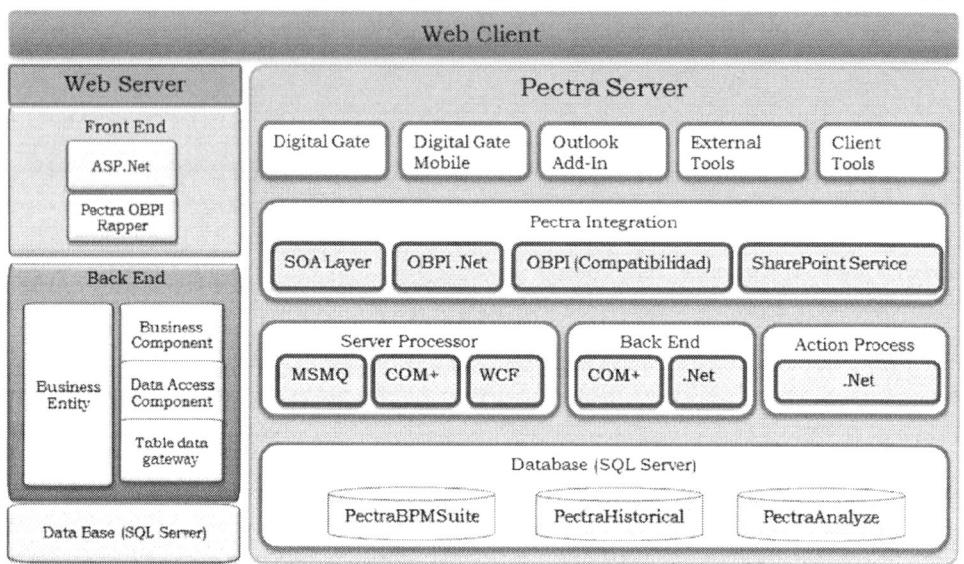

(*) Presentation Layer: Microsoft Visual Studio. Net (C #, VB and ASPX), ASP, HTML, jQuery.

4.2.3 – After BPM Project

After the implementation of the BPM project, CONAGUA dramatically changed the way of working by offering users access to the system in a remote way via the Internet to upload data from any place, being the sending of documents and data carried out exactly as stipulated in the main process. Since the pattern, which prioritizes transparency, is on-line and available for public consultation, it contributed to the modernization of public entity's performance, eliminating the above-mentioned factors that hindered an efficient management.

Today, the system makes it possible the monitoring of all the stages in each work, from its bidding to the handing over, under a systematic and permanent record. Said record contributes to the unification and formalization of criteria for the control and monitoring of public work process under the terms of the Law, and thus becoming an innovative practice completely based on processes management.

When analyzing the 2004-2011 period a greater range is noted, at the institutional and geographical levels, and greater adoption of the concept of BPM which results in more processes, users, profiles, states, regions and towns. In the same period, the BPM project has expanded throughout the organization, growing from 1 to 18 implemented processes with a 700% growth in the number of users.

As a result of the decentralization of the processes the project has also grown geographically, incorporating new states (+23), regions (+13) and towns (+15) in Mexico.

The following table gives details of the evolution of BPM project for the above-mentioned period.

Table 1. Evolution of the BPM Project. 2004 Versus 2011.

Indicator	2004	2011	Evolution (Q)	Evolution (%)
Number of Processes	1	18	+17	1700%
Number of Users	50	400	+350	700%
Number of States	9	32	+23	256%
Number of Central Managers	1	5	+4	400%
Number of Regions	5	18	+13	160%
Number of Local Offices	5	20	+15	300%
Number of *Distritos de Temporal Tecnificado*	21	22	+1	5%
Number of Irrigation Districts	0	85	+85	-
Number of Irrigation Units	0	31	+31	-
Number of Civil Associations	33	33	0	0%

It is important to clarify that although the processes were targeted to public works, now they also serve to manage the substantive associated products and services or investment, as well as current expenditure.

In addition to the above, during 2004-2011 the system improved its operation, with actions such as:

1. Improving the technical and administrative capacity of users.
2. The identification of critical issues, improvement activities and reengineering in the design of processes.

3. Incorporation into the system's database of the rates catalogues for technical advice; water management and soil preservation; rehabilitation and acquisition of machinery and the hydro-agricultural infrastructure inventory complementation for the *Distritos de Temporal Tecnificado*.

4. Improvements of the operation of the two processes integrated into the system, including the Indicators Evaluation System.

5. Adaptation of Management process of the Population Centers Protection Pro-gram (PCP) to the Hydro-agricultural Management System (SGH).

6. Improvements to the process *"Schedule - Budget for 2009"*. Hydro-agricultural infrastructure programs that require registration with the *Secretaría de Hacienda y Crédito Público*.

Figure 4. Before and After BPM Project.

Without BPM	With BPM
• Different data bases. • No determination of client/supplier activities. • Heterogeneity of formats and procedures. • Diversity and doubling of functions and reports. • Generally estimated data and figures. • Delays and incongruity in the physical-financial progress information. • Lack of process global view • Lack of standardized guidelines and criteria about information handling.	• Overall data base. • Processes Management. • Standardized technological platform. • Formats and procedures' standards. • Unique and equal activities with criteria and guidelines standardized at national level. • On-line and real time information transmission and capture. • Information consistency. • Allocation of operation profiles and responsibility. • On-line regulation. • Remote accessibility via Internet under a transparency pattern. • On-line interaction of all the process participation stages.

4.4 Organization

Currently, the BPM project has more than 400 users spread over many Management Offices, Agencies and Local Offices that make up the CONAGUA Subdirección General de Infraestructura Hidroagrícola, located in different geographical areas in Mexico:

- 22 *Distritos de Temporal Tecnificado* Management Offices (GDTT) that interact with 33 civil associations, which are made up of 115,000 beneficiary citizens.
- Hydro-agricultural Infrastructure Construction Management Offices (GCIH).
- Hydro-agricultural Infrastructure Projects Management Offices (GPIH).
- 85 Irrigation District Management Offices (GDR).
- 31 Irrigation Unit Management Offices (GUR).
- 13 River Basin Organizations within regions of Mexico.
- 20 Local Offices in the interior of Mexico.
- CONAGUA staff at each site from the Portal of the *Subdirección de Infraestructura Hidroagrícola:*.

In all the above areas there are several user profiles: Directors, Managers, Assistant Managers, Chiefs, Residents, Supervisors, and others.

It is important to mention that all personnel associated with *Distritos de Tem-poral Tecnificados* were involved since the beginning of the BPM project, from management to operational level staff.

"The system now has a high degree of innovation due to encouraging all staff to know the key processes, which motivates and stimulates efficient operations, and by being available on the Internet, it promotes the active participation of users", says Juan Carlos Garcés.

In addition, the adoption of a process-oriented management philosophy and the implementation of BPM technology allowed streamlining of the activities of those responsible for the execution of contracts for each of the different Mexican towns, helping them to focus on higher value added activities and control information related to the projects and public works, from the moment a need is identified until the physical closure of the public works. With respect to this, Garcés notes: *"The staff has achieved significant skills development through specialized training in processes as well as in administrative proceedings and team management."*

The BPM project have allowed them to employees of the General Department of Irrigation Infrastructure to automate operational tasks, increasing productivity and efficiency of public employees, as well as fostering communication and cooperation between the different participating areas of the processes involved. In other words, doing more in less time, as well as reducing the use of paper and administrative costs.

Roughly speaking the results of surveys administered to users and operational staff demonstrates an increased user satisfaction level: from 50% to 76%.

5. HURDLES OVERCOME

In general terms there were no important hurdles when implementing the BPM project, "mainly due to the great job carried out by BPM Vendor's consultancy area as regards Change Management, key aspect, in my view, for the incorporation of such technologies into an organization", sums up Garcés.

"It was a necessary work since people were used to defining all the activities in very long stages, so that fact obliged us to summarize the tasks and activities each one carried out. This was the most tortuous part of the implementation", Gaytán says.

"The practice was designed from a processes perspective, thus in a first stage a multi-disciplinary and inter-functional group was created, including suppliers and internal clients of the public work process, in order to update and change the Distritos de Temporal Tecnificado' administrative methods and operation", he con-firms.

However, the cultural transformation to carry out a shared view among the headquarters and the offices located in rural areas has made it necessary to establish ways of rewarding staff taking part. National and regional systematic meetings are held twice a year to share experiences with the aim to keep contact at a personal and not just virtual level, creating in this way an intellectual synergy. Besides, training diplomas and certifications are given to all the participants as well as recognition in different fields: participation, consistency and improvement contributions.

6. BENEFITS

The implementation of BPM provided important benefits to CONAGUA. Said benefits are related not only to the observance of laws and rules (due to its Governance character) but also to aspects concerning the efficient resource administration and the improvement of the community's perception of the organism's image.

Nowadays, on-line and real time information is available at site http://sgh.cna.gob.mx and it offers a complete panorama about aspects of public work programming, budgeting, procurement, follow-up and investment closing, thus giving complete transparency to investment management and use.

In this way, it is possible to have access from any place to the information about: investments; contract awards; suppliers; goals; follow-up of public work's physical-financial progress in all the districts, contract closing and management indicators.

- With the implementation of BPM, CONAGUA has succeeded in:
- Standardizing processes and local, regional, and state technology.
- Maximizing the performance of the existing technological systems.
- Defining, designing, and monitoring processes with a digital system and -cording them on- line.
- Measuring, analyzing and creating processes' statistics.
- Improving processes' efficiency and having an Integral Information System.
- Having management indicators for decision-making.
- Reducing time and cost of information processing, capture and analysis.
- Reducing duplicities and improvisations in the execution of activities.
- Having clear process guidelines, shared at all levels.

As a result, CONAGUA has achieved the following proposed goals:

- Centralizing the information from entities and organisms, making easier the administrative procedures and reducing the associated costs.
- Adhering to the agreement for control, accountability and verification of the transparent management of federal public resources.
- Strengthening the transparency of governmental procurement by implementing a mechanism of community's participation, by means of which the processes of governmental performance are assessed, making known the way in which all and each of the procurement stages took place.
- Promoting, through the study, analysis and debate about the corruption phenomenon, the observance of some recommendations derived from commitments undertaken by Mexico at international level and directly related to fighting corruption.
- Strengthening the development of a service, honesty, ethics, accountability, precaution and corruption-fighting culture.
- Improving public function by promoting the exercise of the right to information and citizens' participation.
- Encouraging co-responsibility.
- Promoting citizens' participation to improve the governmental policies and programs, by generating the interchange of successful experiences among states, municipalities and Federation

CONAGUA has also obtained successful results concerning operative efficiency:

6.1 Cost Savings

Savings of USD 340,000 in materials and supplies and of USD 238,000 of current expenses were recorded during the year. Cost reduction:

- Of postal messenger and fax. (Total reduction).
- Of telephone calls (60% reduction).
- Of data transmission.
- Of supplies used for the elaboration of reports (paper, equipment, etc).

6.2 Time Reductions

- The hours spent by the district authorities to elaborate reports were reduced from 50% to 5%, and that time was better spent improving the super-vision of works and increasing the time for intellectual work related to technical consultancy, assessment, analysis and prospecting work.
- The integration with existing information systems made it possible to accelerate 40% the involved processes.

6.3 Increased Revenues

The recovery period for the whole of the investment was of 18 months.

6.4 Productivity Improvements

CONAGUA has shown a significant 67% reduction in administrative activities by eliminating those that create no value such as report multiplicity, filling forms and sending them by courier or fax.

6.5 Other Benefits

6.5.1 - Management control and transparency

CONAGUA has acquired more control on public work delivery, reception, and execution follow-up, making the processes more transparent by presenting complete information about each work's execution stages. Said transparency caused an increase in the citizens' trust in the government's actions.

6.5.2 - Continuous improvement

Through BPM project, CONAGUA produces complete documents in an automatic way, with the support of operation, guideline and procedure manuals for its use, including the Total Quality Management System, certified under ISO 9001. Additionally, it has been achieved the integral standardization of all the elements that the Treasury Department and Public Credit establishes for the execution follow-up of the federal government's public work and to keep them on-line for public consultation. The results obtained after the implementation show a significant reduction of non-conformities in the bidding procedures.

6.5.3 - Modernization and efficiency

The implementation of a BPM project gives the organism the possibility of data and images transmission by means of modern technological platforms, allowing the creation of a link with a data base for the updating of users' register from Districts of more than 118,000 producers. The information generated in the system is the same used for institutional decision-makings and it can be consulted and checked simultaneously by the community and users

In this way, CONAGUA has changed the task management and organization methods, using a practice that has made it possible to overcome the geographical dispersion barrier, the format diversity and the difficulty of means and time to send the reports. Above all, CONAGUA has succeeded in:

- Optimizing the interactive communication management among local and central offices.
- Improving the interconnection with information systems established by CONAGUA.
- Complying with the rules of both Acts.
- Defining performance indicators.
- Making commitments and links transparent.
- Identifying and linking work instruments.
- Identifying and taking advantage of best practices.

The common citizen benefits in various ways:

- The reduction of the contracts' follow-up costs has an impact at the end of the production chain, in that the resulting public work is carried out in a proper and functional way. In this way, the application of public resources is more efficient.
- The reduction of waiting-time for the delivery of restored infrastructure, since it is carried out in a faster way and with better quality.

6.5.4 - Innovation

The innovation development implied by the Hydro-agricultural Management System – CONAGUA identified the technological tool based on a BPM Suite–whose core goal is the management and transparency of public work processes, includes the adoption of modern IT and processes management technologies. The practice has achieved the establishment of a system that goes beyond an administrative improvement with short-term aims. It is a change in the way of working, which updates the investment resources management methods to make them transparent for the citizens, granting efficiency and effectiveness to keep performance indicators on-line and in real time. It is a technological development that returns priority to substantive functions in hydro-agricultural subjects, meeting the users' needs and, in general, the needs of the beneficiaries' communities, in every place where it is applied.

The technological development starts from the experience and knowledge of the operators of substantive processes from the General Sub-directorate of Hydro-agricultural Infrastructure of CONAGUA, who make possible the fulfillment of the Institutional Mission, around which it makes sense. In this subject, innovating by means of technological development has multiplying effects, offers all the benefits derived from knowledge and experiences -an accumulated intellectual capital that, added to the technological tools applied, produce dramatic improvement and boost. Due to the mentioned facts, in benchmarking terms, the practice stands at a higher level than that of emerging economies. The system with platform – feasible to be replicated in any entity of the FPA – gives options to the federal government for the use of information technology, telecommunications, the overall view provided by the processes approach which, in case of being adopted, creates economies of scale and a greater integration and link between the services provided by the development programs of the TSDs.

6.5.5 - Benefit for the community

The system as innovative practice has an approach mainly oriented to the users (internal and external to the Commission) that also includes the possibility of public consultation for a transparent management. The Districts administration and development give as a result the control of water surplus and the exploitation of agricultural lands of the Humid and Sub-humid Tropical areas. The set up infrastructure is not limited to the production activity. Its impacts and effects are systemic; for example, the roads get better with the soil dug up from draining channels and they are used for carrying the agricultural production and any other type of goods, thus increasing the commercial activity in the area near the District, as well as the improvement of the access to schools, health centers and sport facilities.

Other benefits are:

- Know directly and immediately the management of federal resources that are allocated to the CONAGUA for the benefit of society;
- Give functional preference to those process systems that make up CONAGUA and that are fundamental to quality of the results obtained on the basis of the objectives and goals that are defined year by year;
- Take advantage of e-government to bring down costs and time benefiting users; and
- Allow the development of digital information, as well as the distribution and use in the various parts of the country, whereby the speed of consultation by the public is a matter of utmost importance.

The following figure summarizes and outlines the main benefits mentioned above.

Figure 5. Diagram of Benefits achieved with the BPM project at the CONAGUA Subdirección General de Infraestructura Hidroagrícola.

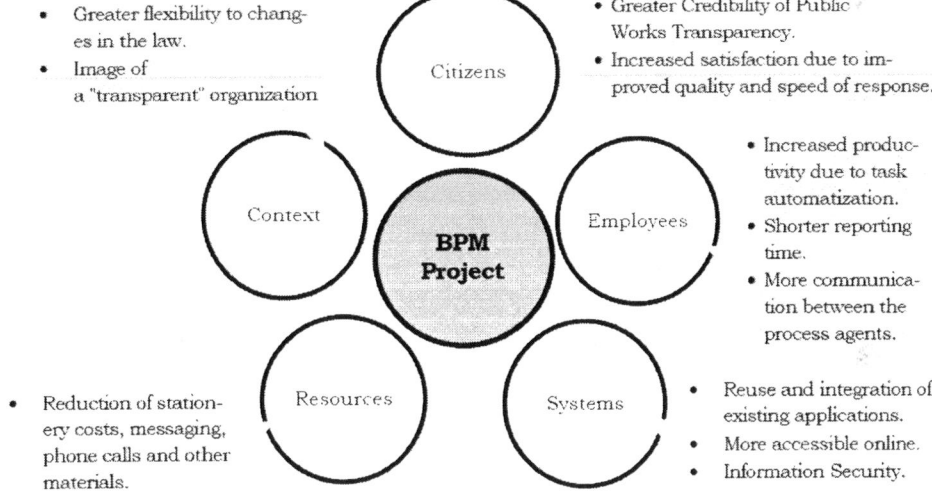

7. BEST PRACTICES, LEARNING POINTS AND PITFALLS

Due to its transparency, the SGH won two awards in 2005: Honorary Mention of the National Transparency Award, and the Innova Acknowledgment awarded by the President of the Republic given that it is a technological tool that had an impact on the 6 strategies for good governance.

The entity was awarded the important mention due to the practice named: *"Hydro-agricultural Management System: Transparency in the use of Public Resources for the Development of the Distritos de Temporal Tecnificado".*

Besides, in the year 2005, the System also obtained the Innova Acknowledgement, awarded by the National Presidency, since it was instituted as a process improvement exemplary tool, with management transparency and administration savings and feasible to be used in other stages, both from the government and the private sector.

The General Assistant Manager of Hydro-agricultural Infrastructure, Sergio Soto Priante, highlighted: *"the implementation of the Hydro-agricultural Management System with a BPM suite gives full assurance to users from TSDs and to the population in general, that the resources for public works are executed with transparency in the various projects under way"*.

Another of his achievements is that the System success case was incorporated, as one of the best improvement practices at the federal regulatory level on the website of the Ministry of Public Administration in the Normateca section. In addition, the System became a reporting element for the Operational Program for Transparency and Combating Corruption in the CONAGUA (POTCC) within the critical process called Public Works.

8. COMPETITIVE ADVANTAGES

Thanks to the BPM project, the *Subdirección General de Infraestructura Hidroagrícola* of the *Comisión Nacional del Agua* can analyze in real-time activities that are underway in order to implement the necessary adjustments on existing processes in an agile and simple manner. This flexibility makes it is possible to adapt to the constantly changing social, political, economic and regulatory environment, improving their responsiveness and image as perceived by broader society. This translates into better services to the community and lower response time to citizens' demands, which in turn maximizes their satisfaction.

Regarding the impact that the BPM project had on citizens, renowned professor and researcher at the faculty of social sciences at the *Universidad Nacional Autonoma de Mexico*, Dr. Ricardo Uvalle Berrones, analyzed the Hydro-agricultural Management System and wrote an article about it, where he noted that: *"Given that the hydro-agricultural management system is a transparent tool within the CONAGUA and before the citizens, it is a matter which falls totally in the public realm of the federal government, which means that the citizen has the opportunity of getting to know the areas that are directly in charge of generating, structuring, recording, distributing and updating information that is of interest because it summarizes the behavior of government policies that intervene in the utilization of public resources"*.

9. TECHNOLOGY

The Technology used was PECTRA BPM Suite, in order to simplify the implementation of process management in organizations, facilitating the analysis, surveying, design, implementation, automation, monitoring and optimization of the processes of Public Works.

The BPM suite allowed us to:

- Integrate existing CONAGUA applications, such as the back office solution Compranet-through which bidding processes are concentrated of over 6,500 procurement and public works units- and Microsoft Office tools (Word, Excel, and Outlook, among others). The integration with the Commission´s portal has helped generate a robust database with figures from previous budget years, and has generated the ability to extract information from internal and external users.
- Handle different types of workflows based on process, documents - allowing any attached document at any moment of the work flow, messaging -allowing us to send messages or notifications (Outlook Add-In).

- To establish performance indicators for monitoring of organizational processes, to detect bottlenecks and support decision-making. Additionally, the graphics provided by the solution will allow society to understand the behavior of the flow of substantive information.
- Management Offices, Organizations and Local Offices that make up the CONAGUA *Subdirección General de Infraestructura Hidroagrícola*, located in different parts of Mexico.
- Having remote access via Internet and does so under a scheme that favors transparency, for being online and available for public consultation.
- Maintain links to the website of the Commission, Compranet (which has a record of tenders and contracts), the *Secretaría de la Función Pública* - Ministry for the Civil Service, *Secretaría de Hacienda y Crédito Público*, the *Secretaría de Medio Ambiente y Recursos Naturales* and the *Portal Ciudadano del Gobierno de la República* -Citizen Portal of the Government of the Republic.
- Streamline activities at all operational levels of the Commission, because it manages online information officially, in a timely and reliable fashion, for compliance with the core operating functions and programs of the Districts.
- Replicate the process in any unit of the Federal Public Administration, and extend these benefits to the entire management of the federal government in public works.
- Have search engines, an option for creating reports, help functions, spaces for comments and observations.
- Have a database with figures from previous budget years, from the whole of investment initiatives in the Districts, with information from different stages of data updates (day, week, month), with the option that information be obtained by internal and external users.
- Plot data according to the requirements provided by users through so-called *"cubes"*. With all this timely decision-making, based on measurement of actual events, is strengthened.
- Be 100% supported by Web technology, with a minimum of implementations in workstations, and by 100% Microsoft platform.
- Have a processes graphic designer, independent of the main engine.
- Generate ASP forms and the ability to generate forms easily and without the use of code in other tools such as Excel or Word.
- Have tools to manage users, roles, profiles, allowing easy management and incorporation of information security already existent in the organization.
- Have a security diagram for users which includes: control of minimum length of password; control of erroneous logins; registration of successful and erroneous logins; password expiration; encryption of password and user data; re-quest for change of password after the first successful logging; block account after strange or incorrect logins.

10. THE TECHNOLOGY AND SERVICE PROVIDERS

The project was developed by PECTRA Technology and its Business Partner Cencade.

- **PECTRA Technology Inc.:** a company specializing in Process Management, with over 12 years of experience in the market and 120 successful implementations in the USA, Argentina, Mexico, Panama, Colombia,

Spain and Chile. We have an extensive network of partners in the entire Latin American region and we provide services to more than 50,000 end users who, in turn, serve 6,000,000+ users/customers. For more information, please visit: www.pectra.com.

- **CENCADE:** Cencade is a management consultancy dedicated to promoting the development of competitive capabilities of both people and organizations. For more than 30 years we have served the Mexican market in different fields of economic activity and we have contributed to the success of our customers to obtain both certifications of their quality management systems and recog-nitions such as: Innova Award (recognition to government quality) and the Transparency Award. For further information, please visit: www.cencade.com.mx.

This document was created by CONAGUA's IT Department along with PECTRA Technology's Marketing and Software Architecture Departments and CENCADE's Commercial Area. Different techniques were used to collect the information. Interviews to the people in charge of the solution's design and implementation were carried out (in an average of two hours each); and also a performance evaluation was carried out in the entire company to respond appropriately to the requirements demanded by the Global Awards for Excellence in Business Process Management and Workflow.

Grupo Hospitalar Conceição, Brazil

Silver Award: Nominated by H&R Consultores, Brazil

1. OVERVIEW

Grupo Hospitalar Conceição (GHC) is the largest hospital complex in the State of Rio Grande do Sul, Brazil, and responsible for the admission of 59,900 people, 2.2 million appointments, and 36,100 annual surgeries. The group comprises four hospital units, twelve health clinics, and three psychosocial care centers.

GHC pursues excellence in providing healthcare to the population as we supply state-run health services given that we are connected to the Ministry of Health and are totally dedicated to users of *Sistema Único de Saúde* – SUS (the public healthcare system). SUS was created in 1988 by the Brazilian Federal Constitution and today is considered one of the largest public healthcare systems in the world. It is an unparalleled social project that materializes by means of actions that foster healthy living, prevent diseases, and provide healthcare to Brazilians in an egalitarian manner.

Besides providing the population with healthcare, Grupo Hospitalar Conceição is also dedicated to fostering education and research, thus becoming a center of knowledge and people training for SUS. To reach our mission of developing full healthcare actions with organizational excellence and efficacy, our group employs technological and human resources and education and research programs.

One of our strategic processes is the supply and service procurement process used by the entire hospital complex. At GHC, purchases are made according to Law 8666/93, which regulates the acquisitions of goods and service and construction contracts by entities making use of public funds in Brazil.

The instances of this process used to be manually controlled and could take up to 3.5 months to complete, depending on the type of purchase. Some of the difficulties found in that work format are highlighted below:

1. Lack of systematization and standardization of all stages involved in the process;
2. Difficulty to trace information related to processes underway;
3. Slow process execution;
4. Difficulty to make process-related information publicly available, a principle set forth by Law 8666/93;
5. High costs related to storage and physical transportation of process-related documents.

To solve those issues, our group adopted BPM (Business Process Management) technical and management principles in the course of an implementation process that lasted approximately 12 months between 2009 and 2010. The work was carried out by an outside consulting firm along with the team in charge of the procurement process at GHC.

It was decided that the process flow would be designed by those involved along with outside support; therefore, in the initial phase of the project several workshops were held with the work groups; in such workshops the process was reviewed, redesigned, and in later phases, automated. That way, the cultural and technological bases were created to set up a new management approach focused on operating quality and efficiency.

Optimizing the process allowed us to cut execution time by 20% to 70%, according to the type of purchase. Additionally, the automated process afforded monthly savings in the amount of BRL 10,000 right in the first months after the process was automated, besides eliminating the use of paper. The application was based on the BPMS Orquestra BPM, by Brazilian company Cryo Technologies. Such BPM application allows us to trace and monitor the entire process cycle, making it possible not only to optimize costs but also to make information transparent.

2. BUSINESS CONTEXT

The procurement process involves the phases of purchase requests by GHC departments, market research, legal opinions, budget and financial clearances, publication of the purchase public notice, receipt and review of proposals from potential suppliers, supply authorizations, contracts, and monitoring the delivery of materials and services provided. All those procedures used to be carried out manually, involved many people, and required large amounts of resources such as time and paper.

Excessive efforts were required to manage and control the instances in this process, considering there were no standards for carrying out the activities and that the information was decentralized, under the responsibility of each department involved in the process. Those issues made it impossible to supply precise information and provide transparent services to clients in an effective manner.

Also, it was difficult to control the history of processes and to define and monitor performance indicators, which made it hard to manage the work and carry out improvement actions. However, in public service, one of the ever-pressing issues regards compliance with deadlines and fulfillment of its activities. Therefore, implementing the BPM technical principles has made it possible to identify all the deadlines of the tasks involved and control and monitor them.

3. THE KEY MOTIVATIONS

Grupo Hospitalar Conceição is under the great responsibility of providing healthcare services to the Rio Grande do Sul population because we are the largest hospital complex in the state and dedicate 100% of our services to patients of *Sistema Único de Saúde* – SUS (the public healthcare system). The purpose of our management and knowledge-generating actions is to turn them into a benchmark for SUS services, and consequently a benchmark for the other hospitals that also provide health services through this healthcare system.

The monetary volume of GHC purchases is close to BRL 150 million a year. The procurement process is responsible for purchasing all the materials and services required by our hospital complex's units. Such units include four hospitals dedicated to general and emergency, pediatric, and physical trauma care, besides services specific for women.

Some of the goals for implementing BPM technical and management principles are highlighted below:
- Systematize and standardize all the tasks involved in the procurement process;
- Shorten the deadlines involved in the procurement process and expedite the work;

- Make the process more transparent for the population, according to the legal principle of publicly supplying procurement-related information set forth by Federal law 8666/93;
- Make the procurement process fully traceable;
- Decrease the costs inherent to each purchase and ensure greater environmental sustainability by cutting back on the use of paper.

4. THE KEY INNOVATIONS

Public management, especially in terms of its resources, is seen across the world as a vital factor to increase the efficiency of governmental actions serving the population. The adoption of BPM by GHC has made it possible to optimize and automate our procurement process, actions which are still restricted to few public institutions in Brazil. It has also given us greater ability to generate results for the population, be transparent, and make improvements that positively impact the environment by eliminating the use of paper.

Business

While the project was being carried out, there were great efforts to get all those involved in the process engaged in the stages of flow chart review and redesign. We were able to see everyone's motivation and commitment to pursuing our goals to standardize and improve our procurement process.

It is a strategic process for GHC, at the same time relatively complex and comprehensive, given it includes activities ranging from the request to the receipt of materials, besides involving several of our hospital group's departments responsible for, for instance, planning the purchases, managing the materials, managing the contracts, clearing budgets and financial issues, and legal matters. The participation of most of the operating team was essential to improve the quality of team work and get everyone committed to our organization's strategic plans.

The procurement procedures adopted by GHC were identified, analyzed, optimized, and automated on an online BPM application. The online BPMS software allowed those involved to access the process, receive and carry out activities, and monitor reports via the Internet.

Process

The procurement process was originally performed manually and the forms and documents related to each purchase were physically processed at GHC. Transporting documents from one unit to the other used to take one day, on average, and considering such transportation could take place several times while the process was underway it took a long time to complete a purchase.

Besides requiring too much time and too many human resources, the process used up a large amount of paper. Using paper considerably helped increase the costs associated with each purchase process and negatively impacted the environment.

After the mapping, we were able to identify 700 activities that were then optimized or excluded after the processes were reviewed and modeled so the process could be implemented in the BPMS. Today, the set of processes comprises 566 human activities. The procurement macro process was split into three processes, according to the type of purchase (Price Registration, Tender, Exemption and Unenforceability).

- Flow of Adherence to another institution's Price Registration;
- Flow of Procurement via Exemption/Unenforceability;
- Flow of Procurement via Tender.

Fluxo de Compras por Licitação v. 1

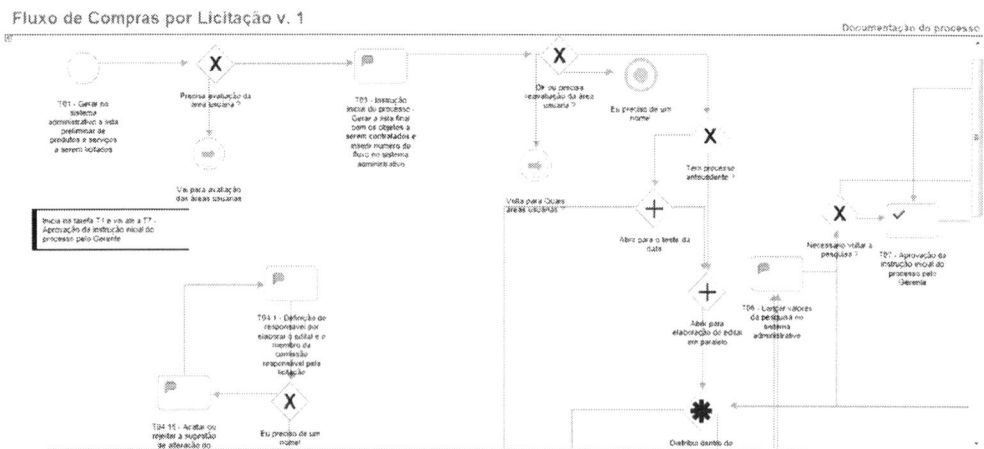

Figure 1 Diagram of the initial part of the Flow of Procurement via Tender.

Now that the technology platform has been implemented, the procurement process for each type of purchase is requested via an electronic form by those responsible for the Materials Management department. They concentrate all the needs for materials and services and are in charge of organizing and prioritizing such needs before they start each one of the three processes mentioned above.

All the documents that used to be printed out are now attached to such electronic form in all stages of the automated processes. In other words, emails containing requests for materials, certificates from suppliers, and market research files, for instance, are now digitally sent to the other people involved in the process activities. Once a request is submitted, the GHC team immediately starts analyzing the information.

Fluxo de Adesão a um Registro de Preços de outra instituição v.1
T01 - Solicitação de adesão a um Registro de Preços de outra instituição

Figure 1: Electronic form requesting the Flow of Adherence to another institution's Price Registration

Those involved in the processes receive and perform activities via a simple, intuitive interface that highlights the list of pending activities. As defined in the process design, each instance started will proceed along a sequence of activities automatically sent to those in charge, who will have deadlines to complete them.

Figure 3 List of tasks to be performed by a process player.

Organization

The BPM implementation project allowed us to generate knowledge and conduct our management through a systemic view of the procurement process. Through the flowcharts defined for the material and service procurement processes we were able to detect improvement opportunities and optimize the activities and procedures involved.

Using the BPMS has significantly decreased the number of manual operations and allowed the GHC team to have greater control of and monitor the performance of process instances. It has also made it possible for the population and audit agencies to view the information, which resulted in greater transparency for the services we provide to society.

Since the project was completed in 2010, over 2560 processes involving more than 300 GHC employees have been carried out. Such executions are now monitored through the process execution average time indicator, which has shown a decrease of up to 70%.

5. HURDLES OVERCOME

While the project was being carried out, we came across a few challenges on our way to reaching the goals we had set, as follows:

Lack of Knowledge regarding the Procurement Process

In the early stages of project development, the procurement process was yet to be defined and standardized by GHC. So, the flowchart was designed with help from the people involved in the process.

Starting from the initial work flow generated and a first optimization cycle, said flowchart was implemented and today is adjusted following continued improvement cycles.

Organizational Culture

Some people involved in the process operating activities resisted the implementation of the project. They opposed some changes that were to be implemented in the way they used to do their activities and operations.

To overcome such hurdles, we tried to get as many people as possible engaged in helping design the process and collectively put together the work flows to be automated on the BPMS. That action got those involved in the process committed to the project and has ensured it is properly put into operation every day after it was implemented.

Adoption by the Organization

Another challenge we faced was getting GHC employees to adopt new software after having spent years performing their work manually. Training sessions were held to educate BPMS users on its application.

The success of the project and of the BPMS implementation was also largely influenced by the constant support from the institution's senior management and the existence of a permanent planning and implementation team assigned to the project and to supply the IT infrastructure resources necessary to accommodate the new work format.

6. BENEFITS

Lower Costs and Increased Earnings

Because we are a public institution that provides healthcare services to Brazilians, increasing our earnings is not among our goals. Our focus is on providing complete healthcare with excellence, on the efficiency and efficacy of our strategic processes, and on shortening the time it takes us to cater to our inner and outside clients.

Nevertheless, given our commitment to sustainable development, our hospital group monitors the cost indicator related to the use of paper in our manually performed processes: since the BPM system-featuring procurement process was implemented, we have been saving approximately BRL 10,000 a month. By decreasing the use of paper, we have also cut back on print-outs and on the use of ink cartridges.

It is also fair to assume that, by eliminating procurement processes processed physically, we have cut costs associated to their transportation and storage. Likewise, the optimized work flow and fewer errors and less rework have positively impacted the costs associated to the process.

Time Savings

One of the project's goals included shortening the time to complete procurement process instances so as to allow GHC to more swiftly meet our units' and departments' needs in terms of goods and service acquisition.

By using the Flow of Procurement via Exemption/Unenforceability we have found the average time to complete the procurement process via the Exemption mode has decreased by approximately 70%. Regarding tender-based purchases, completed through the Flow of Procurement via Tender, we have found a decrease of approximately 22.5%.

Productivity Gains

After the procurement process was automated, GHC employees that perform activities in this process have seen their work gain in productivity. The BPM system automatically forwards the activities defined in the procurement macro process flows to those responsible for them, who have defined deadlines to complete them.

We have seen a considerable drop in the need for rework and also the elimination of actions replaced with automated BPMS tasks, such as emailing and exchanging documents between our institution's departments. Consequently, after the project was completed, the GHC team has been able to dedicate a larger portion of their time to actions that continuously improve the process. Problems related to procurement process traceability and information transparency have also been solved.

7. BEST PRACTICES, LEARNING OPPORTUNITIES AND PITFALLS

Best Practices and Learning Opportunities

Some of the best practices identified in the project that implemented BPM technical and management principles into the GHC procurement process are listed below:

✓ *Understanding the expectations of the people involved in the BPM implementation project, clearly stating the goals we wish to reach and how important cooperation is for us to achieve good results;*

✓ *Getting all those involved in the process to participate in the early phases of the mapping project. Their input was essential to define the work flow, and their involvement minimized hurdles related to project opposition;*

✓ *The senior management's support for the project to be carried out, which especially helps overcome the initial resistance and cultural barriers.*

Pitfalls

✗ *The main pitfall we found was the lack of a deadline set for GHC to adopt automated flows at 100% of our procurement processes. Consequently, in the first few months, while the process was carried out via the BPMS, some instances were still being physically processed at the institution.*

Therefore, setting deadlines for the adoption of changes resulting from the BPM implementation project is seen as a lesson learned for future projects.

8. COMPETITIVE ADVANTAGES

The project implementation and the use of process automation software represent an innovative initiative for the Brazilian public management, given that such practices are adopted by only a handful of public institutions. Additionally, because of GHC's great reputation in terms of catering to the population via SUS, our initiatives may become a benchmark for the other Brazilian hospitals.

Another advantage lies in how society sees the services provided by our hospital complex. Today, the information related to the instances of our procurement process is available to all those who wish to view it, which enables transparent public management.

By analyzing performance indicators, we have been able to see more efficient management in our everyday operations. After the project was completed, tracing and monitoring the procurement process have become permanent operations, and so has carrying out continuous improvement actions.

Long-Term Plans to Sustain the Competitive Advantages

The GHC team continuously identifies opportunities to improve the procedures related to procuring goods and services and optimizing the process. Therefore, in order to sustain the competitive advantages obtained from the project, continuous improvement cycles are going to be carried out.

There is also the possibility of taking BPM practices into the other strategic processes at GHC, all the while following the best practices and lessons learned in this project.

9. TECHNOLOGY

The Orquestra BPM tool from Brazilian company Cryo Technologies was chosen to automate the procurement macro process flows. Some of the reasons for choosing this BPMS are highlighted below:

- Geographical proximity to the manufacturer;
- Product focused on human, collaborative processes;
- Support for human and computer activities;
- Report generation and performance indicator updates;
- Simple, intuitive interface.

Regarding the hardware and software features used to put the solution together, such information is provided below:

Software

Category	Model	Version
OS	Windows	2008 R2 Standard
BD	SQL Server	2008 R2 Standard
BPMS	Orquestra BPM	2.5.9

Hardware

Category	Configuration
Processor	Dual Processor: Dual-Core AMD Opteron Processor 2218 HE 2.60 Ghz
RAM	8GB
HD	200GB

10. TECHNOLOGY AND SERVICE PROVIDERS

The consulting firm hired to implement the project was H&R Consultores, a company specializing in Organizational Management and Business Process Management catering to companies and government agencies. H&R Consultores is a partner company of Cryo Technologies, the supplier of the BPMS we use.

Contact: www.herconsultores.com.br and www.cryo.com.br.

Appendix

Awards Contact Directory

Introduction

Layna Fischer, Future Strategies Inc.
http://www.FutStrat.com

Evolution of BPM: Combining Business Architecture, Intelligence, Case Management to Accelerate Process Implementations

Meera Srinivasan and Linus Chow, Oracle USA
www.oracle.com

Transforming the Business for a new Customer Segment: The Role of BPM in the New Business Model

J. Bryan Lail, Raytheon
www.raytheon.com

BPM Change Management: Some Considerations

Jaisundar Venkat, Wipro
www.wipro.com

Innovation in Health Care: Insight from First Federal Health Care Center

Paul Lam, Captain James A. Lovell Federal Health Care Center
http://www.lovell.fhcc.va.gov/

Linus Chow, Oracle USA
www.oracle.com

Case Studies

1. EUROPE

Silver Award

Roberto Merotto, Avio SpA
www.aviogroup.com

Nominator

Angelo Dimartino, Università del Salento, Centro Cultura Innovativa d'Impresa
www.eka-systems.com

Gold Award

Dr. Horst Karaschewski, HanseMerkur Insurance Group
http://www.hansemerkur.de/home

Nominator

Elena Lucas, Bosch Software Innovations
http://www.inubit.com/en/home

Finalist Award

Paul Swinson, Homeloan Management Limited (HML)
http://www.HML.co.uk

Nominator

Steve Smythe, IBM, USA
www.ibm.com

Gold Award

Chris Ryan, Jardine Lloyd Thompson Group PLC
www.jltgroup.com

Nominator

Garth Knudson, HandySoft
www.handysoft.com

Finalist Award

Inmaculada de Celis Loaiza, Toyota Spain
http://www.toyota.es/

Nominator

Pablo Trilles, AuraPortal USA
www.auraportal.com

2. MIDDLE EAST-AFRICA

Silver Award

Ecobank LLC, Senegal
http://www.ecobank.com

Nominator

Sandipan Chakraborty, Newgen Software
http://www.newgensoft.com

3. MIDDLE EAST-AFRICA

Gold Award

Dr. Adnan A. Al-Tunisi, Riyadh Military Hospital
http://www.rmh.med.sa

Nominator

Marcel Manser, Bizagi
http://www.bizagi.com

4. NORTH AMERICA

Silver Award

Martin Weightman, Danfoss Power Electronics
www.danfossdrives.com

Nominator

Artur Siurdyban, Aalborg University
www.aau.dk

Finalist Award

John Harris, National Institute of Mental Health
www.nimh.nih.gov/index.shtml

Nominator

Marti Colwell, BP Logix, Inc.
www.bplogix.com

Gold Award

Shakir Awan, San Joaquin County Information Systems Division
http://www.co.san-joaquin.ca.us

Nominator

Linus Chow, Oracle
www.oracle.com

Silver Award

Commander Eric Miller, U.S. Navy, Naval Special Warfare Group Four
http://www.navsoc.socom.mil/

Nominator

Garth Knudson, HandySoft
www.handysoft.com

5. PACIFIC RIM

Gold Award

Aaron A Llop, Audi Japan KK
http://www.audi.co.jp

Nominator

Marcel Manser, Bizagi
http://www.bizagi.com

Silver Award

Venkataramanan K.B, Viteos Capital Market Services Ltd.
www.viteos.com

Nominator

Jerry Silver, EMC
www.emc.com

6. SOUTH AND CENTRAL AMERICA

Finalist Award

Hernando Consuegra, Carbones de Cerrejón
http://www.cerrejon.com

Nominator

Marcel Manser, Bizagi
http://www.bizagi.com

Gold Award

Juan Carlos Garces del Angel, Comisión Nacional del Agua
www.conagua.gob.mx

Nominator

Daniel Torea PECTRA Technology Inc
www.pectra.com

Silver Award

Cléber Garbin, Grupo Hospitalar Conceição
http://www.ghc.com.br

Nominator

Cristiano Schuch, H&R Consultores
http://www.herconsultores.com.br

Additional Resources

NEW E-BOOK SERIES ($9.97 EACH)

- Introduction to BPM and Workflow
  http://store.futstrat.com/servlet/Detail?no=75

- Financial Services
  http://store.futstrat.com/servlet/Detail?no=90

- Healthcare
  http://store.futstrat.com/servlet/Detail?no=81

- Utilities and Telecommunications
  http://store.futstrat.com/servlet/Detail?no=92

NON-PROFIT ASSOCIATIONS AND RELATED STANDARDS RESEARCH ONLINE

- AIIM (Association for Information and Image Management)
  http://www.aiim.org
- BPM and Workflow online news, research, forums
  http://bpm.com
- BPM Research at Stevens Institute of Technology
  http://www.bpm-research.com
- Business Process Management Initiative
  http://www.bpmi.org *see* Object Management Group
- IEEE (Electrical and Electronics Engineers, Inc.)
  http://www.ieee.org
- Institute for Information Management (IIM)
  http://www.iim.org
- ISO (International Organization for Standardization)
  http://www.iso.ch
- Object Management Group
  http://www.omg.org
- Open Document Management Association
  http://nfocentrale.net/dmware
- Organization for the Advancement of Structured Information Standards
  http://www.oasis-open.org
- Society for Human Resource Management
  http://www.shrm.org
- Society for Information Management
  http://www.simnet.org
- Wesley J. Howe School of Technology Management
  http://howe.stevens.edu/research/research-centers/business-process-innovation
- Workflow And Reengineering International Association (WARIA)
  http://www.waria.com
- Workflow Management Coalition (WfMC)
  http://www.wfmc.org
- Workflow Portal
  http://www.e-workflow.org

Read More Unique Books
Future Strategies, Publishers (www.FutStrat.com)

TAMING THE UNPREDICTABLE

http://futstrat.com/books/eip11.php

The core element of Adaptive Case Management (ACM) is the support for real-time decision-making by knowledge workers.

Taming the Unpredictable presents the logical starting point for understanding how to take advantage of ACM. This book goes beyond talking about concepts, and delivers actionable advice for embarking on your own journey of ACM-driven transformation.

Retail #49.95 (see discount on website)

HOW KNOWLEDGE WORKERS GET THINGS DONE

http://www.futstrat.com/books/HowKnowledgeWorkers.php

How Knowledge Workers Get Things Done describes the work of managers, decision makers, executives, doctors, lawyers, campaign managers, emergency responders, strategist, and many others who have to think for a living. These are people who figure out what needs to be done, at the same time that they do it, and there is a new approach to support this presents the logical starting point for understanding how to take advantage of ACM.

Retail $49.95 (see discount offer on website)

DELIVERING BPM EXCELLENCE

http://futstrat.com/books/Delivering_BPM.php

Business Process Management in Practice

The companies whose case studies are featured in this book have proven excellence in their creative and successful deployment of advanced BPM concepts. These companies focused on excelling in *innovation, implementation* and *impact* when installing BPM and workflow technologies. The positive impact to their corporations includes increased revenues, more productive and satisfied employees, product enhancements, better customer service and quality improvements. **$39.95 (see discount on website)**

DELIVERING THE CUSTOMER-CENTRIC ORGANIZATION

http://futstrat.com/books/Customer-Centric.php
The ability to successfully manage the customer value chain across the life cycle of a customer is the key to the survival of any company today. Business processes must react to changing and diverse customer needs and interactions to ensure efficient and effective outcomes.

This important book looks at the shifting nature of consumers and the workplace, and how BPM and associated emergent technologies will play a part in shaping the companies of the future. **Retail $39.95**

BPMN 2.0 Handbook SECOND EDITION

(see two-BPM book bundle offer on website: get BPMN Reference Guide Free)

http://futstrat.com/books/bpmnhandbook2.php

Updated and expanded with exciting new content!

Authored by members of WfMC, OMG and other key participants in the development of BPMN 2.0, the BPMN 2.0 Handbook brings together worldwide thought-leaders and experts in this space. Exclusive and unique contributions examine a variety of aspects that start with an introduction of what's new in BPMN 2.0, and look closely at interchange, analytics, conformance, optimization, simulation and more. **Retail $75.00**

BPMN MODELING AND REFERENCE GUIDE

(see two-BPM book bundle offer on website: get BPMN Reference Guide Free)

http://www.futstrat.com/books/BPMN-Guide.php

Understanding and Using BPMN
How to develop rigorous yet understandable graphical representations of business processes.

Business Process Modeling Notation (BPMN) is a standard, graphical modeling representation for business processes. It provides an easy to use, flow-charting notation that is independent of the implementation environment. **Retail $39.95**

BPM & WORKFLOW HANDBOOK: HUMAN-CENTRIC BPM

http://www.futstrat.com/books/handbook08.php

Spotlight on Human-Centric BPM

Human-centric business process management (BPM) has become the product and service differentiator. The topic now captures substantial mindshare and market share in the human-centric BPM space as leading vendors have strengthened their human-centric business processes. Our spotlight this year examines challenges in human-driven workflow and its integration across the enterprise. **Retail $95.00 (see discount on website)**

Social BPM

http://futstrat.com/books/handbook11.php

Work, Planning, and Collaboration Under the Impact of Social Technology

Today we see the transformation of both the look and feel of BPM technologies along the lines of social media, as well as the increasing adoption of social tools and techniques democratizing process development and design. It is along these two trend lines; the evolution of system interfaces and the increased engagement of stakeholders in process improvement, that Social BPM has taken shape. **Retail $59.95 (see discount offer on website)**

Get 25% Discount on ALL Books in our Store.

Please use the discount code SPEC25 to get 25% discount on ALL books in our store; both Print and Digital Editions (two discount codes cannot be used together).
http://store.futstrat.com/servlet/Catalog

16110377R00119

Made in the USA
Charleston, SC
05 December 2012